Divine Descent and the Four World-Ages in the *Mahābhārata* – or, Why Does the Kṛṣṇa *Avatāra* Inaugurate the Worst *Yuga*?

Simon Brodbeck

Cardiff University Press | Gwasg Prifysgol Caerdydd

Published by
Cardiff University Press
Cardiff University
PO Box 430
1st Floor, 30-36 Newport Road
Cardiff CF24 0DE

https://cardiffuniversitypress.org

First published 2022

Cover design by Hugh Griffiths
Front cover image from Arthur M. Sackler Gallery, Smithsonian Institute

Print and digital versions typeset by Siliconchips Services Ltd.

ISBN (Paperback): 978-1-911653-39-4
ISBN (PDF): 978-1-911653-43-1
ISBN (EPUB): 978-1-911653-40-0
ISBN (Mobi): 978-1-911653-41-7

DOI: https://doi.org/10.18573/book9

The full text of this book has been peer-reviewed to ensure high academic standards. For full review policies, see https://www.cardiffuniversitypress.org/site/research-integrity/

Suggested citation: Brodbeck, S. 2022. Divine Descent and the Four World-Ages in the *Mahābhārata* – or, Why Does the Kṛṣṇa *Avatāra* Inaugurate the Worst *Yuga?* Cardiff: Cardiff University Press. DOI: https://doi.org/10.18573/book9. Licence: CC-BY-NC-ND 4.0

To read the free, open access version of this book online, visit https://doi.org/10.18573/book9 or scan this QR code with your mobile device:

Contents

Acknowledgements v

List of Figures vi

List of Abbreviations vii

Chapter 1. Preliminaries **1**

Expanded table of contents 2

Methodology 5

Chapter 2. The Yuga Cycle in the *Mahābhārata* **13**

The *Manusmṛti* account 13

The *Mahābhārata* accounts 16

The complex variable 26

The structure of the cycle 29

The twilight periods 35

Measurement in divine years 38

Chapter 3. The Title Problem **47**

Transition to the *kaliyuga* in the *Mahābhārata* narrative 47

Why does the Kṛṣṇa *avatāra* inaugurate the worst *yuga*? 56

Chapter 4. *Avatāras* and *Yugāntas* **63**

Three senses of *yugānta* 68

The instability theory 75

The *yuga* machine 83

Chapter 5. The Kurukṣetra *Avatāra* and the Divine Plan **89**

The two functions of the *avatāra* 89

The earth and death 94

Three accounts of the earth's problem 101

The view from the gods 116

The two *avatāra* functions in the Kurukṣetra story 130

Chapter 6. Transition to the *Kṛtayuga* **141**

Janamejaya and the *yugas* 141

The king and the *yugas* 146

Vyāsa's transition account 149

The ancient audience and the *yugas* 157

Chapter 7. Conclusion **165**

Avatāra revisited 166

Time 171

Return to the title question 173

Glossary of Sanskrit Words 177

Bibliography 181

Index of Passages Cited 197

Acknowledgements

For personal assistance with this monograph I am grateful to Max Deeg, Laxshmi Greaves, Ed Kaneen, Julius Lipner, Kate Tinson, Christophe Vielle, and many others not named, including those who responded to two papers presented in the Cardiff University Religious Studies Seminar Series in February and November 2020.

I am especially grateful to Lynn Thomas and Adam Bowles, both of whom, as well as assisting in other ways, commented on a full first draft; Alice Percival at Cardiff University Press, for her interest and encouragement; three anonymous reviewers, whose comments have led to many improvements; Hugh Griffiths, for the beautiful cover design; Kirsty Harding, for help with the figures; and my parents, Jan and Tim Brodbeck.

Acknowledgements of a different kind are due to Luis González-Reimann (1948–2022), the Indologist without whose publications the research reported on here would have been least likely to have been pursued. Paul Dundas lent me *The Mahābhārata and the Yugas* (2002) as soon as he had read it. I was charmed by Luis's warmth and collegiality on a visit to Atlanta in 2010, and just before the coronavirus I was looking forward to seeing him again at the Canberra World Sanskrit Conference in January 2021, in a panel on 'Cosmology, Cosmography and Time in the Sanskrit Epics and Purāṇas' convened by Ruth Satinsky; but the conference, and with it England's regaining of the Ashes, was postponed. Luis kindly attended the second of the aforementioned Cardiff seminars online from a distant time-zone, and I regret that I will be unable to discuss this research with him, or to discover what he thinks of my translations from his Spanish. The monograph is dedicated to Luis, who would have been its most appropriate audience, and to my father, who loves mathematics and graphs.

List of Figures

1. *Mahābhārata* Family Tree. 2
2. Stemma of the *Mahābhārata* Textual Tradition (Sukthankar 1933: xxx). 7
3. The Diurnal, Lunar, and Annual Cycles (Sine Wave). 30
4. The Days and Nights of Brahmā. 31
5. The Four *Yugas*. 31
6. The Elision of the Upstroke and the Acceleration of the Downstroke. 32
7. *Dvāpara* to *Kali* Transition (Smooth). 37
8. *Dvāpara* to *Kali* Transition (Steepening). 37
9. *Dvāpara* to *Kali* Transition (Sudden). 38
10. *Dvāpara* to *Kali* Transition (with Trough). 76
11. The *Yuga* Machine. 84
12. Rotating Disc and Groove. 85
13. Side View of the Mechanism. 86
14. Trajectory of Chapter 6. 141
15. *Kali* to *Kṛta* Transition (with Trough). 146

List of Abbreviations

Bhg	*Bhagavadgītā* (Mbh 6.23–40)
Hv	*Harivaṃśa*
Mbh	*Mahābhārata*
Ms	*Manusmṛti* (*Mānavadharmaśāstra*)

What was it Goethe said to Eckermann? Interesting indeed that the 'first European' should have expressed himself thus: 'Men will become more clever and more acute, but not better, happier, and stronger in action – or at least only at epochs. I foresee the time when God will break up everything for a renewed creation. I am certain that everything is planned to this end, and that the time and hour in the distant future for occurrence of this renovating epoch are already fixed ...'

(Miller 1952: 105; see Eckermann 1850: 97–98)

IN THE BLACKNESS NNVSNU THE TSRUNGH TRANSMITS THE MOTHERCODE; SPINNING HIS MIND LIKE A PRAYER WHEEL HE REVOLVES CONTINUALLY THE NUMINOSITIES AND NEXIALITIES THAT COMMUNICATE THE UNIVERSE TO ITSELF.

What does Nnvsnu the Tsrungh actually look like?

ACTUALLY HE'S NOT PROPERLY A HE AND HE'S NOTHING YOU COULD PICTURE IN YOUR MIND. WHAT WE'RE TALKING ABOUT HERE IS A SPACE-TIME SINGULARITY WHICH IS IN FACT A NEURON OF THE COSMIC MIND TO WHICH THIS UNIVERSE HAS OCCURRED.

(Hoban 1987: 132)

CHAPTER 1

Preliminaries

The Sanskrit *Mahābhārata* – one of the longest poems in the world, dating from the last centuries BCE or the early centuries CE – is concerned mainly with the story of a great war, fought on the battlefield of Kurukṣetra (now in the state of Haryana, north of Delhi). The war was between the five Pāṇḍava brothers and their paternal cousins, the one hundred Kauravas, and was ostensibly fought to decide which side of the family would inherit the ancestral Bhārata kingdom. See Figure 1. The junior, Pāṇḍava side won, but huge numbers of allies also fought on both sides, and at the final count 1,660,020,000 were killed, with a further 24,165 missing in action (Mbh 11.26.9–10).

In the *Mahābhārata*'s account of the Kurukṣetra war, the war marked a transition from one age of the world (*yuga*) to another. The war marked the beginning of the *kaliyuga*, the most dismal and immoral age, during which *dharma* – proper behaviour – is at its lowest.

Another prevailing aspect is that some of the war's principal participants were gods who had taken human forms as part of a divine plan to rescue the Earth – personified as a woman – from her oppressions. The text depicts the personified Earth prompting a divine intervention (*avatāra*) for her benefit, which results in the Kurukṣetra slaughter. The intervention is especially associated with Viṣṇu-Nārāyaṇa, and it is one of many such interventions. Viṣṇu famously intervenes repeatedly for cosmic benefit.

This monograph places those two aspects of the *Mahābhārata* account – the *yuga* aspect and the *avatāra* aspect – side by side, and on top of each other. It does so in order to determine the text's overall message about the destiny of the world at that time, and, more generally, in order to investigate the text's theology of time. That message and that theology have implications for King Janamejaya, the direct descendant of the victorious Pāṇḍavas, because the story of the war, as Vaiśaṃpāyana tells it, is told to him, a few generations after the events it narrates. They also have implications for Śaunaka and the seers, because the story of Janamejaya (and how he heard about the war), as Ugraśravas the roving

How to cite this book chapter:
Brodbeck, S. 2022. Divine Descent and the Four World-Ages in the *Mahābhārata* – or, Why Does the Kṛṣṇa *Avatāra* Inaugurate the Worst *Yuga?* Pp. 1–12. Cardiff: Cardiff University Press. DOI: https://doi.org/10.18573/book9.a. Licence: CC-BY-NC-ND 4.0

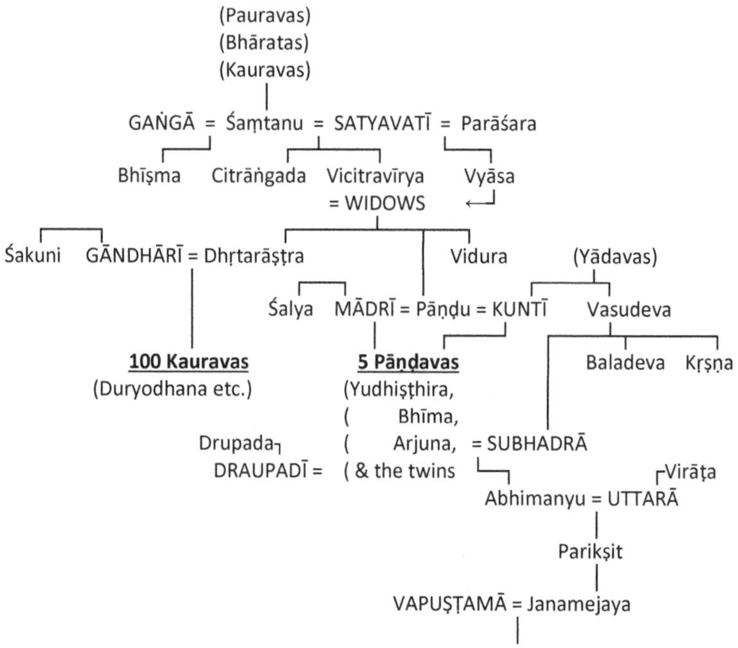

Figure 1: *Mahābhārata* Family Tree.

storyteller tells it, is told to them after that; and they have implications for the *Mahābhārata*'s early audiences, because the text is told to them after that; and they also have implications for us, reading the text in the twenty-first century CE.

The apparent contradiction between the *yuga* and *avatāra* aspects has been noted before, and this monograph is an attempt to explore it directly.

Expanded table of contents

The monograph has seven chapters. This section gives a chapter-by-chapter and section-by-section summary of the argument. Please refer back to it, dear reader, whenever you wish. Overview material is also provided at the ends of Chapters 4 and 5, and in Chapter 7.

The first four chapters are introductory: in an earlier draft, they were one chapter. Chapter 1 consists of this overview and a section on methodology.

Chapter 2 initiates discussion of the cycle of four *yuga*s. The *Manusmṛti* passage on this topic is presented and discussed, as are the various *Mahābhārata* passages. Chapter 2 is a long chapter because the *yuga* cycle is peculiar in various ways, and resists easy conceptualisation. One section discusses the fact that many parameters – notably lifespan, goodness (dharmicness), and length of *yuga* – are part of one complex variable, which is shifted down through levels and up again. One section differentiates this sawtooth cycle of levels (from 4, to

3, to 2, to 1, then right back up to 4 again) from the smooth sine-wave alternations within the diurnal, lunar, and annual cycles. A final section differentiates the *Mahābhārata*'s (and the *Manusmṛti*'s) *yuga* scheme from the longer *yuga* scheme found in various Purāṇas.

The *Mahābhārata*'s *yuga* concept having been set up, Chapter 3 begins by addressing the location of the Kurukṣetra war within it. Multiple short passages are surveyed, cumulatively placing the Kurukṣetra war at the transition between the *dvāpara* and *kali yuga*s. González-Reimann's interpretation of such passages as late ones is discussed and set aside. The Kurukṣetra war having been located to this point in the *yuga* cycle, the second section of Chapter 3 can now elaborate the monograph's basic research question, which is as per the title: Why does the Kṛṣṇa *avatāra* inaugurate the worst *yuga*? How could the world be rescued by divine intervention at that point in the cycle, where things actually get worse?

Chapter 4 begins by discussing the location in time of Viṣṇu's other *avatāra*s, which tend to appear at the end of *yuga*s – that is, at *yugānta*s (*anta* means 'end'), at points of transition between one *yuga* and the next. One section explores the word *yugānta*, which carries a variety of dramatic connotations; the multiple senses of the word *yuga* combine to confer upon some *yugānta*s – including the end of the *dvāparayuga* where the Kurukṣetra war occurs – a poetic register which otherwise they might not have. This is one way of trying to explain why *avatāra*s generally appear at *yugānta*s. Another way is through what I call Thomas's instability theory, the subject of the next section, according to which the end of every *yuga* would be a liminal period of breakdown and chaos, requiring an *avatāra* to appear, defeat the demon, and see the new *yuga* securely in. But although this theory provides a partial answer to our title question, the textual evidence for it is weak. In the final section of Chapter 4 a mechanical analogy is elaborated, evoking an alternative scenario whereby the passage from one *yuga* to another is part of an automatic process, and the idea that God intervenes to change things at that point is a metaphor for the fact that things change at that point.

Chapter 5 tries to understand the *avatāra* concept, as instantiated in the Kurukṣetra *avatāra* at the *dvāpara-kaliyuga* transition, as an encapsulation of the *mahāyuga* cycle as a whole. Its first section presents and discusses a series of *Mahābhārata* passages in search of a general principle of *avatāra*. It is shown that the *avatāra* has two functions: to boost *dharma* and the gods, and to lighten the Earth's burden (Mbh 12.337.29–34). These two separate functions are vital for the argument that follows. The next section studies the *Mahābhārata*'s myth of the origin of Death, in which Death explicitly performs the lightening function for the overburdened Earth, and it links that function with the end of the *kṛtayuga* at one extremity of the *mahāyuga*, the other extremity being the point where *dharma* is rebooted at the end of the *kaliyuga* as per the other function. These matters having now been explored in the abstract, the third section of Chapter 5 – which is, in a sense, the heart of the monograph – focuses on the text's accounts of the specific reason for the Kurukṣetra *avatāra*. In four subsections the accounts are described, discussed, and compared, and their elements are resolved into the two *avatāra* functions, which fit the two extremities of the *mahāyuga* cycle, one of which repeatedly features the Earth.

In the fourth section of Chapter 5, those two extremities are first explored in relation to the notions of *jāmi* and *pṛthak* – 'under-differentiation' and 'over-distinction' (Hegarty 2006a: 59 n. 20), the problems that the two functions of the *avatāra* respectively address – in the Prajāpati myths in the Brāhmaṇa texts. Then those two extremities of the *mahāyuga* are explored in relation to the genders of the female Earth and the male gods in the accounts of the reason for the Kurukṣetra *avatāra*. In a third subsection, and again in terms of the Brāhmaṇa texts, the whole question is raised again, from the end of Chapter 4, of whether, if the Kurukṣetra *avatāra* at the *dvāpara–kaliyuga* transition has a primarily representative or metaphorical effect (representing as it does both functions and both extremities), we might not just as well imagine the shift in levels at *yugānta*s to happen automatically, as years apparently do to us, God willing. Although the Brāhmaṇa texts show the king's ritual making the year, there are no comparable elaborations in the *Mahābhārata* by which we might easily understand the gods' or God's ritual making the *mahāyuga*. That could be ritual only in an oblique sense, as if to dramatise particular moments in an automatic process.

The fifth and final section of Chapter 5 tracks how the two *avatāra* functions – lightening the burden of the Earth, and boosting *dharma* – play out in the *Mahābhārata*'s narration of the Kurukṣetra story at the *dvāpara–kaliyuga* transition. They are seen there combined and differentiable. It is argued that since the descriptions of the problem affecting the Earth describe a time before she complained and prompted its solution, and since that solution requires the gods to be born as humans and grow up to make the war happen, the humans who fight the war are more naturally thought of as part of that collaborative solution than as part of the problem that obtained before they were born. Duryodhana is something of a test case here, for he is issued as part of the collective *avatāra* alongside the many gods, as if Kali were the helpful god of mischief and misfortune, and yet by that very brief he would, as it were, oppose the gods and constitute the problem. This paradox is bridged by the overlay of demonic possession onto divine incarnation: just a few years before the Kurukṣetra war, demons possess characters including Duryodhana, Karṇa, Kṛpa, Droṇa, and Bhīṣma (Mbh 3.240.10–11). The combining of the two *avatāra* functions within the narration of the Kurukṣetra story allows the *avatāra* there to encapsulate the *mahāyuga* as a whole, because it is between the two extremities.

Chapter 6 takes a different tack on the title problem, by focusing on the *dvāpara–kaliyuga* transition as a point just 1,200 years before the great dharmic reboot. This chapter follows the text as it tracks forwards in time from the Kurukṣetra war, thinking about location within the *yuga* cycle. In the first section of the chapter we see how Janamejaya, hearing the Kurukṣetra story, places himself early in the *kaliyuga*. Vyāsa's description to Janamejaya of the *kaliyuga* and the *yugānta* (Hv 116–117) is discussed here, and is compared with Mārkaṇḍeya's accounts of the same (Mbh 3.186–189). In connection with Janamejaya's location within the cycle, the next section explores the idea that the king makes the *yuga* - that in any *yuga* there are bubbles of excellence, even if against the run of play. This is a crucial idea because although it applies to Janamejaya as king, it applies also to everyone else, and allows for the full range of dharmic possibilities, microcosmically, at any time.

Vyāsa tells Janamejaya about a new religious orientation appropriate to the *kaliyuga*; and in relation to the title question, the third section of Chapter 6 focuses on Vyāsa's non-messianic account of the transition from *kaliyuga* to *kṛtayuga*. It is suggested that the *Mahābhārata*, as an ongoing prompt for excellence via the new religious orientation, might eventually cause or constrain that transition to occur. The *Bhagavadgītā*, containing as it does Kṛṣṇa's own - Viṣṇu-Nārāyaṇa's - exposition of the required yogic approach which he himself epitomises, would be the central moment within that prompt. The final section of Chapter 6 discusses the location of the *Mahābhārata*'s ancient audience (and the poets) within the *yuga* cycle, and the drama, for them, of the relative imminence of the *kṛtayuga*. According to the timescale presented within the text, the *kṛtayuga* could have been expected imminently by *Mahābhārata* audiences for a few hundred years, but after that it would be known not to have come as expected; the numbers would break, a crucial aspect of the text would break, and that drama would evaporate. But we would have an answer to our title question: in the *Mahābhārata*, in its own time, the Kṛṣṇa *avatāra* occurred at the *dvāpara–kaliyuga* transition because that is just the right length of time away from the *kali–kṛtayuga* transition for sowing the seed that has since been growing through story, transforming the people, growing with the story's new audience towards sudden fruition at the turn of the *mahāyuga*.

Chapter 7 is a short conclusion. It collects and briefly expands upon the monograph's findings. It returns again to the problem of conceptualising God's action within time. If the *mahāyuga* cycle with its various *yugānta*s and level-shifts just **is** God's action within time, then the specific famous *avatāra*s might as well be myths; but if the next level-shift comes about with and through a groundswell of Kṛṣṇa's *yoga*, then each of us is as much an *avatāra* as any other. The final sections situate our discoveries within the *Mahābhārata*'s overall philosophy of time, and respond summarily to the title question.

Methodology

Mahābhārata scholars have often seen the *Mahābhārata* text as having expanded in phases, and have attempted to separate it into historical layers. Within this frame of analysis, scholars have attempted to place the *yuga* and *avatāra* aspects at particular stages in the *Mahābhārata*'s imagined history of composition or incorporation. For example, González-Reimann has suggested that the *yuga* system was a relatively late addition to the text (González-Reimann 2002); and González-Reimann and many others have also suggested that the theology of Viṣṇu was likewise a relatively late addition to the text (pp. 103–104, 151; Brockington 1998: 255–256; Fitzgerald 2004a: 139–142; Witzel 2005: 66–70; Eltschinger 2020: 50). In English-language scholarship, these and similar opinions resemble that of Hopkins, who in 1901, drawing on German-language scholarship, presented a speculative five-stage scheme of the gradual expansion of 'the epic'. In terms of the *yuga* and *avatāra* aspects, the salient stage in Hopkins's scheme would be the third one:

> Remaking of the epic with Krishna as all-god, intrusion of masses of didactic matter, addition of Puranic material old and new; multiplication of exploits, 200 B.C. to 100–200 A.D.
>
> (Hopkins 1901: 398)

More recently, Hellwig has written:

> While many researchers assume that the Mbh grew over centuries (Hopkins 1901; van Buitenen 1973; J. Brockington 1998), others postulate that the Mbh was composed in a relatively short time and should consequently be read as a literary work (Dahlmann 1899; Hiltebeitel 2001).
>
> (Hellwig 2019: 2)

Note the words 'and should consequently'. As I shall explain, I do not think this is a logical step. But first it should be said that these two basic theses about the text's composition have been with us for over a century now, without anything compelling us to reject either of them. The idea that the *Mahābhārata* 'grew over centuries' is underdetermined by the textual evidence, as is the idea that the *Mahābhārata* 'was composed in a relatively short time'. And this will likely remain the case.

Nonetheless, something crucial did happen in *Mahābhārata* studies in the twentieth century: the production, at the Bhandarkar Oriental Research Institute in Poona, of the *Mahābhārata* critical edition. It is not coincidental that this was also the century in which South Asia achieved freedom from the European yoke (van der Veer 1999). The Poona editors undertook an unprecedentedly and probably unrepeatably wide-ranging survey of Sanskrit *Mahābhārata* manuscripts, and on the basis of that survey they used the stemmatic text-critical method to reconstruct a text which was hypothesised as the most recent common ancestor of all the surviving manuscript versions (Dandekar 1971–1976; Brodbeck 2019a: 8–72). In philological parlance, that most recent common ancestor is the 'archetype' of the surviving versions. Sukthankar, the doyen of the Poona editors, styled this the 'Ur-Mahābhārata' on his stemmatic diagram (Sukthankar 1933: xxx). I reproduce Sukthankar's diagram here in slightly edited form as Figure 2, after removing 'Vyāsa's Bhārata', which Sukthankar places above 'Ur-Mahābhārata'. The words at the bottom are names of scripts.

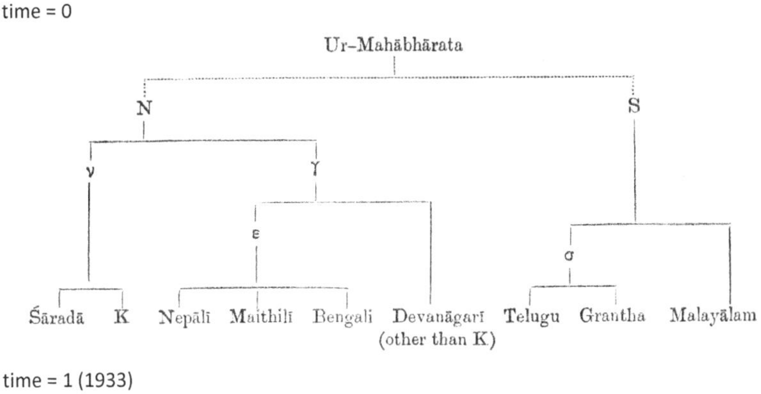

Figure 2: Stemma of the *Mahābhārata* Textual Tradition (Sukthankar 1933: xxx).

Hopkins and Dahlmann only had access to certain manuscript versions, none of which were very old. But we have access to the critically reconstituted *Mahābhārata*, as precisely and singularly formulated as one could wish. This gives us a snapshot of the *Mahābhārata* at a certain point in time, though we do not know exactly when; and we can read it as a literary work, regardless of whether its prehistory was long or short. Since there is no clear basis on which to prefer one type of prehistory over the other, the propriety of a literary approach cannot depend on that issue, despite Hellwig's 'and should consequently'. I do not share Dahlmann and Hiltebeitel's conviction that the text had a short prehistory, but nonetheless I think a literary approach is appropriate. It can lead to discoveries about how the text works as a literary object. Even if the matter of the text's prehistory were settled in favour of Hopkins, a literary approach would still be appropriate. The only decision would be whether or not to pursue it. But if scholars do take a literary approach (whether or not they elsewhere talk about the text's prehistory), they have to take it in relation to the available text. The diachronic and literary approaches do not logically exclude each other, since scholars who take a diachronic approach can and sometimes do imagine the text being, at each stage of expansion, a (different) coherent literary work that could and should be understood on its own terms. But we cannot inspect, and so cannot thus understand, the text at any stage prior to that represented by the reconstituted text.

Hopkins imagines a very specific kind of prehistory for the *Mahābhārata*, since even at the first stage of development he begins with something that he calls 'an epic' (Hopkins 1901: 397–398; see also Witzel 2005: 32). Hopkins traces one particular route through the text's prehistory, and he makes that prehistory out to be singular by identifying 'epic' at both ends of it. If we ask of the river that flows through Kāśī, 'Where is the source of this river?', one obvious answer would be that it has many sources, since it has many tributaries. But because the river at Kāśī is the Gaṅgā, the semiotic dominance of that name over the names of its other tributaries also supplies a singular answer, whereby the source of the river is the source of the Gaṅgā. If, downstream of the Gaṅgā–Yamunā confluence, the name Yamunā had dominated instead, the singular source would be elsewhere. Hopkins preselects a singular route by labelling the extant *Mahābhārata* as 'epic', regardless of the fact that in his opinion a lot of it – presumably including the parts about the *yugas* and the *avatāras* – does not merit that label and is 'pseudo-epic'. But if I were to imagine a prehistory, I would imagine it in the plural.

Insofar as the text is traceable, it is traceable as it develops from the singularity of the archetype into the plurality of the various manuscript versions. The image we have of this is the stemma – that is, through the arboreal metaphor, the image of a branching bush (Figure 2). If we now imagine the text's prehistory, then pursuing the arboreal metaphor, we can imagine a root network covering the period from time = -1 to time = 0. But we might imagine this in any number of ways. Hopkins, by fixing upon the label 'epic', presents us with the image of a tap-root, like a carrot or a parsnip, or, inverted, the kind of tree that has a central dominating trunk throughout its structure. Thus, if one travels forward from the point of origin towards the archetype, the proto-text expands but remains itself throughout. This kind of image is a precondition of imagining something that could be labelled '**the** proto-*Mahābhārata*' at any point between time = -1 and time = 0. But we might instead imagine a root network in which several roots of approximately equal thickness come together just below the ground. Then they would all equally be proto-*Mahābhāratas*.[1]

There is no need to categorise the *Mahābhārata* as 'epic', or to speculate about its origin and development. Those acts could potentially disturb the method by which the text may be understood. Why would we need to imagine an earlier *Mahābhārata* (or earlier *Mahābhāratas*) than the one we have? Even if the Poona *Mahābhārata* were made up entirely of derivative elements, any previous arrangements of those elements (and others) would not compromise the ability of this particular *Mahābhārata* to be, and to know itself as, a distinctive artistic object. A curated exhibition of previously exhibited artworks is itself an artwork (Sathaye 2016: 238–240), as is a piece of music made up entirely of samples, as is a new edition of something presented in other editions before. If we ask whether there is anything particularly special about this *Mahābhārata* as opposed to possible previous others, we can answer: Yes, there is, because we can study this one – provided that, because the previous others that may once have contextualised it are not available for comparison, we study it without and outside the context that they would once have provided.

This implies a heavy self-selection effect. The historical reasons for the reconstructability of **this** text rather than parallel or previous *Mahābhāratas* – that is, the cumulative reasons for the survival of the available manuscript data

[1] Compare the lunar and solar lines of descent in the *Harivaṃśa* and the Purāṇas (Brodbeck 2012; Hv 8–10, 20–29): the lunar lines show plurality (a spreading fan), the solar line singularity (a patriline).

– cannot be discovered and are beyond our imagination. They are not necessarily anything to do with the value of the yielded text. On the one hand, the sheer availability of the surviving manuscript data could prompt an overvaluing of the text that has been reconstituted and retrojected on the basis of them. We must acknowledge that even if we have to privilege this *Mahābhārata*, the survival of this *Mahābhārata*'s descendant versions does not mean it was the best *Mahābhārata*. It is definitive for us, but arbitrarily so. On the other hand, the same situation could prompt an undervaluing of the text that we have.

Thus my approach in this monograph is to think of the text as an integrated whole, as presented in the reconstituted archetype. The *yuga* and *avatāra* aspects are both found in this archetype. The critical-edition project has a philological methodology, and questions about how or in what stages the archetype may have been composed are beyond its scope. This monograph's horizons are thus horizons on one ancient artwork, and on how it works in relation to the *yuga* cycle that it describes.

Many studies of the *Mahābhārata* as an integrated text consider it to end at Mbh 18.5, the end of the *Svargārohaṇaparvan*. But I consider it to include the *Harivaṃśa*, and to end at Hv 118, the end of the *Bhaviṣyaparvan*. I have discussed this approach elsewhere (Brodbeck 2011; Brodbeck 2016; Brodbeck 2021a), but since it informs the monograph's argument to a significant degree, a brief explanation is provided here. The crucial consideration is that in setting out its own contents in its second chapter (1.2.69, 233), the *Mahābhārata* makes it clear that it includes the so-called *khila parvan*s that constitute the *Harivaṃśa*, even though these are not contained within any of its eighteen 'major' books. So if one were to imagine a hypothetical proto-*Mahābhārata* that did not include the *Harivaṃśa*, that proto-*Mahābhārata* would also need not to include these universally attested verses. In other words, a proto-*Mahābhārata* excluding the *Harivaṃśa* could only be produced by picking and choosing from among the universally attested verses according to some higher-critical method, which is exactly the kind of approach that I seek to avoid. It is also the kind of approach that the critical editors, who included the *Harivaṃśa*, sought to avoid. A proto-*Mahābhārata* excluding the *Harivaṃśa* would be of much the same type as a proto-*Mahābhārata* excluding the various substories (*upākhyāna*s), or excluding Bhīṣma's voluminous post-war teachings to Yudhiṣṭhira, or excluding the frame-story of Janamejaya and his snake sacrifice: that is, it would be an unavailable text.

In conceptualising my approach to the text as an integrated whole, I have been helped by the methodological discussion at the beginning of Lipner's book on Hindu image worship (Lipner 2017). Lipner introduces what he calls 'a methodology of respect', which he characterises as follows:

> [A methodology of respect] incorporates the psychological, moral and intellectual readiness – the cultivated readiness – we must bring to our inquiry ... if we are to have a fair hope of achieving some measure of

> success with regard to true understanding and proper evaluation. It is not an optional extra, but an integral requirement for the success of the inquiry.
>
> By 'respect' here, then, I am not talking specifically about some emotion or feeling that may or may not be present in the inquirer with reference to the object of inquiry; I am talking about a disposition, an attitude, which, as the result of a certain disciplined approach, always accompanies the process of inquiry from start to finish, irrespective of how the object of understanding initially presents itself, i.e. as either attractive or repellent.
>
> (Lipner 2017: 11)

Lipner then gives examples of the absence of this disciplined approach, one being that of the missiologist who approached Hinduism in certainty of the completeness of the Christian revelation, and who hence failed to understand certain aspects of Hindu religiosity when writing about Hinduism. 'Such an approach ... arises from lack of proper methodological respect for its object of inquiry' (p. 15). Lipner then speaks of the conceptual research tool of 'constructive empathy', 'our inherent, indeed well-attested, capacity to imaginatively enter the world of the other, to assume his or her perspective' (p. 17, quoting Lipner 1993: 158). Lipner is here speaking of giving individual human beings their due, as his use of personal pronouns indicates. But his approach can be applied where the 'other' in question is not a person. In our case, it is a text.

> A consequence of this approach is that one takes the other's – whether an individual's or a community's – self-description seriously, so long as the other comes across as serious, tractable and sincere in intent. ... [M]ethodological respect for the other's self-description and its relevant implications becomes integral to one's starting point.
>
> (Lipner 2017: 19)

In this way, 'proper trans-cultural understanding of the "other" can be gained across boundaries of incommensurability pertaining to gender, place, time and upbringing' (ibid.). Although the word 'proper' is problematic here because a respectful approach cannot guarantee reliable research results, nonetheless 'proper trans-cultural understanding' is desirable in respect of the *Mahābhārata* as 'the other', and it seems to me that this approach – this research *yoga* – has much to recommend it. In studying the *Mahābhārata*, the issue of tractability recurs. But the other will not go away, so one has to be patient. As Black says, 'the first Western scholars to research the *Mahābhārata* often treated the text with contempt' (Black 2021: 18); but now that we have a critically reconstituted text, we must do our best to respect it. I come at this project in light of the broadly improper transcultural understanding of South Asia by Europe, and more specifically I come at it in light of British colonial history.

At some points in this monograph I slip from talking about Viṣṇu-Nārāyaṇa, with a masculine pronoun, to talking about God, with no pronoun, and back again. Although to some extent this constitutes a departure from the text, nonetheless I have not suppressed it. It seems to be a natural aspect, for me, of attempting to engage respectfully with the theology of the text. I am not sure that I could explain it, or properly discuss the relevant implications of my own positionality; and nor do I think it would help the reader if I were to try. God has been a basic idea for me ever since I had ideas, and my own positionality in relation to God is the same as yours. We are all the most large and the most small. The issue here seems to be not so much to do with where in space and time I culturally am, or the poets who wrote the *Mahābhārata* were. It seems to be to do with the subject matter. Although the God Viṣṇu who intervened as Kṛṣṇa at the *dvāpara-kaliyuga* transition is in the first instance a character in a text – 'the author creates God in his literary work, and in a closed textual world we can know of no God other than that vouchsafed to us by the author' (Dhand 2004: 52) – nonetheless theological questions cannot just be questions about a character in a text or a series of texts. They are live questions and always have been. So I cannot undertake to engage with theological ideas non-confessionally – it would be evasive of me to try to – but at the same time, I do not feel I have anything theological in particular to confess.

The question that this monograph attempts to address is a theological question, but any number of non-theological questions about the text could be addressed using a similar methodology. The monograph is theological by dint of the subject matter, not by dint of the methodology. It is important to be clear about this at the outset, because in the history of *Mahābhārata* interpretation, theological methodologies have often been applied that are similar in some respects to my own non-theological methodology. This is not a circumstance peculiar to the interpretation of the *Mahābhārata*, but is rather to do with its position as a religious text. In common with other religious texts, it has sometimes been assumed by interpreters that the God discussed and described within the *Mahābhārata* is the God that exists outside the text; that the *Mahābhārata* is, at some important level, true; that whatever else it might be, it is a vehicle or a tool for the human understanding of ultimate reality; that this characteristic is not shared by most other texts, which accordingly are less authoritative; and that the text thus has a coherence that it is the faithful interpreter's task to unpack and expound. As a corollary of such assumptions, the interpretation of religious texts has often featured apologetics and creative exegetical strategies in order to 'explain away' apparent inaccuracies, contradictions, or incoherence.

I do not share those assumptions with regard to the *Mahābhārata*. I do not credit the text in advance with any particular level of internal coherence.

Rather, the frame that I set up is an experimental one, justified by the methodology of respect mentioned above. Respect entails an interpretive generosity, so I want to explore what, if the text did all make sense, that sense could possibly be. One way of responding to the title question would be to set it up and explain it in the way I have tried to do in Chapters 1–3, conclude at that point that the text is incoherent in this respect, and then either stop there, or try to account for the perceived incoherence in other terms, for example by making historical speculations that might account for the co-presence, in this text, of such a range of ideas. I think that however interesting it might be, the latter strategy is unreliably speculative, and I would like to see if more sense can be made of the text on its own terms. This does not mean making sense of it at all costs; it means making sense of it if possible. Thus I do not seek to contribute to the developmental history of Indian ideas, which would entail the presentation of conclusions that would be either true or false, depending on whether I was right or wrong. Rather, I seek to contribute an interpretive appreciation of the *Mahābhārata* to the extent that that is possible on this topic, based on my own reflections, closely informed by the text and known prior texts and, where applicable, by the secondary literature upon them.

I said 'to the extent that that is possible', and I realise that different readers will make different judgements on this score. Consequently, although I am at least convinced enough by two main interpretive suggestions (made in Chapters 5 and 6 respectively) to think it worthwhile making them properly and setting them out so that they can be shared, nonetheless I do not imagine the monograph's success to depend upon the reader finding them particularly convincing or satisfying. I only hope that they are as convincing and satisfying as the material permits. As Piatigorsky wrote in the foreword to his *Mythological Deliberations*, 'I have no point to prove and no incentive to be convincing. I simply want to share my thoughts on myth with those also wishing to reflect on it' (Piatigorsky 1993: ix).

I do not argue that the *yuga* and *avatāra* ideas arose together, or that they were features of any particular proto-*Mahābhārata*, or that they fit together particularly well. The salient fact is simply that they are simultaneously present in our text. I am conscious that others will and do think of these ideas, in the form that the *Mahābhārata* presents them, as aspects of Vaiṣṇava theology that were in the process of formation at this point, and that were only systematised later, in various Purāṇas. But I am interested in these ideas as the *Mahābhārata* presents them, and I do not want to see them as steps towards something else – not least because, as discussed in Chapters 2 and 6, the *Mahābhārata*'s *yuga* scheme differed significantly from the standard Purāṇic *yuga* scheme, and that difference permitted a radical view of the reasonably near future. My narrow focus on the *Mahābhārata* itself, as if to remove it from the history of the ideas it contains, is not prompted by a prior belief that it must be coherent or that it carries some particular special truth, but by a desire to do it justice, to acknowledge and honour its presentation as such, and to enquire what it could have meant to its ancient audiences.

CHAPTER 2

The Yuga Cycle in the *Mahābhārata*

The *Mahābhārata*, like many other old Indian texts, presents time in terms of four *yugas*. In order of diminishing *dharma*, they are the *kṛta*, *tretā*, *dvāpara*, and *kali yugas*. The *kṛta* is also known as *satya*, and the *kali* is also known as *puṣya*, *tiṣya*, and *kaṣāya*.

In certain passages, the *Mahābhārata* presents these *yugas* as if they might occur at any time, depending on how good the current king happens to be (Biardeau 1976: 157–171; Thomas 2007). This presentation is perhaps in keeping with the origin of the names of the *yugas* in the names of the four throws of dice (González-Reimann 1988: 59–73; González-Reimann 1989; González-Reimann 2002: 53–62, 122–126). Dicing was a traditional activity of ancient Indian kings (Lüders 1907; de Vreese 1948; Falk 1986; Bowlby 1991). In other passages, the *yugas* are said to occur in an invariable succession, from *kṛtayuga* through *tretā* and *dvāpara* to *kali*, and then returning back to *kṛta* to run through the same sequence again and again. We shall return to the connection between the king and the *yugas* in Chapter 6; but to start with, and for most of what follows, our attention is on the four *yugas* as a fixed and repeating cycle.

The *Manusmṛti* account

In the *Mahābhārata* there are many descriptions of the four-*yuga* cycle. These occur in specific narrative contexts, and I shall survey them below, before moving on to discuss the cycle in some theoretical detail. But first, and as a kind of paradigm (Trautmann 1995: 168), I present and explain the description of the four-*yuga* cycle in the *Manusmṛti*.

brāhmasya tu kṣapāhasya yat pramāṇaṃ samāsataḥ |
ekaikaśo yugānāṃ ca kramaśas tan nibodhata ‖ Ms 1.68 ‖
catvāry āhuḥ sahasrāṇi varsāṇāṃ tat kṛtaṃ yugam |

How to cite this book chapter:
Brodbeck, S. 2022. Divine Descent and the Four World-Ages in the *Mahābhārata* – or, Why Does the Kṛṣṇa *Avatāra* Inaugurate the Worst *Yuga*?. Pp. 13–46. Cardiff: Cardiff University Press. DOI: https://doi.org/10.18573/book9.b.

tasya tāvac chatī saṃdhyā saṃdhyāṃśaś ca tathāvidhaḥ ‖ 69 ‖
itareṣu sasaṃdhyeṣu sasaṃdhyāṃśeṣu ca triṣu |
ekāpāyena vartante sahasrāṇi śatāni ca ‖ 70 ‖
yad etat parisaṃkhyātam ādāv eva caturyugam |
etad dvādaśasāhasraṃ devānāṃ yugam ucyate ‖ 71 ‖
daivikānāṃ yugānāṃ tu sahasraṃ parisaṃkhyayā |
brāhmam ekam ahar jñeyaṃ tāvatī rātrir eva ca ‖ 72 ‖ ...
catuṣpāt sakalo dharmaḥ satyaṃ caiva kṛte yuge |[2]
nādharmeṇāgamaḥ kaś cin manuṣyān upavartate ‖ 81 ‖
itareṣv āgamād dharmaḥ pādaśas tv avaropitaḥ |
caurikānṛtamāyābhir dharmaś cāpaiti pādaśaḥ ‖ 82 ‖
arogāḥ sarvasiddhārthāś caturvarṣaśatāyuṣaḥ |
kṛte tretādiṣu tv eṣāṃ vayo hrasati pādaśaḥ ‖ 83 ‖
vedoktam āyur martyānām āśiṣaś caiva karmaṇām |
phalanty anuyugaṃ loke prabhāvaś ca śarīriṇām ‖ 84 ‖
anye kṛtayuge dharmās tretāyāṃ dvāpare 'pare |
anye kaliyuge nṝṇāṃ yugahrāsānurūpataḥ ‖ 85 ‖
tapaḥ paraṃ kṛtayuge tretāyāṃ jñānam ucyate |
dvāpare yajñam evāhur dānam ekaṃ kalau yuge ‖ 86 ‖

Listen now to a concise account of the duration of a day-and-night of Brahmā and of each *yuga* in proper sequence. The *kṛtayuga* is said to last 4,000 years. It is preceded by a twilight lasting 400 years and followed by a twilight of the same length. For each of the three subsequent *yugas*, as also for the twilights that precede and follow them, the first number of the thousands and the hundreds is progressively diminished by one. These four *yugas*, computed at the very beginning as lasting 12,000 years, are said to constitute a single *yuga* of the gods. The sum total of 1,000 divine *yugas* should be regarded as a single day of Brahmā, and his night as having the very same duration ...

In the *kṛtayuga*, *dharma* is whole, possessing all four feet; and so is truth. People never acquire any property through unlawful means. By acquiring such property, however, *dharma* is stripped of one foot in each of the subsequent *yugas*; through theft, falsehood, and fraud, *dharma* disappears a foot at a time.

In the *kṛtayuga*, people are free from sickness, succeed in all their pursuits, and have a lifespan of 400 years. In the *tretā* and each of the subsequent *yugas*, however, their lifespan is shortened by a quarter. The lifespan of mortals given in the Veda, the benefits of rites, and the

[2] Here and elsewhere I indent the Sanskrit line where the translation that follows has paragraph breaks, so that the passage will be easier to read bilingually. The paragraph breaks in the English are interpretive. The indentations are not there in the Sanskrit text.

> power of embodied beings – they all come to fruition in the world in conformity with each *yuga*.
>
> There is one set of *dharma*s for human beings in the *kṛtayuga*, another in the *tretā*, still another in the *dvāpara*, and a different set in the *kali*, in keeping with the progressive shortening taking place in each *yuga*. Ascetic toil, they say, is supreme in the *kṛtayuga*; knowledge in the *tretā*; sacrifice in the *dvāpara*; and gift-giving alone in the *kali*.
>
> (*Manusmṛti* 1.68–72, 81–86, trans. Olivelle 2006: 90–91, adapted)[3]

Each cycle of four *yuga*s is also called a *yuga*: *Manusmṛti* calls this whole-cycle *yuga* a '*yuga* of the gods' (*devānāṃ yuga*, 1.71d) or a 'divine *yuga*' (*daivika yuga*, 1.72a).[4] The *Mahābhārata* does not use the word *mahāyuga*, but to avoid ambiguity in what follows I shall use that word – meaning 'great *yuga*' – as my standard term to indicate *Manusmṛti*'s '*yuga* of the gods', the repeating twelve-thousand-year cycle of the four *yuga*s. Like the *Manusmṛti* (1.71b), other texts also sometimes use the word *caturyuga* for this 'four-*yuga*' unit, but the *Mahābhārata* only uses this term once in this sense (Hv 32.17a).

There are a thousand *mahāyuga*s in every iteration of the universe. That is twelve million years. An iteration of the universe is called a 'day of Brahmā' in the *Manusmṛti* (Ms 1.72) and also in the *Mahābhārata* (e.g. at Bhg 8.17–19). Elsewhere, including in the *Mahābhārata*, a day of Brahmā is often called a *kalpa* (Thomas 1988: 74–75; Sutton 2000: 248; Bhg 9.7; Hv 7.52–54; 23.30; for *mahākalpa* see González-Reimann 2009: 416); but a *mahāyuga* may be called a *kalpa* too (12.291.14).[5] Sometimes a day of Brahmā is called a *yuga* in the *Mahābhārata* (1.1.28, 36–38; 3.81.109; 6.62.40; 12.203.14–17; 12.327.89; 13.14.183; 13.135.11; Biardeau 1976: 125; González-Reimann 1988: 142–143; Sutton 2000: 248; González-Reimann 2002: 72). The word *yuga* has three senses and more, since it generally refers to any long period of time ('yuga seems to have meant any unit of time', Mankad 1941–1942: 211). In this it resembles the word 'age', which has general and various technical senses. At the end of the day of Brahmā there is cosmic dissolution and the 'night of Brahmā' follows, during which the universe is held in abeyance for a similar period of twelve million years, before the next day of Brahmā (identical in type, but not in every detail; see Balslev 1984: 44–47; Thomas 1997). I use the term 'day of Brahmā' throughout this monograph, as per the name of the masculine god Brahmā. But in many such formulations it is not possible to see whether the god Brahmā

---

[3] Compare Lanman 1978: 57–58, 346. On the commentarial interpretations of the last two quoted verses see Lingat 1962, comparing also similar Buddhist formulations (p. 12).

[4] For 'divine *yuga*' see also Mbh 12.201.9, where Soma is said to have performed *tapas* for a thousand *divya yuga*s.

[5] Compare also the scheme at 12.299.1–14, mentioning the day of the *mahābhūta*s (= 3,000 *kalpa*s), the day of the *ahaṃkāra* (= 5,000 *kalpa*s), the day of Brahmā (= 7,500 *kalpa*s), and the day of the *avyakta* (= 10,000 *kalpa*s).

or the neuter *brahman* is intended, and there are indications in some contexts that the latter would be more appropriate (González-Reimann 1988: 138 n. 12; Cherniak 2008: 231–233).

When judged against the timescale of the day of Brahmā, a *mahāyuga* is not really very *mahā* ('great') at all. A *mahāyuga* is only 'great' in comparison with the four individual *yuga*s that comprise it.

As stated in the *Manusmṛti* passage, in the *yuga* cycle the ratio 4 : 3 : 2 : 1 governs the durations of the *yuga*s, the levels of *dharma* during them, and also the durations of human lifespan during them. *Dharma* is said to stand on all four feet in the *kṛtayuga*, three in the *tretā*, two in the *dvāpara*, and one in the *kali*. At Mbh 3.188.10 the quadruped of *dharma* is identified as a bull (Couture 2006: 70–71), and at 3.56.6–7 the bull is mentioned in connection with dicing (Gönc Moačanin 2021: 108–110).

González-Reimann notes that 'when we penetrate into the world of Brahmanical post-Vedic religion – what is commonly known as Hinduism – we are confronted with a complex and elaborate system of temporal cycles that has no obvious antecedents in Vedic religion'[6] (González-Reimann 1988: 85). Similarly, Eltschinger notes that 'Apart from the respective names of the four ages, which are borrowed from the Vedic game of dice ... nothing is known about the prehistory of the doctrine of the four *yugas*' (Eltschinger 2012: 32; see also Barua 1921: 211). But the cycle of *yuga*s presented in the *Manusmṛti* is also presented on various occasions in the *Mahābhārata*. Sutton sums up the situation:

> There is a predestined inevitability about the progression of *yugas* and the influence they have over human behaviour. There is no explanation as to how and why the nature of the world is repeatedly transformed in this way, but it is clear that humanity is subject to all-powerful cosmic forces over which it can have no control.
>
> (Sutton 2000: 259)

The *Mahābhārata* accounts

I now give an overview of the main *Mahābhārata* accounts: Mbh 1.57; 3.148; 3.186–189; 6.11; 12.200; 12.224; 12.230; 12.327; and Hv 117 (compare Sutton 2000: 255–260, omitting the Mbh 6 passage; Eltschinger 2012: 35–41 and Hudson 2013: 151–155, focusing primarily upon the Mbh 3 passages). There is

[6] 'cuando penetramos en el mundo de la religión brahmánica postvédica, aquella que es conocida comúnmente como hinduismo, nos encontramos con un complejo y elaborado sistema de ciclos de tiempo que no tiene antecedentes obvios en la religión védica'. Footnotes such as this one, which provide the French, Spanish, or German of quotations translated in the main text, are pinned to the end of the quotation, not to the end of the sentence.

some repetition from one account to another, but the overview will be effective in highlighting the most salient features of the cycle, and as a resource to refer back to. It should be borne in mind that in these accounts the use of the word *yuga* is sometimes ambiguous.

1.57. Vaiśaṃpāyana says, while introducing his teacher Vyāsa, author of the tale:

> *pādāpasāriṇaṃ dharmaṃ vidvān sa tu yuge yuge* ǀ
> *āyuḥ śaktiṃ ca martyānāṃ yugānugam avekṣya ca* ǁ 1.57.72 ǁ
> *brahmaṇo brāhmaṇānāṃ ca tathānugrahakāmyayā* ǀ
> *vivyāsa vedān yasmāc ca tasmād vyāsa iti smṛtaḥ* ǁ 73 ǁ

> Knowing that in each successive *yuga* the *dharma* is crippled in one foot, perceiving that the life and vigor of the mortals follow the rules of the *yuga*, and being desirous of showing his grace to both *brahman* and brahmins, he divided the Vedas, and is therefore remembered as Vyāsa ['divider, compiler'].
> (1.57.72–73, trans. van Buitenen 1973: 134, adapted)

3.148. This and the following account occur while the Pāṇḍavas are living in the forest, their kingdom having been lost in a dice match. This account is part of an episode where Bhīma Pāṇḍava goes on an expedition to fetch flowers for his wife Draupadī (3.146–150; for translation, see Laine 1989: 79–100; for discussion, Sullivan 2016). Bhīma meets his elder half-brother, Hanūmat, famous from the story of Rāma (both Hanūmat and Bhīma are sons of Vāyu, the Wind). After they have introduced themselves, Bhīma asks to see the form that Hanūmat assumed when he leaped across the ocean to Laṅkā, and in his response Hanūmat introduces the idea of the *yugas*. Hanūmat says that he cannot show the requested form, because the event to which Bhīma refers occurred in a different *yuga*, and for all beings 'strength, size, and capacity decrease and rise again', depending on the *yuga* (*balavarṣmaprabhāvā hi prahīyanty udbhavanti ca* ǁ 3.148.7ef, trans. van Buitenen 1975: 504). That is perhaps why Hanūmat is huge (*mahākāyo*, 3.146.59).[7]

[7] The stepped descent through four different *yugas* might make us think about change through the passage of prehistoric time. We might think of something like 'punctuated equilibria', with evolutionary developments made in fits and starts rather than as a linear process (Eldredge and Gould 1972): then the punctuations might be like transitions from one *yuga* to another. What about the dinosaurs, who really lived on this very planet? Dinosaur remains have surely been being discovered and discussed by humans for a very long time, and there could be a connection between megafauna remains and the idea of reduction of creature size through the *yugas*. In an interesting article on *Mahābhārata* geomythology, van der Geer, Dermitzakis, and de Vos (2008) have linked the abundant fossil and bone remains in the Siwalik hills with the *Mahābhārata* tale of the great battle at Kurukṣetra. They say that among those said to have died at Kurukṣetra were 'Tens of thousands of heroes twice the size of ordinary men, with

bhīma uvāca |
yugasaṃkhyāṃ samācakṣva ācāraṃ ca yuge yuge |
dharmakāmārthabhāvāṃś ca varṣma vīryaṃ bhavābhavau ‖ 3.148.9 ‖

Bhīma said:
Tell me the number of *yuga*s and the manner of each of them, the state therein of Law, Profit, and Pleasure, of size, power, existence, and death.
(3.148.9, trans. van Buitenen 1975: 504, adapted)

So Hanūmat describes each of the four *yuga*s in turn, focusing upon the progressive decay of *dharma* and the signs of that decay in each *yuga* (3.148.10–39). Along the way he gives an explanation for why the *kṛtayuga* is so called: because 'At that time, in that best of *yuga*s, things are done, not left to be done' (*kṛtam eva na kartavyaṃ tasmin kāle yugottame* ‖ 3.148.10cd, trans. van Buitenen, adapted; see González-Reimann 1988: 63–64).

3.186–189. This episode is partially translated in Laine 1989: 175–190. Yudhiṣṭhira Pāṇḍava asks the visiting and famously long-lived seer Mārkaṇḍeya about the destruction and re-creation of the universe, since Mārkaṇḍeya is known to survive this (3.186.2–12). In response, Mārkaṇḍeya first briefly enumerates the four *yuga*s, mentioning their durations, the durations of their dawns and dusks, the duration of the *mahāyuga* as a whole, and the number of *mahāyuga*s in a day of Brahmā (3.186.17–23). All the figures are as per the *Manusmṛti* passage.

Then, beginning at 3.186.24, Mārkaṇḍeya gives a detailed description of the conditions that obtain 'then, when little remains, at the end of the *yuga*, at the end of the thousand' (*alpāvaśiṣṭe tu tadā yugānte* ... | *sahasrānte*, 3.186.24). Van Buitenen translates as follows: 'at the end of the Eon ... when little time remains of the last thousand years' (van Buitenen 1975: 586). In adding the word 'years' and running *alpāvaśiṣṭe* together with *sahasrānte*, van Buitenen suggests that this is a reference to the end of the *kaliyuga*. But this is not clear from the verse, since *sahasra* ('thousand') could be the thousand years of the

---

arms as thick as elephant trunks' (p. 81). They effectively argue that 'the legendary hot spots concerning the *Mahābhārata* are tightly woven into the landscape of the Siwalik Hill Range' because 'the entire Siwalik Hill Range constitutes a rich fossil deposit, covering the period from middle Miocene to the latest Pleistocene' (pp. 82, 85). They mention 'local myths about remains of giants and [giant] demons who were destroyed by epic heroes' (p. 85, referring to Mayor 2000). They do not mention the *yuga* cycle, or the location of the Kurukṣetra war within it, or the notion that creatures decrease in size as the *yuga*s succeed each other. But those ideas can make sense of megafauna remains, since those who fought at Kurukṣetra would have been born in the *dvāparayuga*, when, according to some accounts, people would have been twice as big as they are now. The variation in size from *yuga* to *yuga* is also used by Nīlakaṇṭha and Sūrya Paṇḍita to explain divergent accounts of the size of the earth, since the units of measurement are derived from the dimensions of the human being (Minkowski 2000: 33, 36, 38 n. 46).

kaliyuga as per van Buitenen, or it could be the thousand *mahāyugas* that make up a day of Brahmā (see further below).

In the following verses Mārkaṇḍeya often gives a locative. He says he is describing conditions *tasmin kāle* ('at this time', 3.186.25), *gate yuge* ('when the *yuga* is spent', v. 26), and then *kalau yuge* ('in the *kaliyuga*', v. 27). When he says *kalau yuge*, this would tend to indicate that what are being described in this multi-verse passage are the general conditions within the *kaliyuga*, rather than the specific conditions near its end. If this were the case, then van Buitenen's translation 'when little time remains of the last thousand years [i.e. of the *kaliyuga*]' would be a misleading introduction to the passage. But within the passage the *kalau yuge* at v. 27 is the only such locative to specify *yuga* as *kaliyuga*: thereafter we find *pūrvarūpaṃ kṣayasya tat* ('that foretells the end', v. 29), *yugānte* ('at the end of the *yuga*', vv. 33, 34), *yugakṣaye* ('when the *yuga* is waning', vv. 35, 36, 43, 48), and *kṣīṇe yuge* ('when the *yuga* is worn out', v. 54), all of which are ambiguous. I quote some pertinent verses from this passage:

alpāyuṣaḥ svalpabalā alpatejaḥparākramāḥ |
alpadehālpasārāś ca tathā satyālpabhāṣiṇaḥ ‖ 3.186.32 ‖ ...
tathā ca pṛthivīpāla yo bhaved dharmasaṃyutaḥ |
alpāyuḥ sa hi mantavyo na hi dharmo 'sti kaś cana ‖ 45 ‖ ...
alpāyuṣo daridrāś ca dharmiṣṭhā mānavās tadā |
dīrghāyuṣaḥ samṛddhāś ca vidharmāṇo yugakṣaye ‖ 48 ‖ ...
bhavanti ṣoḍaśe varṣe narāḥ palitinas tathā |
āyuḥkṣayo manuṣyāṇāṃ kṣipram eva prapadyate ‖ 53 ‖

People are short-lived, enfeebled, of little vigor and valor, weak-bodied, short on substance, and rarely speaking the truth. ...

The one who observes the Law can be reckoned to live but briefly, for no Law survives then, king.

The Law-minded become short-lived and impoverished, and the lawless long-lived and rich, at the close of the Eon. ...

People turn gray in their sixteenth year, and quickly live out their lives.

(3.186.32, 45, 48, 53, trans. van Buitenen 1975: 587–588, adapted)

After this detailed description of the *yugānta* (3.186.24–55), which is presented in a mixture of the present and future tenses, Mārkaṇḍeya describes what happens at the end of the day of Brahmā, 'when the close of the thousand Eons has come' (*yugasahasrānte saṃprāpte*, 3.186.56ab, trans. van Buitenen). The recurrence of *sahasrānte* suggests, against van Buitenen's interpretation at 3.186.24, that what has been described up to now has been the last portion of the thousandth *mahāyuga*. Now there is terrible environmental destruction. There is drought, and the whole world is attacked by wind and devastating fire, and then by wind and clouds and protracted hard rain, flooding everywhere so that everything is underwater (3.186.56–78).

Mārkaṇḍeya reports what he has himself experienced. He survives beyond this dissolution, into the night of Brahmā, and as a result he has a personal encounter with God (3.186.81–187.48). God in the *Mahābhārata* is, to most intents and purposes, Nārāyaṇa, Viṣṇu-Nārāyaṇa himself; and Mārkaṇḍeya finds him in the form of a child, on a branch of a tree in the waters. Mārkaṇḍeya is invited to enter Nārāyaṇa's small body through the mouth, and within that tardis he explores the whole universe extended, as if in potential form. When he finds no end and throws himself upon Nārāyaṇa's mercy, he is expelled again through the mouth. He pays homage to Nārāyaṇa again, asking him what he is doing and why. And Nārāyaṇa tries to explain himself (3.187.1–47).

After Mārkaṇḍeya has described this encounter, he certifies to Yudhiṣṭhira that Viṣṇu-Nārāyaṇa is in fact Kṛṣṇa Vārṣṇeya, Kṛṣṇa of the Vṛṣṇis (3.187.48–55) – that is, he is the human being Kṛṣṇa Vāsudeva who is present there on this very occasion, having arrived to visit the Pāṇḍavas in the forest shortly before Mārkaṇḍeya himself (3.180).

The Pāṇḍavas and Draupadī pay homage to Kṛṣṇa. Then Yudhiṣṭhira says to Mārkaṇḍeya:

āścaryabhūtaṃ bhavataḥ śrutaṃ no vadatāṃ vara ǀ
mune bhārgava yad vṛttaṃ yugādau prabhavāpyayau ǁ 3.188.4 ǁ
asmin kaliyuge 'py asti punaḥ kautūhalaṃ mama ǀ
samākuleṣu dharmeṣu kiṃ nu śeṣaṃ bhaviṣyati ǁ 5 ǁ
kiṃvīryā mānavās tatra kimāhāravihāriṇaḥ ǀ
kimāyuṣaḥ kiṃvasanā bhaviṣyanti yugakṣaye ǁ 6 ǁ
kāṃ ca kāṣṭhāṃ samāsādya punaḥ saṃpatsyate kṛtam ǀ 7ab

We have heard from you, eloquent Bhārgava seer, about wondrous events at the beginning of the *yuga*, and about the appearance and disappearance. Now, I am curious about the *kaliyuga* too: what will be left when all the Laws are confused? What vigor will people possess, what diets and pleasures will they have, how long will they live, what dress will they wear at the end of the *yuga*? After what end mark will the *kṛtayuga* rise again?

(3.188.4–7b, trans. van Buitenen 1975: 593, adapted)

Before providing a further description of the *yugānta* in response to this question, Mārkaṇḍeya runs quickly through all four *yugas*:

kṛte catuṣpāt sakalo nirvyājopādhivarjitaḥ ǀ
vṛṣaḥ pratiṣṭhito dharmo manuṣyeṣv abhavat purā ǁ 3.188.10 ǁ

adharmapādaviddhas tu tribhir aṃśaiḥ pratiṣṭhitaḥ |
tretāyāṃ dvāpare 'rdhena vyāmiśro dharma ucyate ‖ 11 ‖
tribhir aṃśair adharmas tu lokān ākramya tiṣṭhati |
caturthāṃśena dharmas tu manuṣyān upatiṣṭhati ‖ 12 ‖
āyur vīryam atho buddhir balaṃ tejaś ca pāṇḍava |
manuṣyāṇām anuyugaṃ hrasatīti nibodha me ‖ 13 ‖

Of yore, in the *kṛtayuga*, the Law was potent among people, intact in all its four quarters, without guile and devoid of obstruction. In the *tretāyuga* the Law lost one quarter, but was still established; in the *dvāparayuga* the Law, it is said, was mixed half and half. Now lawlessness has overcome the world, three-quarters rampant, but a quarter of the Law has stayed with people.

Learn this from me: *yuga* after *yuga*, people's lifetime, virility, wisdom, strength, and influence shrink by one-fourth, Pāṇḍava.
(3.188.10–13, trans. van Buitenen 1975: 594, adapted)

There follows another extended description of the *yugānta*, in a mixture of the present and future tenses (3.188.14–84). As with the previous such description, this one has an early indication that it would be about the *kaliyuga* in general, since that is what Yudhiṣṭhira has asked about in 3.188.5. But as with the previous description, apart from this, the indicators are ambiguous. Mārkaṇḍeya uses the locatives *yugānte paryupasthite* ('when the end of the *yuga* has set in', vv. 19, 35, 36, 37, 39, 43, 44, 47, 54, 76, 81, 82, 83), *yugakṣaye* ('when the *yuga* wanes', vv. 20, 21, 22, 23, 25, 33, 41, 78, 85), *yugasyānte* ('at the end of the *yuga*', v. 32), *yugānte* ('at the end of the *yuga*', vv. 49, 53, 73, 79), *saṃprāpte yugasaṃkṣaye* ('when the waning of the *yuga* has set in', v. 55), *yadā ... tadā saṃkṣepsyate yugam* ('when ... then the *yuga* is soon to end', vv. 59, 67, 68), *yugasaṃkṣaye* ('at the waning of the *yuga*', vv. 62, 64), *yuge kṣīṇe tad yugāntasya lakṣaṇam* ('that's the mark of the end of the *yuga*, when the *yuga* is worn out', v. 66), *gate yuge* ('when the *yuga* is spent', v. 69), and *paryākule loke* ('when the world is out of order', v. 72). Again I quote some pertinent verses:

satyaṃ saṃkṣepsyate loke naraiḥ paṇḍitamānibhiḥ |
satyahānyā tatas teṣām āyur alpaṃ bhaviṣyati ‖ 3.188.15 ‖
āyuṣaḥ prakṣayād vidyāṃ na śakṣyanty upaśikṣitum |
vidyāhīnān avijñānāl lobho 'py abhibhaviṣyati ‖ 16 ‖
lobhakrodhaparā mūḍhāḥ kāmasaktāś ca mānavāḥ |
vairabaddhā bhaviṣyanti parasparavadhepsavaḥ ‖ 17 ‖ ...
paramāyuś ca bhavitā tadā varṣāṇi ṣoḍaśa |
tataḥ prāṇān vimokṣyanti yugānte paryupasthite ‖ 47 ‖

> People who think of themselves as learned will abbreviate the truth, others will kill the truth; hence their lifetime will be shortened. Their shorter lives will not allow them to teach knowledge in full, and those who fall short in knowledge will be beset by greed because of their ignorance. A prey to greed and ire, confused, addicted to pleasures, people will be locked in rivalry and wish each other dead. ...
>
> Life will at most last sixteen years, then they will give up the breath, when the end of the *yuga* is at hand.
>
> (3.188.15–17, 47, trans. van Buitenen 1975: 594–595, adapted)

Biardeau quotes parts of this passage and then says: 'It is clear: it really concerns an end of Kaliyuga that leads into a new Kṛtayuga'[8] (Biardeau 1976: 133). This time around, what is being described is not the end of the thousandth *mahāyuga*, since beginning at 3.188.85, and in accordance with Yudhiṣṭhira's question, Mārkaṇḍeya describes the return of the *kṛtayuga*, which is aided by 'a brahmin by the name of Kalkin Viṣṇuyaśas' (*kalkir viṣṇuyaśā nāma dvijaḥ*, 3.188.89ab, trans. van Buitenen, adapted). The stem of this name is sometimes *kalkin*, sometimes *kalki*; for simplicity I have standardised to 'Kalkin' throughout. Kalkin 'will be king, a Turner of the Wheel, triumphant by the Law ... the revolver of the *yuga*' (*sa dharmavijayī rājā cakravartī bhaviṣyati* | ... *yugasya parivartakaḥ*, 3.188.91–92, trans. van Buitenen, adapted). Kalkin will destroy the barbarians, perform the horse sacrifice, and re-establish perfect *dharma*, and it will be *kṛtayuga* again (3.188.85–189.13; on Kalkin's home village see Fleet 1911: 697–698, following the interpolation Hv *481, Vaidya 1969: 231).

Mārkaṇḍeya then closes his account:

> *eṣa dharmaḥ kṛtayuge tretāyāṃ dvāpare tathā* |
> *paścime yugakāle ca yaḥ sa te saṃprakīrtitaḥ* ‖ 3.189.13c–f
> *sarvalokasya viditā yugasaṃkhyā ca pāṇḍava* |
> *etat te sarvam ākhyātam atītānāgataṃ mayā* |
> *vāyuproktam anusmṛtya purāṇam ṛṣisaṃstutam* ‖ 14 ‖
>
> Such is the Law in the *kṛtayuga*, the *tretā*, the *dvāpara*, and the last phase of the *yuga*, which I have proclaimed to you. The numbers of the *yuga* are known to all the world, Pāṇḍava: I have declared to you all that is past and future, as I remember the Lore, lauded by the seers, that was promulgated by the Wind God.
>
> (3.189.13c–14, trans. van Buitenen 1975: 598, adapted)

6.11. In this passage, which is set just before the Kurukṣetra war, King Dhṛtarāṣṭra, the Pāṇḍavas' blind uncle, asks his aide Saṃjaya to tell him 'about the duration of life, and about the good and bad rewards in this land of the

[8] 'C'est clair: il s'agit bien d'une fin de Kaliyuga qui débouche sur un nouveau Kṛtayuga'

Bhāratas ... the future, the past, and the present' (*bhāratasyāsya varṣasya ... | pramāṇam āyuṣaḥ ... phalaṃ cāpi śubhāśubham || anāgatam atikrāntaṃ vartamānaṃ ca*, 6.11.1–2b, trans. González-Reimann 2002: 211; the word *varṣa*, here 'land', also means 'year'). Saṃjaya lists the *yugas*, and specifies the order in which they come. He does not specify their durations, nor does he mention their dawns and dusks. He specifies the length of lifespan in each of them, and the type of people who live in them (6.11.3–14).

Saṃjaya's account departs from the lifespan details given in the *Manusmṛti* and elsewhere in the *Mahābhārata*. According to Saṃjaya:

> *catvāri ca sahasrāṇi varṣāṇāṃ kurusattama* |
> *āyuḥsaṃkhyā kṛtayuge saṃkhyātā rājasattama* || 6.11.5 ||
> *tathā trīṇi sahasrāṇi tretāyāṃ manujādhipa* |
> *dvisahasraṃ dvāpare tu śate tiṣṭhati saṃprati* || 6 ||
>
> Truest of Kurus, truest of kings, leader of the people. Four thousand years is counted as the duration of life in the *kṛtayuga*, then it is three thousand in the *tretā*, two thousand in the *dvāpara*, and one hundred at the present time.
>
> (6.11.5–6)

Saṃjaya also says in the next line that lifespan has no fixed length in the last *yuga*. This latter detail presumably means that premature death is more common in the *kaliyuga*. But Saṃjaya's lifespan figures for the first three *yugas* are aberrant by a factor of ten (González-Reimann 1989: 201 n. 22; González-Reimann 2002: 213 n. 1). Only the M1 manuscript has lifespan in these *yugas* reckoned in hundreds instead of thousands of years here (M1 has *śatāny eva* instead of *sahasrāṇi* at 6.11.5a and 6a, and *dve śate vai* instead of *dvisahasraṃ* at 6.11.6c; Belvalkar 1947: 60). By reckoning lifespan in thousands of years for the first three *yugas*, Saṃjaya gives the numbers that are elsewhere given for duration of *yuga*, but he himself gives no numbers for duration of *yuga*. Saṃjaya's four *yugas* could all be of the same duration; or it is as if he partially mixes up lifespan with duration of *yuga*.

In his account of the inhabitants of the *yugas*, Saṃjaya places powerful sages (*munayo*) in the *kṛta*, powerful *kṣatriyas* in the *tretā*, powerful people of all classes (*sarvavarṇā*) in the *dvāpara*, and weak, miserable people in the *kali* (6.11.8–14). These details reflect the standard idea that *dharma* decays through the *yugas*, since by implication the higher the class, the better the *dharma*.

Finally, Saṃjaya notes that 'The land of Himavat surpasses Bhārata-varṣa in virtues, and Hari-varṣa is superior even to that land' (*guṇottaraṃ haimavataṃ harivarṣaṃ tataḥ param* || 6.11.14cd, trans. Cherniak 2008: 85). This comment is in keeping with Dhṛtarāṣṭra's specific question, which asked about those two other lands too. All three were previously mentioned together at 6.7.6; by implication, the land of the Bhāratas is **our** world (indeed, according to

Viṣṇupurāṇa 2.3.19, the land of the Bhāratas is the only place where the *yuga* cycle operates; Gombrich 1975: 132). Saṃjaya's account of the *yugas* in Mbh 6 is nested within a geographical scheme which it resembles: the four *yugas* are graded into an order just as the three lands are. Slippage between geographical and temporal aspects is also evident elsewhere, when Lomaśa says, in connection with the prospect of the Pāṇḍavas bathing in it (*avatīrya*), that the River Narmadā is the junction between the *tretā* and the *dvāpara* (*saṃdhir eṣa naraśreṣṭha tretāyā dvāparasya ca* | 3.121.19ab).

12.200. This and the next several passages occur within the extensive teachings that are provided to the victorious King Yudhiṣṭhira by Bhīṣma, the mortally wounded family patriarch, after the Kurukṣetra war (12.56–13.151). More specifically, these passages are found within the *Mokṣadharmaparvan* (12.168–353), where Bhīṣma's general topic is salvation. In Mbh 12.200 Yudhiṣṭhira asks about Viṣṇu, and, introducing his reply, Bhīṣma says that he knows what he knows about this subject from Rāma Jāmadagnya, Nārada, and Vyāsa, and that Asita Devala, Vālmīki, and Mārkaṇḍeya have also discoursed about it.

The chapter focuses largely upon the process of creation. After the four classes (*varṇas*) have been created from the four body-parts of Viṣṇu (in the manner of *Ṛgveda* 10.90), Bhīṣma says:

> *yāvad yāvad abhūc chraddhā dehaṃ dhārayituṃ nṛṇām* |
> *tāvat tāvad ajīvaṃs te nāsīd yamakṛtaṃ bhayam* ‖ 12.200.34 ‖
>
> So long as men believed they could hold on to their bodies, they lived: there was no fear of Yama [Death] back then.
>
> (12.200.34, trans. Wynne 2009: 301)

He then says that at that time, and in the *tretāyuga*, children were produced just by wishing for them (*saṃkalpāt*, vv. 35c, 36b); that sex (*maithuno dharmaḥ*) originated in the *dvāparayuga*; and that coupledom (*dvaṃdvam*) is a feature of the *kaliyuga* (vv. 35–37).

Bhīṣma then speaks about miscreants (*pāpakṛtas*, v. 41a). He lists various ethnic groups of undesirables, and says they arose only in the *tretāyuga* (v. 42).

> *tatas tasmin mahāghore saṃdhyākāle yugāntike* |
> *rājānaḥ samasajjanta samāsādyetaretaram* ‖ 12.200.43 ‖
>
> Then, in that terrible twilight period at the end of the *yuga*, the kings assailed each other and made battle.
>
> (12.200.43)

Both Ganguli and Wynne here gloss *saṃdhyākāle* ('twilight period') as the *tretā–dvāparayuga* transition, presumably because the *tretāyuga* was mentioned in the previous verse (Ganguli 1970: Santi Parva CCVII, 83–84; Wynne 2009:

303). But the description of combat between kings does not fit that juncture, and it seems that this verse instead refers to the recently concluded Kurukṣetra war, and thus to the *dvāpara–kaliyuga* transition.

12.224. This chapter begins with a question from Yudhiṣṭhira about the *yugas*:

> *ādyantaṃ sarvabhūtānāṃ śrotum icchāmi kaurava* |
> *dhyānaṃ karma ca kālaṃ ca tathaivāyur yuge yuge* || 12.224.1 ||
>
> Kaurava, I would like to hear about the start and finish of all beings, and about meditation, activity, time, and lifespan in each of the *yugas*. (12.224.1)

In answer, Bhīṣma relays to Yudhiṣṭhira a conversation between Vyāsa and his son Śuka (12.224–247). Near the beginning of this conversation, Vyāsa tells Śuka about the four *yugas*, and there is considerable verbatim overlap between his account and the *Manusmṛti* account quoted above (Gombrich 1975: 120–122; for a detailed comparison, see Bühler 1886: lxxxiii–xc). Vyāsa states the names of the four *yugas*, their durations, and the durations of their dawns and dusks (12.224.18–20).

Vyāsa specifies the duration of lifespan in each *yuga*, describes how *dharma* decreases in the same proportion, specifies what the supreme virtue is in each successive *yuga* (*tapas* - *jñāna* - *yajña* - *dāna*, i.e. asceticism - knowledge - sacrifice - charity, 12.224.27, as per Ms 1.86 above), and says that there are a thousand cycles in each day of Brahmā, with Brahmā's night being the same length (12.224.22–30). The theme of the decrease of *dharma* through the *yugas*, and the consequent change in appropriate forms of religiosity, is reprised briefly later in the chapter (12.224.62–69; sacrifice originated in the *tretāyuga*, v. 62). In these latter verses, Vyāsa mentions that the dharmic decline from one *yuga* to another is a consequence of the decrease in lifespan (*saṃrodhād āyuṣas tv ete vyasyante dvāpare yuge* | 12.224.65cd).

12.230. Later in the same conversation, Vyāsa revisits the topic of the *yugas* (12.230.7–18). The theme here is the different capacities of people of different *yugas* and the consequent status of Veda, *tapas*, and *dharma*, with particular focus on the ideal scenario of the *kṛtayuga*. Repeating verbatim the line that he spoke at 12.224.65cd, Vyāsa mentions again that the dharmic decline from one *yuga* to another is a consequence of the decrease in lifespan (*saṃrodhād āyuṣas tv ete vyasyante dvāpare yuge* | 12.230.14cd).

12.327. This passage is in the *Nārāyaṇīya* section of the *Mokṣadharmaparvan* (Mbh 12.321–339). Janamejaya has interrupted Vaiśaṃpāyana's account of what Bhīṣma taught Yudhiṣṭhira, and has asked Vaiśaṃpāyana 'how it is that the same blessed Nārāyaṇa who favours disengagement [*nivṛtti*] has also established engagement [*pravṛtti*]' (Smith 2009: 662, de-italicised; on *pravṛtti* and *nivṛtti* see Bailey 1985). In his response, Vaiśaṃpāyana relates what Vyāsa once told his disciples (including Śuka and Vaiśaṃpāyana himself). After the creation of the universe, Nārāyaṇa instructed two groups of seers to concentrate on *pravṛtti* and *nivṛtti*, respectively. As he instructed the gods and seers, he told them that the *kṛtayuga* would be followed by the *tretā*, *dvāpara*, and *kali yugas*, with *dharma* decreasing by a quarter each time, but that *dharma* would always survive somewhere (12.327.73–78).

Hv 117. There are no systematic accounts of the *yugas* in the *Harivaṃśa*, although in the closing *Bhaviṣyaparvan*, while Vyāsa is in conversation with Janamejaya after the end of the latter's snake sacrifice, he provides an extended description of the *yugānta* (Hv 116–117). This description largely resembles the two descriptions previously given by Mārkaṇḍeya in Mbh 3. Among other things, Vyāsa says that lifespan at the *yugānta* is thirty years at the most (Hv 117.38). Vyāsa's description resembles most particularly the second of Mārkaṇḍeya's *yugānta* descriptions (3.188–189), in that it ends with a description of the transition from the end of the *kaliyuga* to the beginning of the following *kṛtayuga*. But it differs from that description in that it envisages the *kṛtayuga* coming about without the intervention of Kalkin. We shall discuss this passage in some detail in Chapter 6.

The complex variable

The various passages surveyed above present roughly the same picture of the *yuga* cycle. But they contain differing lists of exactly which parameters constitute the complex variable that decreases from *yuga* to *yuga* in the 4 : 3 : 2 : 1 ratio. The basic parameters are *dharma*, lifespan (*āyus*), and duration of *yuga*. The various passages additionally indicate the following parameters: *satya* 'truth', and general health and efficacy (*arogāḥ sarvasiddhārthāś*, Ms 1.81–83); *śakti* 'vigor' (Mbh 1.57.72, trans. van Buitenen 1973: 134); *bala* 'strength', *varṣman* 'size', and *prabhāva* 'capacity' (3.148.7, trans. van Buitenen 1975: 504); *bala* 'strength', *tejas* 'ardour', *parākrama* 'energy', *deha* 'body', *sāra* 'firmness', and *satya* 'truth(fulness)' (3.186.32, trans. Eltschinger 2012: 38); *vīrya* 'virility', *buddhi* 'wisdom', *bala* 'strength', and *tejas* 'influence' (3.188.13, trans. van Buitenen 1975: 594; see also 3.188.31); and 'good and bad rewards' (*phalaṃ cāpi śubhāśubham*, 6.11.1d, trans. González-Reimann 2002: 211). Some additional parameters are mentioned in questions but are not necessarily confirmed by the responses that follow, as if the questioner is extrapolating, rightly or wrongly, from what has already been said: Bhīma asks how the *yugas* affect 'Law, Profit, and Pleasure ... size, power, existence, and death' (*dharmakāmārthabhāvāṃś ca varṣma vīryaṃ bhavābhavau* ‖ 3.148.9cd, trans. van Buitenen 1975: 504); and Yudhiṣṭhira asks how the *kaliyuga* affects 'vigor ... diets and pleasures ... [and] dress' (*kiṃvīryā mānavās tatra kimāhāravihāriṇaḥ* ǀ *kimāyuṣaḥ kiṃvasanā bhaviṣyanti yugakṣaye* ‖ 3.188.6, trans. van Buitenen 1975: 593), and how 'meditation, activity, and time' vary from *yuga* to *yuga* (*dhyānaṃ karma ca kālaṃ ca*, 12.224.1c). These various parameters are usually mentioned as if their effects are upon human mortals, but at 3.148.7 Hanūmat says that 'Earth, rivers, trees, and mountains, Siddhas, Gods, and great seers adjust to time from *yuga* to *yuga*, as do the creatures' (*bhūmir nadyo nagāḥ śailāḥ siddhā devā maharṣayaḥ* | *kālaṃ samanuvartante yathā bhāvā yuge yuge* | 3.148.7a–d, trans. van Buitenen 1975: 504, adapted).

I have spoken of 'parameters', as if these are continuous variables such as mass, volume, extension, and so on – as if they are primarily quantitative, and so would submit easily to arithmetical reduction. But the repeated questioning suggests a narrative genre whereby an arithmetical reduction in a particular aspect of operations is presented in qualitative terms, so that four levels or four segments of the range are generalised as four types. This is something like the basic theory of *varṇa* and *dharma* (Smith 1994: 26–57, 201 n. 31). It is also something like what happens when the continuously variable frequency of visible light is neurolinguistically resolved into a limited selection of colour words whose basic meanings are absolute. Concepts of colour do not invoke any relative positions on a scale, but in the general case of *dharma* quantitative and qualitative measures stand parallel, with 4, 3, 2, and 1 reading off as *tapas*, *jñāna*, *yajña*, and *dāna* respectively.

What is the relation between lifespan and *dharma*? In the line that Vyāsa speaks twice to Śuka, the decline of the Vedas, sacrifices, *varṇa*s, and *āśrama*s from the *tretāyuga* to the *dvāpara* is presented as a simple consequence of the decrease in lifespan (*saṃrodhād āyuṣas tv ete vyasyante dvāpare yuge* ‖ 12.224.65cd and 230.14cd). Taking these four as a bundle of *dharma*, it is perhaps appreciable that longevity would favour general propriety, on the grounds that through learning and memory, age could help to confer wisdom (for the importance of memory, see the story of the seven brothers at Hv 14–19). People might be less wise if they have less time to become wise in, and if they are supervised by elders who are younger (and so less wise). From this perspective, any reduction of lifespan would reduce *dharma*, and that would be why humans are less dharmic than gods in the first place.[9]

A causal relationship in the opposite direction is indicated at Hv 41.16, where, since human beings are behaving so very dharmically, they do not fear Death, and so there is an overpopulation problem. Here it is as if by being dharmic one can stave off death, as if by karmic fruition within one lifetime.

Mārkaṇḍeya too mentions the relation between lifespan and *dharma*, in these verses already quoted above, which could be a comment on the *yuga* cycle in general:

> People who think of themselves as learned will abbreviate the truth, others will kill the truth; hence their lifetime will be shortened. Their

---

[9] This perspective can also help us to appreciate why the *kṛtayuga* and the other *yuga*s would have dawns (on which see below), during which *dharma* could, as it were, catch up (or down) with the shift in lifespan.

> shorter lives will not allow them to teach knowledge in full, and those who fall short in knowledge will be beset by greed because of their ignorance. A prey to greed and ire, confused, addicted to pleasures, men will be locked in rivalry and wish each other dead.
>
> (3.188.15–17, trans. van Buitenen 1975: 594)

At first this account is as per the *Harivaṃśa* passage (on which more in Chapter 5): the change in truthfulness causes the change in lifespan. But in the next verse, shortened lifespan means less time to conquer desire and anger, which is as per our interpretation of Vyāsa's version above. So Mārkaṇḍeya indicates that a change in *dharma* causes a change in lifespan, and also that a change in lifespan causes a change in *dharma*.

The role given to truth here is consonant with the alternative name of the *kṛtayuga* as the *satyayuga*, and also with the *Mahābhārata*'s five identifications of truth as the highest *dharma* (Hiltebeitel 2001: 207–208, incl. n. 80 for the references, and p. 211). But the role of desire and anger (here *lobhakrodha*, van Buitenen's 'greed and ire') is also significant. In the *Bhagavadgītā* Kṛṣṇa describes desire and anger as the basic enemies (Bhg 3.36–43), and in the myth of the origin of Death (Mbh 12.248–250) they are linked with death. To help her do her job, Brahmā tells Death that her tears will become diseases, and that she will also use desire and anger: 'Therefore welcome desire; join together and destroy creatures here' (*tasmāt kāmaṃ rocayābhyāgataṃ tvaṃ saṃyojyātho saṃharasveha jantūn* ‖ 12.250.35cd, trans. Doniger O'Flaherty 1994: 42, adjusted). And so Death 'began to destroy the life's breath of creatures that breathe, at the time of their end, bewildering them with desire and anger' (*atho prāṇān prāṇināṃ antakāle kāmakrodhau prāpya nirmohya hanti* ‖ 12.250.36cd, trans. Doniger). Here I think it is not that desire and anger feature most particularly at the end of life, but that their existence is somehow tantamount to the proximity of death. When the people living in the *kaliyuga* are described as being 'prey to greed and ire, confused, addicted to pleasures ... locked in rivalry and wish[ing] each other dead' (3.188.17, quoted above), we should not think, by analogy with the *mahāyuga*, that people would become less dharmic as they get older. Rather, our vulnerability to desire and anger is somehow constitutive of our mortality, in the same way that our vulnerability to disease is.

The apparent mutual causation between levels of lifespan and *dharma* is not very well theorised, but it certainly emphasises the complexity of the complex variable. Perhaps similar relations might be imagined linking each of the various other parameters quasi-causally with each other in both directions. The idea of causality is strained here, because it would imply that the parameters are separate, but they are not. They are aspects of the same single variable.

The frequent mentions of the brevity of life in the *kaliyuga* are part and parcel of the idea of human depravity. Despite some friction between the accounts of how exactly lifespan and *dharma* are connected, their correlation with each other is probably easier to understand than their correlation with *yuga* duration, and with 'strength, size, and capacity', and so on (*balavarṣmaprabhāvā hi*, 3.148.7e, trans. van Buitenen 1975: 504).

The structure of the cycle

In the Hv 117 passage Vyāsa presents an analogy between the *mahāyuga* and the moon, starting off full but progressively losing its lustre:

> *sādhuvṛttiḥ kṛtayuge kaṣāye hānir ucyate* |
> *eka eva tu kālaḥ sa hīnavarṇo yathā śaśī* ‖ Hv 117.45 ‖
> *channo hi tamasā somo yathā kaliyuge tathā* |
> *pūrṇaś ca tapasā hīno yathā kṛtayuge*[10] *tathā* ‖ 46 ‖

> They say that there is good behaviour in the *kṛtayuga* and ruin in the ochre [i.e. *kaliyuga*], but that time itself is always the same. It just loses its lustre, like the moon does. In the *kaliyuga* it is as if the moon is hidden by darkness. In the *kṛtayuga* it is as if the moon is full, but without burning heat.
>
> (*Harivaṃśa* 117.45–46)[11]

This analogy is nice poetry, and it is effective. But if we push the metaphor we will find it significantly imperfect in terms of time-scale, because the lunar process is continuous rather than proceeding in stages, and because it reverses at the same rate. The lunar cycle is in fact more akin to the succession of days and nights of Brahmā, where the day would be when the moon is more than half full, and the night would be when it is less than half full. We shall return to the *Harivaṃśa*'s analogy between moon and *mahāyuga* in due course below, after first exploring some other analogies à propos the moon, with some graphs.

The lunar cycle is like the diurnal cycle (at the equinox) and the annual solar cycle (at any place apart from the equator) in being proportional in both directions: that is, it splits, as it were naturally, into four sections of equal size. If the diurnal cycle is forenoon, afternoon, and double-night, then the lunar cycle is waxing gibbous, waning gibbous, waning crescent, and waxing crescent, and the annual cycle is spring equinox to summer solstice, summer solstice to autumn equinox, autumn equinox to winter solstice, and winter solstice to spring equinox. For the year judged as a 360-day cycle in four parts, see for example *Ṛgveda* 1.155.6 (Parpola 1975–1976: 372). These three natural functions – day, lunar month, and year – are in the sine-wave pattern: see Figure 3 (two cycles). The peaks in Figure 3 are full moon, high noon, and summer

---

10 Here at Hv 117.46d Vaidya has *kaliyuge* (as in *pāda* b), as does Dandekar (1971–1976, vol. 5: 221), but this must be a typographical error, because as *pāda* d variants the apparatus lists *kaliyuge* and '*kṛtayugaṃ* (for °*yuge*)' (Vaidya 1969: 777). I have emended *kaliyuge* to *kṛtayuge*.

11 All *Harivaṃśa* translations are adapted from Brodbeck 2019b.

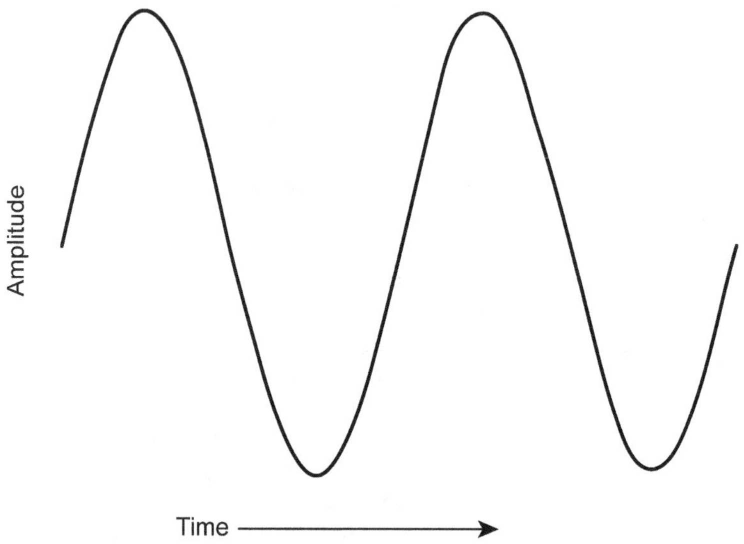

Figure 3: The Diurnal, Lunar, and Annual Cycles (Sine Wave).

solstice; the troughs are new moon, midnight, and winter solstice. In these cycles the amplitude is continuously variable.

In the cycle of days and nights of Brahmā, the analogue form is digitised. The *mahāyugas* near the start of a day of Brahmā seem to be qualitatively identical to the ones midway through a day of Brahmā (none is more intense than another), and likewise things are identical at every point during the night of Brahmā (nothing is happening in equal measure). It is as if Brahmā's days and nights were just on and off, like a light that is switched full on for twelve hours and full off again for twelve hours, as per Figure 4 (two cycles). The *mahāyuga* cycle, however, is more like Figure 5 (two cycles; Figure 5 represents only the main body of each *yuga*, omitting the dawns and dusks).

Returning to the analogy at Hv 117.45–46: if the *kṛtayuga* were the full moon and the *kaliyuga* were the new (dark) moon, then the *mahāyuga* cycle would be as if the moon was full for four times as long as it was new, and as if it changed from full to new with just two intermediate steps, and then changed back to full again with **no** intermediate steps. And although the idea of full moon fits the plenitude of *dharma* in the *kṛtayuga*, at the other extremity the idea that 'the moon is hidden by darkness' (Hv 117.46) does not quite fit, because in the *kaliyuga* there is still some *dharma* (as Nārāyaṇa points out in Mbh 12.327).

My intention in interrogating the lunar metaphor to this extent is not to criticise it, but to show that the *mahāyuga* cycle is strange, because in significant ways it does not reflect the available natural cyclic models. This is in contrast

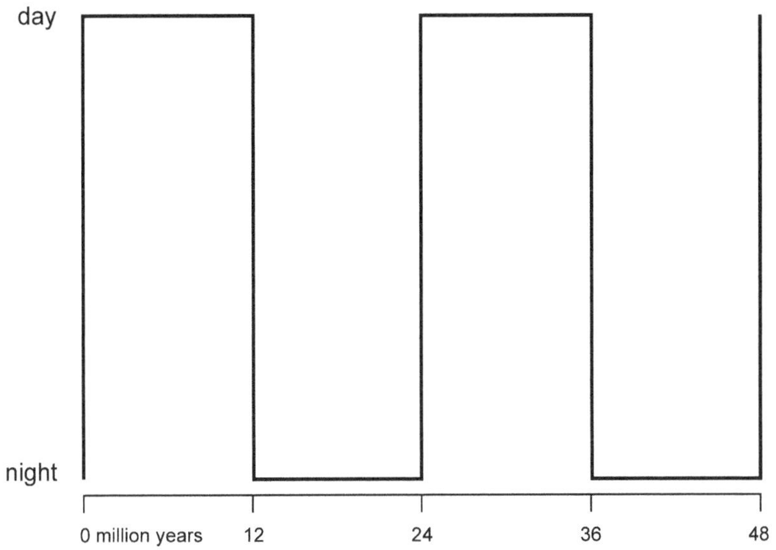

Figure 4: The Days and Nights of Brahmā.

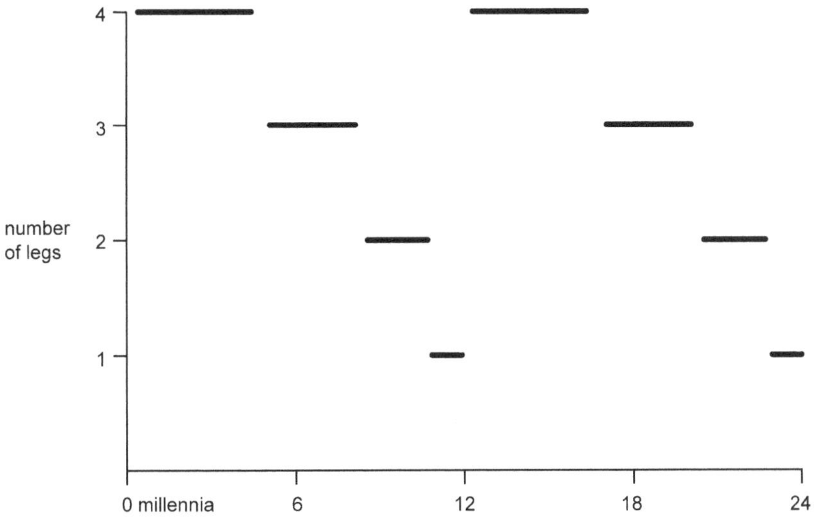

Figure 5: The Four *Yugas*.

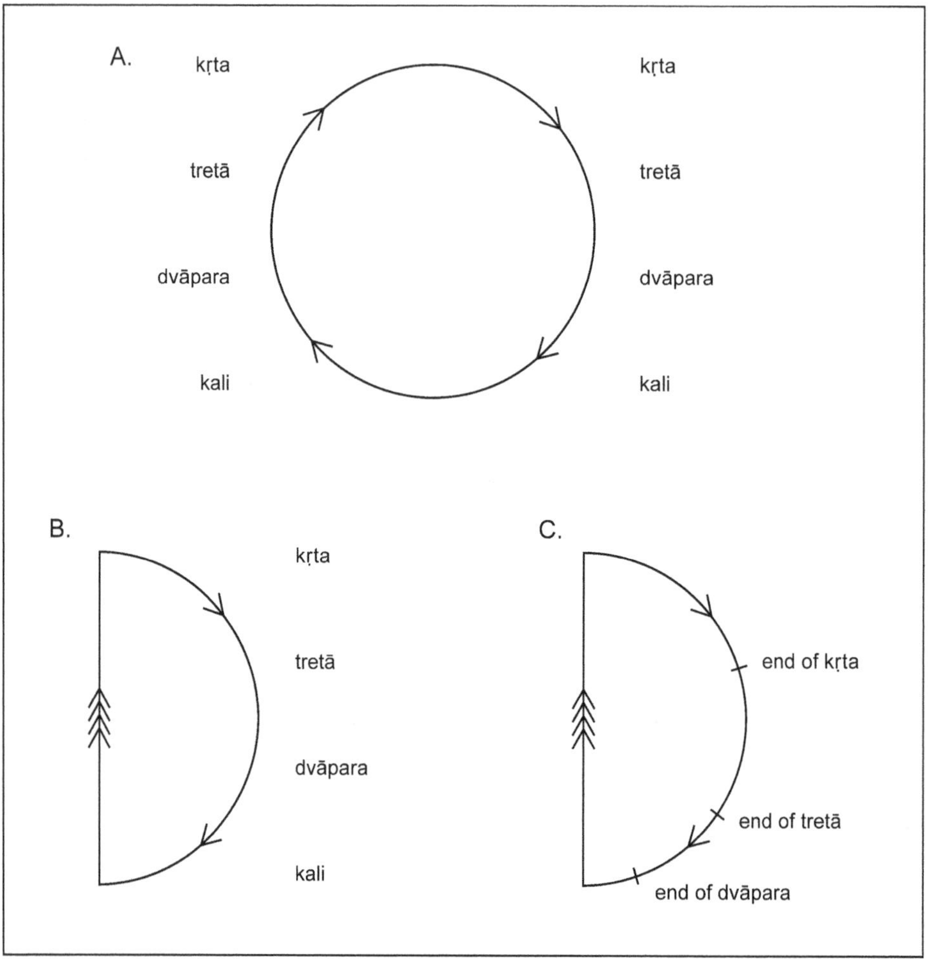

Figure 6: The Elision of the Upstroke and the Acceleration of the Downstroke.

to Jain and Buddhist schemes of graded temporal cyclicity (González-Reimann 1988: 113–116; González-Reimann 2002: 198 n. 98). In the Jain system, the cycle is divided into ascending and descending halves (*utsarpiṇī* and *avasarpiṇī*; Dundas 2002: 20; compare *Āryabhaṭṭīya* 3.9). The Buddhist system incorporates the names of the four Hindu *yuga*s, and has *yuga*s occurring from *kali* in steps up to *kṛta* and then back down again, with lifespan and *dharma* increasing and then decreasing from *yuga* to *yuga*, before repeating (Jacobi 1908: 202 col. 1; Gombrich 1975: 137).

The Hindu *yuga* cycle differs from the natural model in accelerating the downstroke, and in eliding the upstroke. In this it has no astronomical analogue.

The elision of the upstroke is nicely presented in González-Reimann's diagrams (1988: 112–113), adapted here as Figures 6A and 6B. Figure 6A represents the expected picture as per the sine-wave and the Jain and Buddhist systems, and Figure 6B elides the upstroke, with *kṛtayuga* following immediately after *kaliyuga*. The acceleration of the downstroke is not reflected in Figure 6B, which shows each *yuga* with the same duration. In Figure 6C, however, as per the Hindu system, the ends of the *kṛta*, *tretā*, and *dvāpara yuga*s are indicated at points that are respectively four-tenths, seven-tenths, and nine-tenths of the way along the descending arc.

(The downstroke is not **really** accelerated, since in Figure 6C the speed of travel along the semicircular arc is constant, only increasing, effectively to infinity, in the straight section between the bottom of the arc and the top. If the downstroke were really accelerating, then the distance along the arc occupied by each *yuga* would be constant – as in Figure 6B – but the speed of travel would increase at the ends of the *kṛta*, *tretā*, and *dvāpara yuga*s. This would be as if each *yuga* were to last the same number of years, but time were to go faster in each subsequent *yuga*, and then slower again for the next *kṛtayuga*. But that is not how it works.)

Why the Hindu *yuga* system would diverge from the natural model in these ways is a complicated question to which there is probably no single answer. One factor is the influence of the ancient Indian game of dice and the names of the various throws.

> We do not know for sure how the game was played; it is even possible that in time the rules may have changed or that the ritual game may have been different from the popular one. But, if many details are obscure, it seems clear that the 4-3-2-1 sequence was an integral part of the game (MacDonell and Keith, 1912, vol. 1, pp. 3–4). The number four was related to Kṛta, three to Tretā, two to Dvāpara, and one to Kali. Of these, Kṛta was the winning throw and it was followed by the others in descending order down to Kali, the worst throw of all.
>
> (González-Reimann 1989: 196)

González-Reimann points out that this connection helps to explain why the second *yuga* would have a name that is related to the word for 'three', and the third *yuga* would have a name that is related to the word for 'two' (ibid.). The image of the leggèd bull also helps here, since the bull is on three legs in the second *yuga* and on two legs in the third.

Another possible factor is provided by etymology. Parpola proposes that the bovine image is connected to the notion of a four-part time-cycle through the etymology of the Sanskrit word for 'time', *kāla* (which occurs in the *Ṛgveda* only once, at 10.42.9). In contrast to scholars who have attempted to derive this word from an Indo-European root, Parpola argues that it is of Dravidian origin and that it derives from the word *kāl*. The primary meaning of this Dravidian word is 'leg' or 'foot', but by extension, through the analogy of the bovine quadruped, it also means 'quarter', and it is thus particularly applicable to fourfold entities – of which time, as naturally presented through the cycles discussed above, is a salient example (Parpola 1975–1976). Thus, in Parpola's view, the image of the quadruped in connection with the *yugas* (Ms 1.81–82; Mbh 3.188.10; 12.224.22; 12.327.73) is a play on the original identity of the word for 'time' (or 'season' as a **part** of time) and the word for 'leg' (Parpola 1975–1976: 375–376). In connection with this etymological argument, Parpola also suggests that the myth of the four *yugas* goes back, in germinal form, to pre-Vedic times, as a development of the fourfold conception of the year (pp. 376–378). If Parpola's etymology is correct, then it might constitute a strong encouragement for any temporal cycle to be envisaged in four sections, even if the ascending half of the normal cycle-type is elided.

Different etymological suggestions have been made by Przyluski, linking the Sanskrit word *kāla* – which has two mature senses, 'black' or 'dark', and 'time' or by implication 'death' – with the names Kālī, Kalkin, Kālika, Mahākāla, and Mahākālī, and with the words *kalka* ('impurity'), *kaluṣa* ('dirty'), and *kali* ('misfortune', which functions also as the name of a dice throw and a *yuga*), and with the dark (i.e. waning) fortnight or the latter part of a temporal cycle (Przyluski 1938). Przyluski's speculations have in common with Parpola's that they involve the Sanskrit word being derived from a Dravidian word, though in Przyluski's case the root is *kār*, not *kāl*. Although some etymological arguments should probably be taken with a pinch of salt, the constellation of concepts explored by Parpola and Przyluski is very suggestive in terms of the various features of the *yuga* system.

With some uncontroversial recourse to etymology (*yuga*, like *yoga*, is from the Sanskrit root *yuj*, to yoke), González-Reimann traces Vedic usages of the word *yuga* (González-Reimann 1988: 55–59). Its earliest stable usage seems to be as a (human) 'generation'. In the Brāhmaṇas there is a tendency for it to refer to a period of five years, but there are diverse other specific usages, in these and other texts (Kloetzli 2013: 646–647).

Neither the possible etymological connections of the word *kāla* nor the Vedic connections of the word *yuga* really helps us to understand why the downstroke would be accelerated. The downstroke is accelerated in the *yuga* cycle because the four *yugas* are of steadily decreasing durations. In Āryabhaṭṭa's astronomical system (Āryabhaṭṭa lived in the fifth and sixth centuries CE), the four *yugas* are of equal lengths (Mankad 1941–1942: 215–216; Shukla and Sarma 1976: xxxi; González-Reimann 1988: 106; Plofker 2009: 70–71).

Though it is somewhat artificial, the analogy between the *mahāyuga* and the bull standing on its varying number of legs fits the *mahāyuga* better than the sine-wave analogy does. Although it may be hard to envisage a bull standing on just one leg, certainly if a bull **were** to stand on just one leg, he would not wish to hold the position for long; so this analogy nicely brings out the discomfort of the latter phases in the cycle. Thus, to understand the acceleration of the downstroke, the bovine image helps. But then perhaps this image seems to accelerate the downstroke too fast. The *kaliyuga* is one-tenth of the duration of the *mahāyuga*, but a bull could not stand on one leg for one-tenth of the time. Again, my purpose here is not to criticise the analogy, but to explore which aspects of the *yuga* cycle it helps (and does not help) us to understand.

A possible correlate of the accelerating downstroke – the decreasing durations of successive *yuga*s within one *mahāyuga* – can be extrapolated from the connection with dicing and gambling. In the dice game, the four *yuga* names are names of throws. One wants to throw a *kṛta*. One does not want to throw a *kali*. Chance is involved, so perhaps throwing a *kali* is not avoidable altogether. But it is a place that one would wish to be in rarely, and not for long. And the way gambling works is often such that you **cannot** stay there for long. There are amazing comebacks, but the basic pattern is that soon you simply lose. If you cannot afford your opponents' raise but they can afford yours, then the playing field is not level. This is, in a way, the basis of capitalism. As Jesus said, 'Whoever does not have, even what they have will be taken from them' (ὃς οὐκ ἔχει, καὶ ὃ ἔχει ἀρθήσεται ἀπ' αὐτοῦ, *Gospel According to Mark* 4.25; par. *Gospel According to Matthew* 13.12).[12]

The twilight periods

In the four-*yuga* cycle, each *yuga* includes a twilight period at its beginning and end – a dawn (*saṃdhyā*) and a dusk (*saṃdhyāṃśa*). Strictly speaking, the Sanskrit terms *saṃdhyā* and *saṃdhyāṃśa* do not mean 'dawn' and 'dusk', they

[12] I have often tried to find natural models that could fit the structure of the *mahāyuga* cycle. Here I mention just two – not as suggested inspirations for the cycle, but simply as points of possible interest.

The first model is the human menstrual cycle, which is approximately the same length as the lunar cycle (Knight 1995). Male householders are instructed to have sex with their wives according to the menstrual cycle, beginning after the woman has bathed at the end of her period (Ms 3.45–47 and Olivelle 2006: 257). At this point, fertility – and, for dutiful couples, sexual activity – is high. But towards the other end of the cycle, there is pre-menstrual tension; then there is the bleeding, the bath, and the restart (Slaje 1995). In this analogy, the bleeding period, during which sex is prohibited (Ms 4.40–42; *Gautama Dharmasūtra* 23.32–34; 24.4–5; *Vāsiṣṭha Dharmasūtra* 12.5), would correspond to the *kaliyuga*. The *kaliyuga* is one-tenth of the *mahāyuga*'s duration, whereas the bleeding period is of variable length; but the Dharmaśāstra regulations pertaining to the bleeding period last for just three days, regardless of whether bleeding continues thereafter (Leslie 1996: 92–93, 98–102). The analogy with the menstrual cycle facilitates a focus on the *dvāpara–kaliyuga* transition, which brings with it the knowledge of non-pregnancy and another cycle to come.

The second model is the human lifetime. One of the earliest Vedic meanings of the word *yuga* was 'generation' (González-Reimann 1988: 55–59), and Jacobi sees the four *yuga*s as 'analogous to the four ages of man, viz. childhood, youth, adult life, and old age' (Jacobi 1908: 201 col. 2). On this model death is the end of the cycle, and the idea of reincarnation supplies another *mahāyuga* to follow (beginning again from age zero, with the upstroke elided). The acceleration of the downstroke – the earlier *yuga*s being longer than the later ones – can here be explained phenomenologically: as one gets older, time seems to speed up (as described by Pink Floyd in 'Time'; see also Adams 2021). We might wish to adjust Jacobi's scheme and begin with conception instead of birth; then the *yuga*s would be the unborn state (birth would occur at the end of the *kṛtayuga* in response to a situation that cannot continue), childhood, adulthood, and old age.

mean 'junction' and 'junction portion'; but the diurnal metaphor is very close by, because *saṃdhyā* also means 'twilight' (Fleet 1911: 481 n. 1). The dawn and dusk of a *yuga* are of equal duration, proportional to the duration of the *yuga*. So, for example, the transition (*saṃdhi*) from a *kṛta* to a *tretāyuga* consists of the dusk of the *kṛta*, followed by the dawn of the *tretā*. Thus although the dawn and dusk of any particular *yuga* are of the same duration, in any particular transition between *yuga*s the dusk of one *yuga* and the dawn of the next will be of differing durations, because every *yuga* has its own duration. The transition takes place in two unequal phases.

Although this is nowhere stated in the *Mahābhārata*'s accounts of the dawns and dusks, the double-twilight period at the transition between *yuga*s could potentially mean that the change of level (of *dharma*, lifespan, etc.) from one setting to another would not occur suddenly, but would be smoothed out. At descending transitions, the dusk of the outgoing *yuga* would then see the level falling lower than during the main body of that *yuga*, and the dawn of the incoming *yuga* would, as it were, receive the baton at a level higher than that of the main body of **that** *yuga*.

Because every *yuga* has its own duration, and thus its own duration of dawn and dusk, if the transition in level is extended it is not clear whether we would imagine a smooth passage from one level to another throughout the two-part transition period, or a change in the rate of change when the dusk of the outgoing *yuga* finishes and the dawn of the incoming *yuga* begins. The latter scenario would allow the junction between the dusk of one *yuga* and the dawn of the next to occur when the level is exactly halfway between the levels of the two adjoining *yuga*s. If we were to imagine a change in the rate of change, it would be greatest at the *kali–kṛtayuga* transition, where the dusk of the outgoing *kaliyuga* is one-quarter of the length of the dawn of the incoming *kṛtayuga*.

Figures 7, 8, and 9 represent three possible transition-scenarios in the descending phase. The *dvāpara–kaliyuga* transition has been chosen for these illustrations because in the descending phase the hypothetical change in the rate of change would be greatest at the *dvāpara–kaliyuga* transition, because the *dvāpara*'s dusk is twice as long as the *kali*'s dawn. Thus in Figure 8 the line's gradient is twice as steep in the *kali*'s dawn as it is in the *dvāpara*'s dusk. The *dvāpara–kaliyuga* transition has been chosen also because that is where the Kurukṣetra *avatāra* is set (see below).

The two scenarios sketched in Figures 7 and 8 are both hypothetical, because the general accounts of the *yuga* cycle do not describe the transition between descending *yuga*s; they mention dawns and dusks only in terms of their existence and durations (Mbh 3.186.18–21; Mbh 12.224.19–20 ≈ Ms 1.69–70). The dawns and dusks could have nothing to do with the level (of *dharma*, lifespan, etc.), apart from standing on either side of its sudden change, as per Figure 9. In this case, one might wonder what the dawns and dusks were 'for', as it were; and perhaps the dawn might then be the period during which the quality of

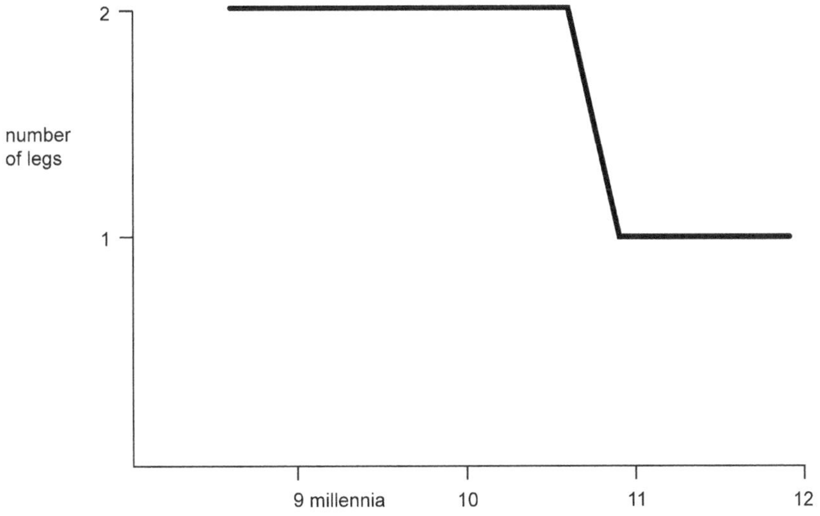

Figure 7: *Dvāpara* to *Kali* Transition (Smooth).

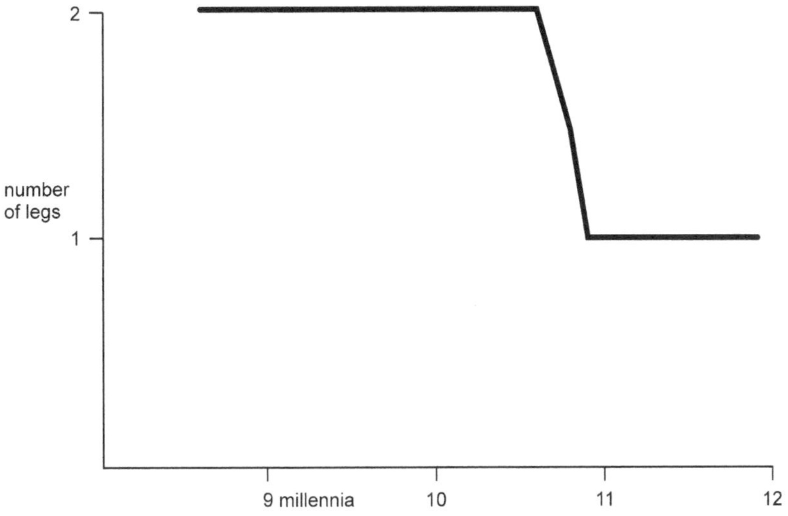

Figure 8: *Dvāpara* to *Kali* Transition (Steepening).

the *yuga* would still be fresh enough to be noticeable (implicitly in comparison with what preceded it), and the dusk might be the period of anticipation of an impending change.

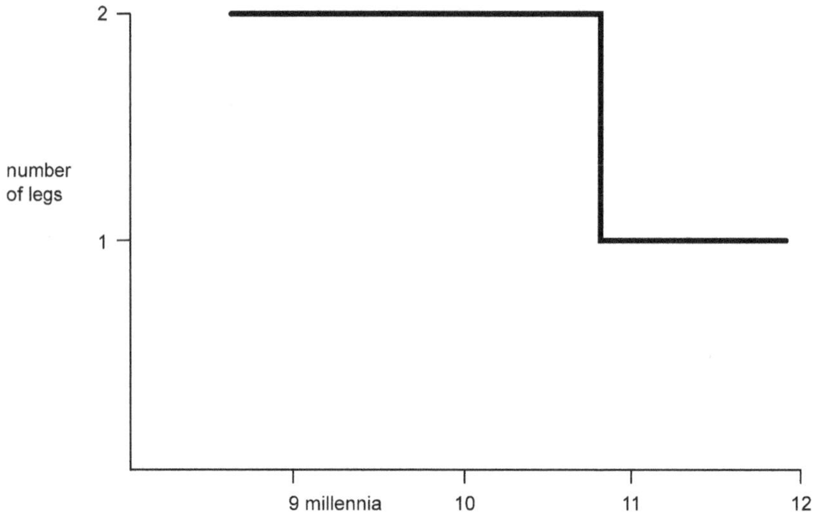

Figure 9: *Dvāpara* to *Kali* Transition (Sudden).

These graphs serve to highlight that at such points of transition there are, in theory, various possibilities; and there are others not yet sketched.

Measurement in divine years

This section discusses a development evident in various Purāṇas, whereby the years specifying the durations of the various *yuga*s (adding up to twelve thousand for the *mahāyuga* as a whole) are interpreted as years of the gods. Since one of our years is just a day-and-night for the gods, in the Purāṇic scheme the length of the *mahāyuga* (and of each of its component *yuga*s) is thus multiplied by 360, and the *mahāyuga* lasts for 4,320,000 human years (González-Reimann 2002: 6).[13] The factor of 360 is the approximate number of days in a year – that is, the number of human days-and-nights (nycthemerons) in a day-and-night of the gods – and also, coincidentally, the number of degrees in a circle. As Pingree wrote to Gombrich, '360 is the number of *saura* days in a sidereal year, where a *saura* day is defined as the time required for the mean Sun to traverse 1° of the sidereal ecliptic' (quoted in Gombrich 1975: 140 n. 10).

[13] According to Bronkhorst, the *Vāyupurāṇa* and *Brahmāṇḍapurāṇa* do not number the *yuga* durations in divine years (Bronkhorst 2015: 34–35; see also Gupta 1969: 307–308).

This development from human to divine years is not evident in the *Mahābhārata* except allegedly on one single occasion, in the passage at Mbh 12.224. Discussing that passage (which is the one largely parallel to the *Manusmṛti* passage quoted earlier), Sutton says 'here it is made clear that the 12,000 year cycle is in years of the gods' (Sutton 2000: 259). Smith shares this interpretation: in his summary of the chapter he says that 'The twelve thousand years of the gods constituting the four ages make up one *yuga*' (i.e. one *mahāyuga*; Smith 2009: 639, de-italicised). The source of this interpretation is presumably the word *daivalaukike* at 12.224.17b (see below). If Sutton and Smith's interpretation were accepted, this would be the only occasion on which the *Mahābhārata* would give any indication that the years numbering the *yuga*s would be years of the gods. Data to the contrary would be every apparently normal usage, in the text, of words for 'year' – including other such usages in Mbh 12.224, such as the detail that human lifespan in the *kaliyuga* is one hundred years (which cannot really be understood to mean 36,000 years). I take the *Mahābhārata*'s view to be that the *yuga*-duration numbers are in normal years. Though these might be thought of as human years (as opposed to divine ones), in truth they are more terrestrial than they are human.

The offending verse, 12.224.17, comes just after Vyāsa's account of various units of time, from short to long, from the *nimeṣa* (the 'blink') to the year, at the end of which he mentions that a month is a day-and-night for the ancestors, and that a year is a day-and-night for the gods (12.224.15–16 ≈ Ms 1.66–67). And the offending verse comes just before Vyāsa's account of the *yuga*s, which gives numbers in years. The junction between these two accounts takes up just one verse in the *Manusmṛti* (Ms 1.68, pp. 13–14 above), but in the *Mahābhārata* it takes up two verses (12.224.17–18), the first of which is the offending verse. González-Reimann has a footnote on it that I quote at length:

> The *MDhŚ* [*Mānava Dharmaśāstra*, = *Manusmṛti*] at no point says that the years for each yuga should be considered as divine years. Nor in the third book of the *Mbh* (3.186.18–23), when Mārkaṇḍeya talks about the yugas and expounds the duration of each one, does he specify that it is a matter of divine years. In the case of book 12 of the Epic, which is where we find the passage parallel to the one in the *MDhŚ*, there is a mention (*Mbh*, 12.224.17) that the day and night of Brahmā should be computed according to days and nights of the world of the gods (*daivalaukika*). This would imply that the measure of each yuga would be considered as expressed in divine years. But the curious fact is that in the *MDhŚ* this phrase was absent, while what is said immediately before and after coincided with what was written in the *Mbh*. Moreover, the word *daivalaukika*, as an indicator that it is a matter of divine time, does not appear in all versions of the text. Although this term was the one chosen by the critical edition, a fair number of manuscripts (almost all of the

northern-recension ones) say *jīvalaukika* in place of *daivalaukika*. This indicates that it is a matter of the contrary situation, to wit, days and nights for humans. That is why the translations of Roy (9, p. 168) and Bühler (p. lxxxiv) say in this passage that it is a matter of human days and nights (even if both of them anyway take it for granted that the duration of the yugas is referred to in divine years). Like Roy so also Bühler uses the Bombay edition, which pertains to the northern recension; also part of the northern recension is the Calcutta version, which is the one consulted by Monier-Williams who, in his dictionary (p. 423), refers to this passage as an example of the use of the term *jīvalaukika*. Elsewhere, Frauwallner surely consulted another version, since his translation (according to Gombrich, 'Ancient Indian Cosmology', in *Ancient Cosmologies*, p. 122) specifies that it is a matter of days of the gods.[14]

It is possible that, although the texts do not say so in explicit form, the years of each yuga should be considered as divine years; in fact, to interpret them in this sense is the generalised custom. But it appears to us more probable that they reflect an earlier stage in the formation of the theory of the yugas, a stage in which the measure was expressed in terrestrial time. With time, the figures could have been expanded by saying that they were in divine years. This type of amplification of figures is common in Hinduism. It is not superfluous to note that elsewhere the Iranian Great Year had a duration of 12 000 years, and in that case it is clear that it is a matter of human years.[15]

(González-Reimann 1988: 81–82 n. 25)

---

[14] Gombrich is referring to Frauwallner 1953. Gombrich claims that 'Frauwallner is using divine years' (Gombrich 1975: 122), but I do not think he is; see p. 43 n. 19 below.

[15] 'El *MDhŚ* en ningún momento dice que los años de cada yuga deban ser considerados como años divinos. En el tercer libro del *Mbh* (3.186.18-23), cuando Mārkaṇḍeya habla acerca de los yugas y expone la duración de cada uno, tampoco especifica que se trate de años de los dioses. En el caso del libro 12 de la Epopeya, que es donde encontramos el pasaje paralelo al del *MDhŚ*, hay una mención (*Mbh*, 12.224.17) de que el día y la noche de brahmā deben ser computados según los días y noches del mundo de los dioses (*daivalaukika*). Esto implicaría que la medida de cada yuga debería considerarse como expresada en años divinos. Pero es curioso el hecho de que en el *MDhŚ* esta frase esté ausente, mientras que lo dicho inmediatamente antes y después coincide con lo escrito en el *Mbh*. Más aún, la palabra *daivalaukika*, como indicador de que se trata de tiempo de los dioses, no aparece en todas las versiones del texto. Si bien este término fue el escogido para la edición crítica, un buen numero de manuscritos (casi todos ellos de la recensión del norte) dicen *jīvalaukika* en lugar de *daivalaukika*. Esto indica que se trata de la situación contraria, es decir de días y noches de los humanos. Es por esto que la traducción de Roy (9, p. 168) y la de Bühler (p. lxxxiv) dicen en este pasaje que se trata de días y noches humanos (aunque de todos modos ambos dan por sentado que la duración de los yugas se refiere a años divinos). Tanto Roy como Bühler utilizaron la edición de Bombay, la cual pertenece a la recensión del norte; también es parte de la recensión del norte la versión de Calcuta, que es la consultada por Monier-Williams quien, en su diccionario (p. 423), se refiere a este pasaje como ejemplo del empleo del término *jīvalaukika*. Por otra parte, Frauwallner seguramente consultó otra versión, ya que

Sutton, Smith, and González-Reimann write as if the word *daivalaukike* at v. 17b in the critically reconstituted text would mean that the numbers are given in divine years. As Thomas puts it, the numbers would be 'by implication (following v.17), but not explicitly, in *divya* years' (Thomas 1988: 68).[16] But it is not so. Here is the verse together with those that immediately precede and follow it, and a translation that gives three options:

daive rātryahanī varṣaṃ pravibhāgas tayoḥ punaḥ |
ahas tatrodagayanaṃ rātriḥ syād dakṣiṇāyanam ‖ 12.224.16 ‖
ye te rātryahanī pūrve kīrtite daivalaukike |
tayoḥ saṃkhyāya varṣāgraṃ brāhme vakṣyāmy ahaḥkṣape ‖ 17 ‖[17]
teṣāṃ saṃvatsarāgrāṇi pravakṣyāmy anupūrvaśaḥ |
kṛte tretāyuge caiva dvāpare ca kalau tathā ‖ 18 ‖

16. A year is a day and night of the gods. Now the division of those two: the day is the [sun's] progress north [i.e. ending at the summer solstice]; the night is the [sun's] progress south [i.e. ending at the winter solstice].

17(1). I will number the extent in years [of the various *yugas*] in terms of the aforementioned day and night that belong to the world of the gods, and then I will tell of the day and night of Brahmā.

17(2). Numbering the extent in years in terms of the aforementioned day and night that belong to the world of the gods, I will tell of the day and night of Brahmā.

17(3). Now that I have numbered the extent of a year as being the aforementioned day and night that belong to the world of the gods, I will tell of the day and night of Brahmā.

---

su traducción (según Gombrich, "Ancient Indian Cosmology", en *Ancient Cosmologies*, p. 122) especifica que se trata de días de los dioses.

'Es posible que, aunque los textos no lo digan en forma explícita, los años de cada yuga deben ser considerados como años divinos; de hecho, interpretarlos en este sentido es la costumbre generalizada. Pero nos parece más probable que reflejan una etapa antigua en la formación de la teoría de los yugas, etapa en la cual la medida estaba expresada en tiempo terrestre. Con el tiempo, las cifras pudieron expandirse al decir que se trataba de años celestes. Esto tipo de aplificación de cifras es común en el hinduismo. No está de más anotar, por otra parte, que el Gran Año iranio tenía una duración de 12 000 años, y en este caso es claro que se trata de años humanos.'

[16] In quotations from Thomas's thesis, I have replaced bold type with italics and standardised the diacritics.

[17] The following variants are recorded for this verse (Belvalkar 1954: 1252): 'a) Ś1 K1.2.4.6 Dn4 T2 G1 M5 *ete* (for *ye te*). Da4 *rātryahani.* K7 D4.8.9 M5 *pūrvaṃ*; B6.7 Da3.a4 *pārtha*; B6 (marg.) *pure*; T2 *pūrvaiḥ* (for *pūrve*). — b) Ś1 K1.4 *kathite* (for *kīrtite*). Ś1 K1.4 *deva-*; K6.7 B0.6–9 Da3.a4 Dn1.n4 Ds D2.3.6.8 M1.6 *jīva-* (for *daiva-*). D2 om. from *valau* up to *saṃyānti* (in 20c). K2 *kathite laukike ca te.* — c) D6 *rātriḥ* (for *tayoḥ*). K7 *sakhyāya*; D7 *saṃkhyā ca* (for *saṃkhyāya*). K6 *vargāgraṃ*; K7 B8 D4.6.9 *varṣāgryaṃ.* — d) B0 Dn4 Ds1 G3.6 *brāhmye*; Da4 *brahmo*; D5 *brāhmyaṃ* (for *brāhme*). Dn4 *vakṣāmi.* Ś1 K1.2 *aha*(K2 °*haṃ*)*kṣaye*; K6 V1 Da4 Dn4 D6 *ahaḥkṣaye*; D4.9 *ahaḥkṣipe*; D5 *aśeṣataḥ* (for *ahaḥkṣape*).'

18. With respect to the *kṛta*, *tretā*, *dvāpara*, and *kali yuga*s, I will state, one after another, their extents in years.

(12.224.16–18)

The skeleton of v. 17 is: absolutive *saṃkhyāya* ('numbering/having numbered') with accusative object *varṣāgraṃ* ('extent of/in year/s'),[18] connected to the relative clause in the first line by the pronoun *tayoḥ*; then main verb *vakṣyāmy* ('I will describe') with accusative object *brāhme ... ahaḥkṣape* ('the day and night of Brahmā').

The line 17ab is composed of six nominative duals. They are duals because *rātryahanī* ('day and night') is dual, as it is in v. 16a; and that is why the pronoun *tayoḥ*, which connects them to the verb *saṃkhyāya*, is dual. Vyāsa says that this day-and-night has been *pūrve kīrtite daivalaukike*, 'previously/already described *daivalaukike*'. This seems to refer back to v. 16, which described the day and night of the gods. According to González-Reimann (in the long quotation above), *daivalaukike* would mean 'of the world of the gods'. Elsewhere *daiva* and *laukika* are often set in contrast to each other as 'divine' and 'terrestrial', and so there is also the option of taking *daivalaukike* as 'divine and terrestrial'; but this is a poorer fit with the previous verse and also with the following ones, where the durations of the *yuga*s are given in one system only, whichever it might be. So I take *daivalaukike* to refer just to 'the world of the gods', as González-Reimann does (for *laukika* as 'belonging to the world of', see Monier-Williams 1899: 909 col. 3).

The three translations differ over the interpretation of the absolutive: does it indicate something that Vyāsa will do before he does the main verb, or something that he will do **as** he does the main verb (Rocher 1980), or something that he has already done? In both of the future-tense options, *varṣāgraṃ* fits with the *saṃvatsarāgrāṇi* ('extents in years') that appears in v. 18, and so the absolutive *saṃkhyāya* in v. 17 announces something that is re-announced in v. 18: the stating of the *yuga* durations, which is indeed included in the general account of the four *yuga*s that then follows beginning in v. 19. The day and night of Brahmā promised in v. 17d are only explicitly returned to after that general account, in v. 30, where Vyāsa says that one thousand *mahāyuga*s constitute a day of Brahmā, each *mahāyuga* being composed of the four *yuga*s he has just described. So in the first future-tense option the account of the *yuga*s is considered separate from the account of Brahmā's days and nights, and in the second one it is considered part of it. If the absolutive *saṃkhyāya* indicates something that Vyāsa has already done, then it would be what he has done in the previ-

[18] The compound *varṣāgraṃ* appears in the *Mahābhārata* just this once. Ganguli takes it with the second verb, *vakṣyāmy* ('I shall speak of the day and night of Brahman and his years also', Ganguli 1970: Santi Parva CCXXXI, 155), but this does not seem right, because there is no *ca* ('and'), and because it is more natural to break the phrasing at the *pāda* boundary.

ous verse, v. 16, which did indeed define the year as a divine day-and-night, as v. 17 states.

All three translations imply that Vyāsa would go on to quantify the *yuga* durations in terms of our normal years, each of which is a day-and-night for the gods. As Frauwallner says, 'Such gods' days are also the units according to which the world-ages (*yugāni*) are reckoned'[19] (Frauwallner 1973: 93, trans. Bedekar). Years of the gods are not mentioned here; Vyāsa only mentions days-and-nights of the gods, which are years. Just before this verse, Vyāsa has relativised (in the approximate ratio 1 : 30 : 360) time for us, time for the ancestors, and time for the gods; and so before he quantifies the *yugas*, he needs to specify what units he will use. And so he does: the units are years, that is, days-and-nights of the gods. So there is no need to interpret the verse, against the rest of the text, as indicating that the *yuga* durations that follow are given in years of the gods, as Sutton and Smith do, and as González-Reimann would seemingly be minded to do were he to accept the critically reconstituted version of the verse.[20]

Thomas says that 'The consistent omission of divine as a qualification of year in all but 12.224.17 ... suggests that the Mbh computations are understood to be in the simpler scheme of human years' (Thomas 1988: 71; see also Gupta 1969: 306). And indeed they are. But divine does not qualify year in 12.224.17; it qualifies day-and-night. Nonetheless, regardless of this verse, we know from nearby texts, even if not from the *Mahābhārata* itself, that there is a method of computing *yugas* in divine years. The *Mahābhārata*'s method for computing *yugas* is out of step with, and apparently contradicts, a wealth of other texts and traditions. And I think it is consistent in doing so.

The computation in divine years is connected with astronomy – as well it might be, since the business of astronomy is the business of the celestial bodies, which are *daiva* ('in the heavens') by definition, and which are involved in the Vedāṅga of *jyotiṣa* or calendrical astronomy (*Āpastamba Dharmasūtra* 2.8.10–11). Various astronomical systems of the mid-first millennium CE identify 4,320,000 as the number of human years in a *mahāyuga* (González-Reimann 1988: 105–107; *Āryabhaṭṭīya* 1.3–4). If we think about empirical cyclicity on a lengthening scale, we can experience and record days, months, and years, but on a longer scale there would be cycles that human beings, being short-

---

[19] 'Solche Göttertage sind nun auch die Einheit, nach der die Weltalter (*yugāni*) berechnet werden' (Frauwallner 2003: 75).

[20] Van der Waerden might seem to interpret this verse in the same way as Sutton and Smith, but he also takes the parallel *Manusmṛti* passage in that way (i.e. as numbering the *yugas* in years of the gods), even though it does not include this verse (van der Waerden 1978: 361–363). So in the case of van der Waerden it seems to be an assumption rather than an interpretation. Trautmann also erroneously states that the *yuga* durations in the *Manusmṛti* are given in divine years (Trautmann 1995: 169). Kane lumps together many texts, including the *Manusmṛti* and the *Mahābhārata*, as reckoning in divine years (Kane 1973: 890–891). Most recently, Taylor characterises the *Manusmṛti* and the *Mahābhārata* as reckoning the *yuga* durations in divine years (Taylor 2022: 77).

lived, could only dimly envisage. The *mahāyuga* is of this longer scale, as are the cycles of the relative configurations of the cyclical celestial bodies – the sun that measures days and years, the moon that measures months, and the various planets, each in its own measured and regular peregrination.

Since the moon, the sun, and the various planets each has its own cyclicity, they go into and out of phase with each other; and there is thus the idea of a longer cycle, sometimes called an *exeligmos* (by the Greeks) or a 'great year' (*annus magnus*, by the Romans), cycling from the time when they are in phase with each other to the next time they are in phase with each other. As Pingree puts it, 'The mean motions of the planets can be described in terms of an integer number of revolutions within a given period as long as that period is fairly long' (Pingree 1963: 239; see also Burgess 1893: 721; Fleet 1911: 489–492). Thinking about such a longer cycle, or something like it, has yielded, among others, an astronomical number that reads, in base ten: 4, 3, 2, many zeroes. This long number shares its first three digits with the number of human years in the Purāṇic *mahāyuga* (converted from divine reckoning via the factor of 360). Those first three digits are also the first three digits in the ratio of descending *yuga* lengths and levels (4 : 3 : 2 : 1).

González-Reimann seeks to separate the two computation methods chronologically, and that is the general trend. The scholarship gives two historical pictures. One of them has the Purāṇic computation method taking over from the *Mahābhārata* computation method through the influence of astronomy (Gupta 1969: 308; González-Reimann 1988: 97, referring to Fleet 1911). The other has the Purāṇic method taking over from the *Mahābhārata* method 'when the period of 1 200 years assigned to the Kali yuga had already expired, and on noting that the catastrophe predicted for that moment did not occur'[21] (González-Reimann 1988: 98, referring to Aiyer and Basham; see also González-Reimann 2009: 417; González-Reimann 2013: 109; Bronkhorst 2015: 33–34). We will return to the second of these pictures in Chapter 6. Regarding the first, is there an origin of the number 4, 3, 2, zeroes?

The number 43,200 occurs in the *Sumerian King List*: En-men-lu-Anna, the third king mentioned, ruled for that many years (Jacobsen 1939: 71–73). Pingree says of the number 432,000: 'This is a Babylonian number: sexagesimally it would be written 2,0,0,0. It is the span of time given to the Babylonian kingdom before the Flood in the histories of Berossos and Abydenus' (Pingree 1963: 238; see also van der Waerden 1978: 360). And the number 432,000 multiplied by ten is 4,320,000, just as the duration of the *kaliyuga* multiplied by ten is the duration of the *mahāyuga*. At some point the number 432,000 was identified as the duration of the 'great year' (Pingree 1963: 239). According to Filliozat, this identification was made by Berossos himself (Filliozat 1970: 327). But Filliozat and González-Reimann point out that the number 432,000 is also

[21] 'cuando el lapso de 1 200 años asignado al Kali yuga ya había expirado, y al constatar que la catástrofe predicha para tal momento no se presentaba'

Vedic, since it is found by implication in the *Śatapatha Brāhmaṇa*'s discussion of the total syllable counts of the various Vedas (*Śatapatha Brāhmaṇa* 10.4.2; Eggeling 1978: 352 n. 2, 353 nn. 2–3; Filliozat 1957: 773; González-Reimann 1988: 38–39, 103, 108). Filliozat says that 'the figures most probably came to Heraklitus and Berossos from India' (Filliozat 1957: 773; see also Geslani et al. 2017: 166–169, questioning the assumption of Babylonian influence on Indian astronomy). González-Reimann says:

> [I]f in reality the Mesopotamian period of 432 000 years was transmitted to India during the reign of the Achaemenids (or in some earlier epoch), it would have acquired importance because it could be identified with a numerical tradition that already existed in Vedic literature. And it is also possible that this native numerical tradition could have given rise to the Purāṇic computation system without any need for external influences which, we repeat, would in any case have done nothing but confirm something already accepted.[22]
>
> (González-Reimann 1988: 103–104)

There are multiple suggested origins for the number 4, 3, 2, zeroes (Rocher 1975: 142), and I do not propose to resolve the issue.

The main points to sum up from this section are: that in contrast to the *Mahābhārata*, the Purāṇic system numbers the *yuga*s in years of the gods, yielding 4,320,000 as the number of human years in a *mahāyuga*; that something closely resembling this number is also known from astronomy in connection with the duration of the 'great year'; and that whatever the connection might be between the Purāṇic system and the 'great year', it is a connection that does not apply to the *Mahābhārata* system. The *Mahābhārata* quantifies the *yuga* durations in normal years.[23]

[22] 'si en realidad el período mesopotámico de 432 000 años fue transmitido a la India durante el reinado de los aqueménidas (o en alguna época posterior), adquirió importancia porque se le podía identificar con una tradición numérica ya existente en la literatura védica. Y también es posible que esta tradición numérica nativa haya dado origen al sistema puránico de cómputo sin la necesidad de influencias externas las cuales, repetimos, en todo caso no hubieran hecho sino confirmar algo ya aceptado.'

[23] This also means that Kloetzli's discussions (Kloetzli 2013) are tangential to our project. Kloetzli proposes that the structure of the *yuga* cycle reflects a combination of three different numbering systems: 'Greek acrophonic, Babylonian sexagesimal and Hindu decimal' (p. 631). Decimal means in powers of ten, sexagesimal means in powers of sixty, and acrophonic means using letters to designate numbers. In particular, in decimal numbering the *yuga* system can encode number of zeroes (4/0/to the next power, 3, 2, 1) in a way that is useful for multiplication. Kloetzli concentrates mainly on the *Viṣṇupurāṇa*, whose link to the sexagesimal system depends upon the multiplication by 360 (yielding the number 4, 3, 2, zeroes). Kloetzli also makes much of the decimal number 10,000 (a myriad), which in years is significantly shorter than a *mahāyuga*, and which can only be related to the *yuga* scheme by adding up the *yuga* durations excluding the dawns and dusks. A decimal number is important to Kloetzli because it is at such a number that the Greek acrophonic system (with twenty-seven letters used in three sets of nine to denote units, tens, and hundreds) requires an extra bit of notation.

In this chapter on 'The *Yuga* Cycle in the *Mahābhārata*', we began with the single account of the *yugas* at *Manusmṛti* 1.68–86. Then we surveyed the various *Mahābhārata* accounts, and we found that together they give effectively the same picture of repeating *mahāyugas*, each containing four *yugas* of descending duration and dharmic character in the ratio 4 : 3 : 2 : 1. We discussed the complex variable that descends in this ratio. We compared this *Mahābhārata* cycle with other cycles of time. We mentioned the dawns and dusks at the beginnings and ends of *yugas*. And we briefly discussed a parallel or later tendency in the Purāṇas, a tendency to interpret the *yuga* durations as numbered in years of the gods, which would make them 360 times longer than they are in the *Mahābhārata* scheme.

Kloetzli also makes much of Saṃjaya's aberrant account at 6.11. He leans on speculations about the ancient Indian game of dice, in terms of a dice-throw being divisible by four with potential remainders three, two, and one, and the skill of computation at a glance (Heesterman 1957: 143–146; Shulman 1992: 351–352). And he speculates further historical developments ('The *Saṃdhyās* could have been added to adapt the decimalization of the Greek acrophonic system to include Babylonian sexagesimal reckoning', Kloetzli 2013: 645). Kloetzli's idea that the *yuga* scheme is somehow the mnemonic for a calculation tool – such as Śakuni might have used – depends on the multiplication by 360; and in any case, most audience members (of this text or any other that describes a *yuga* scheme) would not be using the *yuga* scheme for that purpose.

CHAPTER 3

The Title Problem

Transition to the *kaliyuga* in the *Mahābhārata* narrative

González-Reimann has identified nine instances where *Mahābhārata* characters locate events narrated in the Kurukṣetra story in terms of the transition from a *dvāparayuga* to a *kaliyuga* (González-Reimann 2002: 86–102; González-Reimann 2010: 62–63 and nn. 3–10; see also Thomas 1988: 253–256; Katz 1985: 120 n. 19). There are also such instances in the *Harivaṃśa*. Hudson rather underrepresents the situation when she says that 'There are approximately two passages in the [*Mahābhārata*] text that state explicitly that the war took place at the juncture of the Dvāpara and Kali *yugas*' (Hudson 2013: 154).

González-Reimann, attempting to emphasise 'how fluid and unreliable these assertions are' (González-Reimann 2002: 91), identifies an 'insoluble contradiction' in Saṃjaya's account (Mbh 6.11), between verses that seem to say it is the *dvāparayuga* and others that seem to say it is the *kaliyuga* (pp. 90–91, 213–214). But because each *yuga* includes a dawn and a dusk, the transition from a *dvāpara* to a *kali* potentially takes three hundred years to occur, beginning during the *dvāpara* and ending during the *kali*; and so, bearing Figures 7, 8, and 9 in mind, there would be some uncertainty, at various points during that transition, over which of the two adjoining *yuga*s one were in. This is an important point. There is no *yuga* meter to consult. Nonetheless, the *Mahābhārata* is as certain as can reasonably be about the Kurukṣetra story's *yuga* location. Here below I present a selection of indicative instances, in order of appearance, including most of the ones mentioned by González-Reimann and most of the ones in the *Harivaṃśa*.

In Mbh 1.1, Ugraśravas tells the seers at Śaunaka's twelve-year *satra* in Naimiṣa Forest where he has been. He mentions that

How to cite this book chapter:
Brodbeck, S. 2022. Divine Descent and the Four World-Ages in the *Mahābhārata* – or, Why Does the Kṛṣṇa *Avatāra* Inaugurate the Worst *Yuga*?. Pp. 47–62. Cardiff: Cardiff University Press. DOI: https://doi.org/10.18573/book9.c.

samantapañcakaṃ nāma puṇyaṃ dvijaniṣevitam |
gatavān asmi taṃ deśaṃ yuddhaṃ yatrābhavat purā |
pāṇḍavānāṃ kurūṇāṃ ca sarveṣāṃ ca mahīkṣitām ‖ 1.1.11 ‖

I journeyed to that holy place called Samantapañcaka, which is sought out by the twiceborn, the country where once was fought the War of the Kurus and Pāṇḍavas, and of all the kings of earth.
(1.1.11, trans. van Buitenen 1973: 20)

Accordingly, the seers at 1.2.1 ask Ugraśravas to say more about Samantapañcaka. Ugraśravas says that this is where, in the junction between the *tretāyuga* and the *dvāparayuga*, Rāma Jāmadagnya repeatedly culled the *kṣatriya*s, and their blood made lakes there (1.2.3–8).

antare caiva saṃprāpte kalidvāparayor abhūt |
samantapañcake yuddhaṃ kurupāṇḍavasenayoḥ ‖ 1.2.9 ‖
tasmin paramadharmiṣṭhe deśe bhūdoṣavarjite |
aṣṭādaśa samājagmur akṣauhiṇyo yuyutsayā ‖ 10 ‖

It was at this same Samantapañcaka that at the juncture of the *dvāparayuga* and the *kaliyuga* the war between the armies of the Kurus and the Pāṇḍavas was fought. In that country, innocent of any flaws of the soil and supremely firm in the Law, eighteen armies massed together to wage war.
(1.2.9–10, trans. van Buitenen 1973: 32, adapted)

In Mbh 3, during the Pāṇḍavas' exile, in Hanūmat's discourse on the *yuga*s to Bhīma Pāṇḍava, after describing the *kaliyuga* Hanūmat says:

etat kaliyugaṃ nāma acirād yat pravartate | 3.148.37ab

Such is the yuga called Kali, which will soon begin.
(3.148.37ab, trans. González-Reimann 2002: 92)[24]

In Mbh 6, having described the *yuga*s to Dhṛtarāṣṭra just before the Kurukṣetra war (and having implied that it is now the *kaliyuga*; 6.11.6, quoted above, p. 23), Saṃjaya says to Dhṛtarāṣṭra:

saṃkṣepo vartate rājan dvāpare 'smin narādhipa | 6.11.14ab

The end of this *dvāpara* age is drawing near, Your Majesty, lord of the people.
(6.11.14ab, trans. Cherniak 2008: 85)

[24] This interpretation differs from that of Fleet, for whom 'Hanumat ... observed that the Kali age had recently begun' (Fleet 1911: 677).

During the war, Bhīṣma, discoursing to Duryodhana about Kṛṣṇa-Nārāyaṇa, says:

> *dvāparasya yugasyānte ādau kaliyugasya ca* |
> *sātvataṃ vidhim āsthāya gītaḥ saṃkarṣaṇena yaḥ* ‖ 6.62.39 ‖
>
> [He is] The one who, at the end of the Dvāpara Yuga and the beginning of the Kali Yuga, was praised by Saṃkarṣaṇa (Balarāma) in accordance with *sātvata* precepts.
> (6.62.39, trans. González-Reimann 2002: 89)[25]

The Sātvatas are Kṛṣṇa's people, Saṃkarṣaṇa is Kṛṣṇa's brother Baladeva, and the *sātvata vidhi* is the religion of devotion to Kṛṣṇa-Nārāyaṇa (González-Reimann 2002: 109–110 n. 13).

On the eighteenth day of the war, Kṛṣṇa says to that brother Baladeva, in explanation of Bhīma's having felled Duryodhana with a blow below the belt:

> *prāptaṃ kaliyugaṃ viddhi pratijñāṃ pāṇḍavasya ca* | 9.59.21ab
>
> Know that the Kali Yuga has arrived, and the vow of the Pāṇḍava (Bhīma) has been completed.
> (9.59.21ab, trans. González-Reimann 2002: 100; compare Meiland 2007: 337)

In Bhīṣma's post-war instruction to Yudhiṣṭhira, in the *Nārāyaṇīya*, Bhīṣma describes how Nārāyaṇa told Nārada about his *avatāra* habit. After mentioning the boar *avatāra*, the man-lion, the dwarf, and the two Rāmas, Jāmadagnya and Dāśarathi, Nārāyaṇa says:

> *dvāparasya kaleś caiva saṃdhau paryavasānike* |
> *prādurbhāvaḥ kaṃsahetor mathurāyāṃ bhaviṣyati* ‖ 12.326.82 ‖
>
> In the *saṃdhi* between Dvāpara and Kali, towards the end, I will appear in (the city of) Mathurā, because of Kaṃsa.
> (12.326.82, trans. González-Reimann 2002: 88)

Later in the *Nārāyaṇīya*, we hear of Nārāyaṇa creating boar, man-lion, dwarf, and human forms, and also creating a seer named Apāntaratamas, who will become Vyāsa. Nārāyaṇa tells Apāntaratamas that his job is to divide the Vedas (compare 1.57.72–73, quoted above, p. 17), and continues:

[25] Thomas translates this verse differently (Thomas 1988: 240), but still so as to locate Kṛṣṇa and Baladeva at the *dvāpara-kaliyuga* transition. Ganguli has: 'He it is who, towards the close of the *Dwapara Yuga* and the beginning of the *Kali Yuga*, is sung of with Sankarshana, by believers with devotion' (Ganguli 1970: Bhishma Parva LXVI, 173).

punas tiṣye ca saṃprāpte kuravo nāma bhāratāḥ |
bhaviṣyanti mahātmāno rājānaḥ prathitā bhuvi ‖ 12.337.42 ‖
teṣāṃ tvattaḥ prasūtānāṃ kulabhedo bhaviṣyati |

And when Tiṣya (Kali) comes again, Bhārata kings known as Kurus will be born. They will be noble, famous on earth. They will be your [i.e. Vyāsa's] descendants, and a rift will occur in the family ...
(12.337.42–43b, trans. González-Reimann 2002: 88, adapted)[26]

In the *Harivaṃśa*, Mārkaṇḍeya tells Bhīṣma (and Bhīṣma tells Yudhiṣṭhira) about the ancestors. Acchodā is thrown out of heaven, but while falling, she petitions the ancestors. They say that she will be the mother of Vyāsa, Vicitravīrya, and Citrāṅgada.

tasyaiva rājñas tvaṃ kanyā adrikāyāṃ bhaviṣyasi |
aṣṭāviṃśe bhavitrī tvaṃ dvāpare matsyayonijā ‖ Hv 13.39 ‖
evam uktā tu dāseyī jātā satyavatī tadā |
matsyayonau anupamā rājñas tasya vasoḥ sutā ‖ 40 ‖

You will be the daughter of the aforementioned king [Vasu], by Adrikā. But you will be born from the womb of a fish, in the twenty-eighth *dvāparayuga*.

Then, after being told this, she was born from the womb of a fish, as Satyavatī the fishergirl, the peerless daughter of that King Vasu.
(*Harivaṃśa* 13.39–40)

In due course, Brahmā describes the situation to the gods. Vicitravīrya's posthumous and compromised sons (Vyāsa's genital sons) Dhṛtarāṣṭra and Pāṇḍu have both grown up and married. Brahmā tells the gods:

atra vo 'ṃśā vibhajyantāṃ vipakṣaḥ pakṣa eva ca |
putrāṇāṃ hi tayo rājñor bhavitā vigraho mahān ‖ Hv 43.53 ‖
teṣāṃ vimarde dāyādye nṛpāṇāṃ bhavitā kṣayaḥ |
yugāntapratimaṃ caiva bhaviṣyati mahad bhayam ‖ 54 ‖
sabaleṣu narendreṣu śātayatsv itaretaram |
viviktapurarāṣṭraughā kṣitiḥ śaithilyam eṣyati ‖ 55 ‖

---

[26] These and the following lines may seem to indicate that the *kaliyuga* commences before, or as, the Kuru princes sired by Vyāsa come into prominence. But *tiṣye ... saṃprāpte* at 12.337.42a qualifies several circumstances, including, most saliently, the *kulabheda* (family feud) that is encapsulated by the war. However, *kṛṣṇe yuge ... saṃprāpte* at 12.337.44c certainly qualifies Vyāsa's dark colour (since this is why the term *kṛṣṇa yuga* is used here for the *kaliyuga*), and we do not hear of him changing colour at about the time of the war; he seems always to have been dark (1.99.14d).

dvāparasya yugasyānte mayā dṛṣṭaṃ purātane |
kṣayaṃ yāsyanti śastreṇa pārthivāḥ saha vāhanaiḥ ‖ 56 ‖
tatrāvaśiṣṭān manujān suptān niśi vicetasaḥ |
dhakṣyate śaṃkarasyāṃśaḥ pāvakenāstratejasā ‖ 57 ‖
antakapratime tasmin nivṛtte krūrakarmaṇi |
samāptam idam ākhyāsye tṛtīyaṃ dvāparaṃ yugam ‖ 58 ‖
maheśvarāṃśe 'pasṛte tato māheśvaraṃ yugam |
tiṣyaṃ prapatsyate paścād yugaṃ dāruṇamānuṣam ‖ 59 ‖
adharmaprāyapuruṣaṃ svalpadharmaparigraham |
utsannasatyasaṃyogaṃ vardhitānṛtasaṃcayam ‖ 60 ‖
maheśvaraṃ kumāraṃ ca dvau ca devau samāśritāḥ |
bhaviṣyanti narāḥ sarve loke nasthavirāyuṣaḥ ‖ 61 ‖

Your characters [i.e. theatrical parts] must be distributed here as two rival parties, and there will be a great war between the sons of these two kings. In their war of succession there will be a massacre of kings, and there will be great distress, just as there is at the end of the *yuga*. When the kings and their armies kill each other the earth will be relieved, and her many towns and kingdoms will be spaced out.

As I foresaw in former days, at the end of the *dvāparayuga* the kings on their vehicles of war will go to their destruction by the sword. Then, using fire and the power of his missiles, Śaṃkara's portion [i.e. Aśvatthāman] will burn the remaining people while they are sleeping at night, oblivious. And when this man of cruel deeds - the image of Death - has departed, I shall declare this third *yuga*, the *dvāpara*, to be over. After that, once Maheśvara's portion [i.e. Aśvatthāman] has slunk away, Maheśvara's age will set in: the fourth *yuga*, when men are merciless, and people apply themselves to *adharma*, and there is hardly any *dharma*, and concern for truth vanishes, and the quantity of falsehood increases. The world's entire population will follow the two gods Maheśvara and Kumāra, and no one will live to old age.

(*Harivaṃśa* 43.53–61)

Kṛṣṇa, after withdrawing his people from Mathurā to Dvārakā, engineers the death of his enemy Kālayavana. He does this by having Kālayavana zapped by fire from the eye of Mucukunda, who has slept for many years and was granted the boon of zapping whoever wakes him up (Hv 85.40–45). As the smoke is clearing, 'the king [Mucukunda] now saw [Kṛṣṇa] Vāsudeva, and, noticing that he was a small man, he judged from this evidence that a long time had passed and the age had ended' (*vāsudevam athālakṣya rājā hrasvaṃ pramāṇataḥ* | *parivṛttaṃ yugaṃ mene kālena mahatā tataḥ* ‖ Hv 85.55). Mucukunda asks Kṛṣṇa, 'How long have I been asleep?' (*kaś ca kālaḥ prasuptasya*, 85.56c). Kṛṣṇa says:

> *tretāyuge samutpanno vidito me 'si nāradāt* |
> *idaṃ kaliyugaṃ viddhi kim anyat karavāṇi te* ‖ Hv 85.59 ‖
>
> I learned from Nārada that you were born in the *tretāyuga*, but you should know that it is now the *kaliyuga*. Is there something else I can do for you?
>
> (*Harivaṃśa* 85.59)

Kṛṣṇa's comment seems imprecise, because this is before the Kurukṣetra war. But the point is that Kṛṣṇa looks small to Mucukunda because it is now a different *yuga* from the one in which Mucukunda fell asleep. Nārada is here said to have placed Mucukunda's birth in the *tretāyuga*, but Mucukunda received his boon because 'he had done his duty in the battle between gods and demons' (*purā devāsure yuddhe kṛtakarmā mahābalaḥ* ‖ Hv 85.40cd), which would be in the Tārakāmaya war, placed in the *kṛtayuga* by Hv 32.10 and at the *kṛta–tretāyuga* transition by *Yugapurāṇa* 12–13. Whichever option we take for dating the start or the end of Mucukunda's sleep, he would have slept across at least the *tretā–dvāparayuga* boundary. Given that the twilight periods of the outgoing and incoming *yuga*s are of different lengths and it is not clear at what point or in what manner the level of the complex variable shifts from one setting to another, Kṛṣṇa's exaggerated comment is not good evidence against the proposition that the Kurukṣetra war occurred at around the *dvāpara–kaliyuga* transition. The text's various comments on the dating of events come sometimes from extra-terrestrial characters and sometimes from terrestrial ones, and we might expect the latter to be more approximate in their observations.

Collectively and severally, the above quotations locate the Kurukṣetra generation at the transition from the *dvāparayuga* to the *kaliyuga*. The assembled quotations do not speak in one voice; they are voiced by different characters. But in the Hv 43 passage Brahmā is precise on the matter. In addition to the above extracts there are other, more ambiguous passages that can be interpreted in similar terms (see e.g. *kalidvāram* at 2.45.50; González-Reimann 2002: 54–55). More generally, the identification of Śakuni and Duryodhana as incarnations of Dvāpara and Kali respectively 'makes it clear that the over-riding intention of the epic narrators is to present a personification of the last two *yugas*, a personification that can only be meant to intensify awareness of the *yugānta* setting' (Thomas 1988: 301).

González-Reimann argues that 'As for placing the action [of the *Mahābhārata*, i.e. the Kurukṣetra action] at the beginning of the Kali Yuga ... the internal evidence for this is, at best, weak and meager' (González-Reimann 2002: 206). This conclusion has been questioned by Hiltebeitel (2011a: 125), and it is the opposite of my own conclusion on the basis of much the same 'weak and meager' evidence, and so some further discussion is necessary here.

González-Reimann does not argue that the Kurukṣetra war is located anywhere in the *yuga* cycle other than the *dvāpara–kaliyuga* transition. Rather, he argues that the *Mahābhārata* existed before the *yuga* scheme was introduced into it. He notes Mārkaṇḍeya's reference to 'the Lore, lauded by the seers, that was promulgated by [Vāyu] the Wind God' (*vāyuproktam ... purāṇam ṛṣisaṃstutam*, 3.189.14, quoted on p. 22 above). Vaiśaṃpāyana also cites Vāyu using the compound *vāyuprokta* in connection with the scheme of *manvantara*s at Hv 7.11 and 21, and González-Reimann thinks that the *Mahābhārata* acquired the *yuga* scheme from textual traditions close to those of the *Vāyupurāṇa* and the *Yugapurāṇa* (González-Reimann 2002: 96–99; see also Eltschinger 2012: 41–42; Brinkhaus 2021: 289–290). Once incorporated into the *Mahābhārata*, the *yuga* scheme 'always remained on the periphery of the narrative, never at its core' (González-Reimann 2002: 104). Effectively, González-Reimann thinks that the Kurukṣetra events are not really located within the *yuga* cycle at all. Accordingly, he seeks to downplay the countervailing evidence. The nine instances he singles out for attention are, he says, 'very few'; 'most of them are single verses'; 'they are brief, isolated instances'; 'these mentions generally bear no direct relationship to the story' (p. 86); they are not 'an organic part of the story'; 'the yuga theory is only loosely connected to the Epic' (p. 103); it 'is not central to the poem' (p. 104). Such judgements go hand in hand with the idea that these verses are 'part of the later strata of the text' (p. 86).

González-Reimann envisages a prior text that is somehow more authentically the *Mahābhārata* than the *Mahābhārata* as we have it is. This prior text has a similar story, but without 'foreign material' (2002: 104; see also 92, 95). González-Reimann calls this prior text 'the text as a whole'; 'the main body of the text' (p. 87); 'the main body of the *Mahābhārata*' (p. 91). In common with Hopkins's speculations about the *Mahābhārata*'s development, González-Reimann thinks that this more authentic *Mahābhārata* would contain less material about Viṣṇu (pp. 103–104). But the *Mahābhārata* that González-Reimann imagines cannot be studied. The longstanding tradition within *Mahābhārata* scholarship of labouring under the weight of an imaginary prior text has recently been subjected to sustained critique (see e.g. Adluri and Bagchee 2014: 30–313, following Hiltebeitel 2001). But if we try to study the text that we have, not in order to split it into chronological layers but in order to understand it as a piece of work (Balkaran 2022), then however successive its redactors may have been, we should not sideline parts of it that are relatively difficult to integrate into our understanding.

My approach, as set out in Chapter 1, is to treat all parts of the critically reconstituted *Mahābhārata* as equally authentic, regardless of how many proto-*Mahābhārata*s they might or might not have been part of. As Fitzgerald says, 'the first approach to the received text of a verbal cultural artefact must be synchronic, for whatever history the text may have had prior to its integration of its pre-existing and specially created components, it now exists as a simultaneous fact' (Fitzgerald 2002: 91). Thus although González-Reimann is correct to say that some translators have read the *yuga* scheme into passages that do not necessarily refer to it (González-Reimann 2002: 61), nonetheless his text-historical speculations are not to the present point. Regardless of whether the quoted evidence is early or late, it locates the events of the Kurukṣetra generation at the *dvāpara–kaliyuga* transition. If González-Reimann were to overlook the distinction between hypothetically early and hypothetically late, I think he would agree. This location of the Kurukṣetra generation is a key premise of this monograph.

González-Reimann would perhaps have found it more difficult to downplay the *Mahābhārata*'s integration of the *yuga* scheme had he included the *Harivaṃśa* within his study, because several of the passages quoted above (and others discussed below) that connect the Kurukṣetra generation with the *dvāpara–kaliyuga* transition are found within the *Harivaṃśa*. González-Reimann's decision not to include the *Harivaṃśa* data within the *Mahābhārata* data accords with a text-historical judgement, which was common until recently in *Mahābhārata* scholarship but I hope will be less so in future, to the effect that the *Harivaṃśa* is later than the *Mahābhārata*, and thus that the *Mahābhārata* should be deemed not to include it. As discussed in Chapter 1, the critically reconstituted *Mahābhārata* indicates that it includes the *Harivaṃśa* (Brodbeck 2011; Brodbeck 2016; Brodbeck 2021a), and thus the omission of *Harivaṃśa* data would be akin to omitting, for example, Mbh 3 or Mbh 12 data because they are found in passages thought to have been relatively late additions to an expanding *Mahābhārata*. González-Reimann does effectively do this, because the surmise that many Mbh 3 or 12 passages are late, which is a corollary of the old text-historical approach, is a key factor in his judging that the *yuga* scheme detailed within them is not integral to the *Mahābhārata*; but nonetheless he did have to engage with the Mbh 3 and 12 data as he did so. With the *Harivaṃśa* data, there was no need to do even that. Compare Smith 2009, which purports to encompass the critically reconstituted *Mahābhārata* (p. lxviii), but omits the *Harivaṃśa* without discussion.

So much for the location of the Kurukṣetra war at the *dvāpara–kaliyuga* transition. We are now in a position to present the title problem that orients this monograph. But it is worth noting in passing that the *yuga* cycle, and the location of this great war within it, bear some likeness to Hesiod's account of the successive ages of humanity, as described in *Works and Days* (109–201; Roth 1860; Wulff Alonso 2008: 153–156; Eltschinger 2020: 38–39, 53). After setting out the *yuga* scheme, Gombrich says:

> This basic time-scheme of the four ages reminds us of Hesiod; and, if I may obtrude a personal detail, I distinctly remember being taught in primary school that there were four ages of man, old stone, new stone,

> bronze and iron, and that we live in the iron age. The only difference was that this was progress.
>
> (Gombrich 1975: 121)

In Hesiod's account, the five Greek ages are: the 'golden age', in which humans enjoyed themselves in harmony with the gods; the 'silver age', in which they quarrelled and would not serve the gods, and Zeus killed them; the 'bronze age', in which they fought with bronze weapons and killed themselves off; the nominally anomalous 'heroic age', in which lived legendary heroes such as those who fought in the two famous wars (there are survivors of this age on distant isles); and, finally, the 'iron age' in which Hesiod lived (and we live), in which life is hard and people are shabby and comparatively worthless.

There are obvious similarities with the *yuga* cycle. Where the *Mahābhārata*'s heroic war lies between the third and fourth *yuga*s, the Greek heroic age constitutes itself as a separate *yuga* between the third and fifth. But whereas in the *yuga* cycle the *yuga*s are continuous with each other, such that a person might be born in one *yuga* and die in the next, in Hesiod each variety of humanity is done with at the end of its age, and in the next age another variety is created: 'This is a history not of one humankind, but a story of five humankinds' (Currie 2012: 42; see also Fleet 1911: 488). Most importantly, Hesiod's sequence of ages does not repeat, although there is a hint that the fifth age might not be the last ('would that I were not among the men of the fifth generation, but either had died before or been born afterwards', *Works and Days* 174–175, trans. Evelyn-White).

I am not going to take this comparison further, here or below, and nor am I going to engage in other comparisons between *Mahābhārata* material and material from other parts of the world, except in very brief and impressionistic ways on the basis of my own passing acquaintance. But other comparative paths are certainly available. For example, longevity is a particular feature of the antediluvian patriline in *Genesis* 5.3–32. Adam lived for 930 years, Seth 912, Enosh 905, Kenan 910, Mahalalel 895, Jared 962, Enoch 365, Methuselah 969, Lamech 777, and Lamech's son Noah was 500 when he had his sons, Shem and so on. On these numbers see for example Etz 1993: 'The most important function of the numbers was apparently to show the overall decline of lifespans from the pre-Flood patriarchs to Aaron and Moses' (pp. 181–182). In the first section of genealogy after the flood (*Genesis* 11.10–26) the lifespans are still long, but the range is noticeably lower, and seems to get lower still: Shem lived for 600 years, Arpachshad 438, Shelah 433, Eber 464, Peleg 239, Reu 239, Serug 230, Nahor 148, and Nahor's son Terah was 70 when he had his sons, but thereafter lifespans are not stated. So one might wonder what is going on here, and what kind of indirect historical relationship these *Genesis* lists – which could seem to present something like an 8 : 4 : 2 : 1 ratio (divisions by 2) – might have had with the *yuga* system presented in the *Mahābhārata*.

I cannot advise here. My learning is slight, and is concentrated overwhelmingly onto the *Mahābhārata* side of any comparison. Where such comparisons are pursued, they often turn into questions of who influenced whom, as is evident in the various sources cited above regarding the astronomical lore (the number 4, 3, 2, zeroes, the 'great year', and so on). A common problem with this kind of question, as with the hypothesising of proto-*Mahābhārata*s, is that often any conclusion is underdetermined by the evidence. Arguments for the descent of the *Mahābhārata* and the Mediterranean narratives from a common Indo-European ancestor (e.g. Allen 2019), and for the influence of the Mediterranean material upon the *Mahābhārata* (e.g. Wulff Alonso 2014, 2018), and for the influence of the *Mahābhārata* upon the Mediterranean material, depend upon the same evidence – amazing textual similarities – but differ in their conclusions.

Why does the Kṛṣṇa *avatāra* inaugurate the worst *yuga*?

To anticipate our imminent discussions slightly (as the quotations above and in Chapter 2 have necessarily already done), it is a commonplace in post-Vedic Sanskrit literature that the god Viṣṇu intervenes in the world in order to solve problems. This is stated most famously in the *Bhagavadgītā*, and since the speaker here is Kṛṣṇa, who is Viṣṇu embodied in human form, we have this from the horse's mouth, as it were:

> *yadā yadā hi dharmasya glānir bhavati bhārata* ǀ
> *abhyutthānam adharmasya tadātmānaṃ sṛjāmy aham* ǁ Bhg 4.7 ǁ
> *paritrāṇāya sādhūnāṃ vināśāya ca duṣkṛtām* ǀ
> *dharmasaṃsthāpanārthāya saṃbhavāmi yuge yuge* ǁ 8 ǁ
>
> I send myself forth whenever righteousness declines and unrighteousness is on the rise, Bhārata; age after age I come into being to protect the virtuous, destroy the wicked, and reestablish righteousness.
> (*Bhagavadgītā* 4.7–8, trans. Cherniak 2008: 203)

Given this statement, it is natural enough to imagine that, as Couture says, 'The erosion of *dharma* down through the *yuga*s ... explains the need for the regular manifestation of the supreme god in the human world (cf. *BhG* 4.5–7)' (Couture 2006: 70).

In light of Viṣṇu's special relationship with *dharma* as described here, and in light of the location of the Kurukṣetra war as described above, the question that provoked the research for this monograph is simply this. If Viṣṇu took form as

Kṛṣṇa in order to re-establish *dharma*, then how is it that his appearance ushered in the most adharmic *yuga*?

This problem (Woods 2001: 20 calls it an 'anomaly') has been noticed before:

> It is not very easily understood why the *avatāra*, following the *yuga* where it appears, restores *dharma* more or less completely. In fact, only one situation would be fully comprehensible: the descent of a saviour at the end of a Kaliyuga to bring back a golden age ... It is thus by a sort of artifice that the *avatāras* have been connected with the points of passage between *yugas* other than the Kali and the Kṛta.[27]
>
> (Biardeau 1976: 140, 142)[28]

> It seems to me that the most widespread Indian tradition, which places the Kurukṣetra battle *at the beginning* of the kali age, contradicts the *Mbh*'s deep meaning. If this tradition is accepted, Duryodhana (: Kali) dies just before or at the beginning of the kali age; the victory of the dharmarāja Yudhiṣṭhira, his alliance with Kṛṣṇa, his celebration of the aśvamedha, and the birth of Parikṣit result only in the kali age being inaugurated and our being driven a bit further into adharma.[29]
>
> (Scheuer 1982: 332)

> But the passage of the *Gītā* says that God incarnates when *dharma* decreases and *adharma* increases, and we already know that the cycle that refers to the loss and recuperation of *dharma* is the sequence of the four yugas. In addition, the second of the cited verses [i.e. Bhg 4.8] clearly says that God is born in each yuga.[30] This represents a new problem, since we do not know if it is a matter of the mahāyuga or of each one of the individual yugas. It would be natural for it to refer to the sequence of mahāyugas, and for God's descent to occur when *dharma* had come to its lowest point, that is, at the end of each Kali yuga. In this way, the appearance of the *avatāra* would provide the impulse necessary for the start of a new Kṛta yuga, which is also, after all, the start of

---

[27] 'On ne comprend pas très bien porquoi l'*avatāra*, suivant le *yuga* où il apparaît, restaure le *dharma* plus on [ou?] moins complètement. En fait, une seule situation serait à la rigueur compréhensible: la descente d'un sauveur à la fin d'un Kaliyuga pour ramener un âge d'or ... C'est donc par une sorte d'artifice que l'on fait correspondre des *avatāra* avec des points de passage entre les *yuga* autres que le Kali et le Kṛta.'

[28] For different statements of the same problem, see Biardeau 1994: 102–103; Biardeau 1997: 169.

[29] 'Il me semble que la tradition indienne la plus répandue, qui situe la bataille du Kurukṣetra *au début* de l'âge kali, contredit la signification profonde du *Mbh*. Si l'on accepte cette tradition, Duryodhana (: Kali) meurt à la veille ou au début de l'âge kali; la victoire du dharmarāja Yudhiṣṭhira, son alliance avec Kṛṣṇa, sa célébration de l'aśvamedha, la naissance de Parikṣit, ont pour seul résultat d'inaugurer l'âge kali et de nous enfoncer un peu plus dans l'adharma.'

[30] On the idea that 'God is born in each yuga', see further below.

> a new mahāyuga. The case of Kalkin ... coincides perfectly with this type of incarnation since he will appear at the end of the present Kali yuga. Nonetheless, the other *avatāras*, including Kṛṣṇa, do not fit this pattern. Kṛṣṇa inaugurated our Kali yuga, and the start of the Kali yuga is not the lowest point of the cycle of *dharma*'s ascent and descent.[31]
>
> (González-Reimann 1988: 146)

> [T]he regular descent of an *avatāra* to check or reverse the moral decline of the world is not entirely compatible with the process of inexorable degeneration implicit in the theory of the four *yugas*, for the two systems are based on different theoretical premises.
>
> (Brockington 1992: 27)

> [T]he theory of time affects our evaluation of the war. Despite its being a victory for Yudhiṣṭhira (who is Dharma incarnate), the outcome is (paradoxically) not a better world, but a worse one: we must now endure the *kali yuga*.
>
> ... As Krishna says in the *Gītā* (4.7–8), whenever *dharma* languishes and *adharma* grows, he is reborn age after age (*yuge yuge*), to re-establish *dharma*. How to harmonise this statement with the *yuga* doctrine is, like so many internal doctrinal discrepancies, left to the reader ...
>
> (Allen 2006: 146)

> The myth of the Partial Incarnations [i.e. the Kurukṣetra *avatāra* myth] suggests that *dharma* would be restored after the victory of the gods' side ... [But] If the war was part of the transition from the Dvāpara to the Kali Yuga, then it should, on the contrary, mark a deterioration of *dharma*.
>
> (Reich 2011: 30)

As the above quotations show, this problem has been articulated repeatedly in the scholarly literature (see also Brodbeck 2014: 48–49 and n. 48). This

[31] 'Pero el pasaje de la *Gītā* dice que el dios encarna cuando el *dharma* disminuye y el *adharma* aumenta, y ya sabemos que el ciclo que se refiere a la pérdida y la recuperación del *dharma* es la secuencia de los cuatro yugas. Además, el segundo de los versos citados dice claramente que el dios nace en cada yuga. Esto representa un nuevo problema, ya que no sabemos si se trata del mahāyuga o de cada uno de los cuatros yugas individuales. Lo natural sería que se refiriese a la secuencia de mahāyugas, y que el descenso del dios ocurrise cuando el *dharma* hubiese llegado a su punto más bajo, es decir, al finalizar cada Kali yuga. De esta manera, la aparición del *avatāra* proporcionaría el impulso necesario para el inicio de un nuevo Kṛta yuga, que también es, después de todo, el comienzo de un nuevo mahāyuga. El caso de Kalkin, ya comentado, coincide perfectamente con este tipo de encarnación ya que aparecerá al terminar el actual Kali yuga. Sin embargo, los demás *avatāras*, incluyendo a Kṛṣṇa, no se ajustan a este patrón. Kṛṣṇa inauguró nuestro Kali yuga, y el comienzo del Kali yuga no es el punto más bajo del ciclo de ascenso y descenso del *dharma*.'

monograph dwells upon the title problem as marked by the foregoing series of quotations, and tries to articulate and explore different kinds of solution.

Despite this being a rather obvious problem, neither Janamejaya nor Śaunaka ask about it. Why is this? Addressees within the text often seem to direct the narrative by asking the narrator questions, and sometimes the questions that they ask are in keeping with what other listeners at other narrative levels (or even the audience outside the text) are wondering also. For example, after the Pāṇḍava story has been completed, Śaunaka asks Ugraśravas to tell him more about Kṛṣṇa and his family, and Ugraśravas says that that is just what Janamejaya asked Vaiśaṃpāyana to do (Hv 1.1–14), and so Ugraśravas is able to provide what Śaunaka asked for by relaying what Vaiśaṃpāyana said to Janamejaya, and the audience outside the text are doubly reassured that it is appropriate for them now to hear about Kṛṣṇa in detail. On another occasion, Janamejaya takes up a whole chapter in asking how it could be that the transcendent Viṣṇu-Nārāyaṇa took birth as a lowly human being born from a womb (Hv 30). This gives us some indication of the conceptual obstacles hindering Janamejaya's receipt of the *avatāra* theology. But our title problem for this monograph is not voiced within the text.

Perhaps the poets did not put our question into Janamejaya's or Śaunaka's mouth because if they had, they would have had to put an answer into Vaiśaṃpāyana's or Ugraśravas's mouth, and that might have occasioned a demanding or long-winded tangent. Indeed, it is never directly stated within the text that Kṛṣṇa came to restore *dharma* at a point where *dharma* in fact diminished, and it may be that this is in order not to encourage any character to ask how that could be. Perhaps the poets themselves were concerned to downplay this as a possible problem. As far as I know, there are no interpolations within the manuscript tradition that address it, and no discussion of it by *Mahābhārata* commentaries in Sanskrit. Nonetheless, as we will begin to see immediately below, the problem is addressed by the text at some level. And although we cannot really comment on why the problem is not raised explicitly within the text, it could have been raised by ancient audiences, and it has been raised within the scholarly community, which is reason enough to pursue it. Textual scholars often attempt to answer questions that ancient textual characters never asked.

What has been previously forthcoming by way of a solution? Biardeau calls the *yuga* scenario presented by the text 'a sort of artifice' ('une sorte d'artifice'), and she discovers a different scenario presented in parallel within it, whereby the Kurukṣetra war represents the junction between one *mahāyuga* and another (Biardeau 1976: 151–154). In Biardeau's analogy, the dicing match in Mbh 2, organised by Śakuni and Duryodhana (respectively incarnating Dvāpara and Kali), represents the *dvāpara-kaliyuga* transition; the exile of Yudhiṣṭhira (Dharma) and his brothers in Mbh 3–4, during which Duryodhana (Kali) rules the whole kingdom, represents the *kaliyuga*; and the period after the war, when

Yudhiṣṭhira (Dharma) rules the whole kingdom, represents the *kṛtayuga* of the following *mahāyuga*.

This analogy fits the textual evidence well in many ways, and Biardeau sets it out persuasively. But I do not think it contradicts the fact that the Kurukṣetra war took place at the *dvāpara–kaliyuga* transition. Being on a different scale (since the *kaliyuga* here lasts just thirteen years), it is obviously a different interpretive theme, symbolically suggested rather than stated. This is also Biardeau's assessment: she acknowledges that her analogy operates at 'a second level' ('un niveau second'), although she does also say that 'it is this [second] level, where the *yuga*s become asuric rulers and the cosmic conflagration [becomes a] war, that defines the epic'[32] (Biardeau 1976: 172). This judgement of what 'defines the epic' is gratuitous. From our point of view, the significant feature of Biardeau's analogy is that by reading the war – the war which is the basic purpose of the collective *avatāra* – as the *kali–kṛtayuga* transition where Dharma triumphs over Kali, it places the *avatāra*'s intervention at the point in the cycle where *dharma* is restored, which is the rationale of the *avatāra* as per Bhg 4.7–8 quoted above. One might say that by arranging the text so as to establish this analogy, the text's authors, like Biardeau and the others quoted above, have acknowledged that there is something odd about the actual location of this *avatāra*'s deeds, and have counterbalanced that oddness to some degree. But they have not thereby reduced it; and so by outlining and discussing this analogy, Biardeau has not proposed a solution to our problem. Rather, the kind of satisfying narrative that has a happy ending would naturally be susceptible to this kind of analogy. Similarly, wherever in the *mahāyuga* cycle Rāma Dāśarathi's *avatāra* deeds might be located, the righteous rule following his return from exile would be a *kṛtayuga*, and the period before that would be a *kaliyuga*. Thus the king makes the *yuga* (as discussed further in Chapter 6).

Soifer's approach stresses the textual cross-fertilisation between the idea of the end of a *yuga* and the idea of the end of a *kalpa* or day of Brahmā. This cross-fertilisation, which will be discussed in Chapter 4, means that there is a 'pralayic tendency inherent in the yuga (especially at *yugānta*)' (Soifer 1991: 147). Soifer quotes Biardeau ('It is not very easily understood why the *avatāra*, following the *yuga* where it appears, restores *dharma* more or less completely', quoted above), and then says:

> From an overall, general point of view, her comment seems correct; but by reading each myth, each version, an answer to this complaint begins to appear; and it is subtle, subtle perhaps as the dharma is itself ... [W]e see not really black and white, but varying shades of gray; not really *Adharma* vs. *Dharma*, but a conflict in which the characters are tempered by the times ... [H]ow can we judge the dharmic nature of

[32] 'c'est ce niveau, où les *yuga* deviennent princes asuriques et la conflagration cosmique guerre, qui définit l'épopée'

> Kṛṣṇa's council to the Pāṇḍavas during the *Mahābhārata* battle; does the incredibly 'subtle' nature of Kṛṣṇa's rendering of the dharma not signal the advent of the Kali Age itself? ... The temporal structure, complete with deteriorating dharma, is an absolute ... The descent of Viṣṇu speaks to both yuga and dharma: it maintains the partial and dynamic nature of dharma as regulated by the yugas by allowing neither Perfect Dharma ... nor total Adharma ... [to] prevail.
>
> (Soifer 1991: 148–149)

On this view, we can perhaps understand why, given the constraints of the place in time where it appears, the *avatāra* would 'restore *dharma* more or less completely'. That is, if there were an *asura* or some other disturbance driving *dharma* away from the currently permissible level, the *avatāra* would only return it to that level. But this approach seems to fit better with an intervention mid-*yuga* than it would with an intervention at a transition between descending *yuga*s. If, as Soifer says, 'The temporal structure, complete with deteriorating dharma, is an absolute', then the deterioration at the transition between one *yuga* and another should occur automatically; as Biardeau suggests, 'the succession of *yuga*s can be described without any reference to an *avatāra*'[33] (Biardeau 1976: 123). So I do not think that Soifer proposes a solution to our problem either.

Chapter 5 sketches a kind of solution whereby, at some level, the Kurukṣetra *avatāra* located at the *dvāpara-kaliyuga* transition represents not (or not just) what happens at the switch between those two particular *yuga*s on the descending arc, but (also) what happens across and around the *yuga* cycle as a whole. Insofar as this sketched solution concerns what is 'represented' by the Kurukṣetra *avatāra*, it could be seen as theoretically akin to Biardeau's. In this sense it would not be a solution as such, because regardless of what the Kurukṣetra war might be said to **represent**, the Kurukṣetra war **is** what the *avatāra* effects, in connection with the ongoing Bhārata lineage, at the *dvāpara-kaliyuga* transition. But the solution sketched in Chapter 5 is a solution nonetheless, because it reassesses what the *avatāra* – any *avatāra* – is for. In my view, the blockage in previous attempts to address the problem has been the singular conception of what an *avatāra* does, as conditioned by Kṛṣṇa's statement in the *Bhagavadgītā*. In fact the *avatāra* has two functions. But before exploring that, we must set the scene a bit more fully.

[33] 'on peut décrire la succession des *yuga* sans aucune référence à un *avatāra*'

CHAPTER 4

Avatāras and *Yugāntas*

Viṣṇu's appearance as Kṛṣṇa is contextualised by his earlier appearances as a boar, a dwarf, a man-lion, and various human beings including Rāma Jāmadagnya and Rāma Dāśarathi (Soifer 1991: 4–5; Sutton 2000: 156–181; Matchett 2001: 28–32, 183; Couture 2010; Coleman 2017). Lists of Viṣṇu's various forms are provided at 3.100.19–23; 12.326.71–97; 12.337.35–36; and Hv 31. The *Mahābhārata* does not use the word *avatāra* for these forms – it uses the words *aṃśa* 'part', *bhāga* 'portion', *avataraṇa* 'crossing-down', and *prādurbhāva* 'manifestation'. I use the word *avatāra*, cognate and synonymous with *avataraṇa*, because it is well known.

The usage of the word *avatāra* is potentially problematic when discussing the *Mahābhārata*, since apart from its one appearance at 3.146.33 (Sullivan 2016: 191), the word *avatāra* is used only in later texts. When meeting the word *avatāra* in this monograph, readers should really substitute the word *prādurbhāva*. In routinely using the word *avatāra* I do not intend to allow the importing into the *Mahābhārata* context of theological aspects only later associated with the word. The danger is not so much one of anachronism as of the fact that the same word *avatāra* is used with slightly different connotations in different contexts. Even if the word *avatāra* were used routinely by the *Mahābhārata*, using it in this monograph would be dangerous because readers might thereby think that in the *Mahābhārata* it means everything that it means in some other Vaiṣṇava context with which they are more familiar. But that is a general danger with using words. The word *avatāra* has a basic meaning in keeping with its etymology; it passed into English as 'avatar' in the nineteenth century, and it is now used in computing contexts, where it retains the theatrical sense that Couture has emphasised (Couture 2001: 319–323). It may be summed up as an appearance in character, as theorised by Snout the tinker:

How to cite this book chapter:
Brodbeck, S. 2022. Divine Descent and the Four World-Ages in the *Mahābhārata* – or, Why Does the Kṛṣṇa *Avatāra* Inaugurate the Worst *Yuga*?. Pp. 63–87. Cardiff: Cardiff University Press. DOI: https://doi.org/10.18573/book9.d.

In this same interlude it doth befall
That I, one Snout by name, present a wall ...
This loam, this roughcast, and this stone doth show
That I am that same wall; the truth is so. ...
  Thus have I, Wall, my part dischargèd so;
And, being done, thus Wall away doth go.
(*A Midsummer Night's Dream*, act 5 scene 1)

Hacker's article on 'the evolution of the *avatāra* theory' ('Zur Entwicklung der Avatāralehre', Hacker 1960) has been criticised for overlooking this theatrical connotation (Couture 2001: 313) and for its allegedly circular argument (Adluri and Bagchee 2016: 82 n. 13), but it is important for us nonetheless, as it discusses the ambiguity of the word *avataraṇa*. In Hacker's view, this word originally described the descent of various gods to earth on one specific occasion (as described in 1.58 and Hv 40–45, discussed in Chapter 5 below), but it did not describe Viṣṇu in particular, still less did it describe a repeating tendency of his. Later, the word *avataraṇa*, which already had the sense of descending or crossing down, was also used, somewhat artificially (Hacker 1960: 58), to describe the 'taking down or removal' of, in particular, the Earth's burden (Monier-Williams 1899: 753 col. 1), and was thus able to serve in a double sense to indicate both the gods' method and their objective. Later still, this double sense was restricted to apply to Viṣṇu in particular, and was generalised to cover his multiple appearances within the world. This developmental sequence of ideas is speculative and from our point of view largely unhelpful, since its effect is to recontextualise specific usages away from the synchronically reconstituted text in which they occur; but nonetheless it highlights the wordplay that we see there. The compound *bhārāvataraṇa* occurs seven times in the text, almost always in connection with Viṣṇu (3.45.21; 12.326.92; 12.328.33; 12.337.31; 16.9.29; Hv 41.29; Hv 42.39), with it being either implied or explicitly stated that the burden is the earth's burden (Couture 2001: 319).

The Kurukṣetra *avatāra* is not the only *avatāra* that is located at a specific point in the *yuga* cycle (Huntington 1964: 16–30; Kloetzli 2013: 636). Kalkin is specifically located, as he oversees a transition to the next *mahāyuga* at the end of a *kaliyuga* (González-Reimann 2013: 107–108). Kalkin and his deeds are described at 3.188.85–189.9. There he is not explicitly identified as an *avatāra*; but he is identified as an *avatāra* at Hv 31.148. Where in the *yuga* cycle do the various other *avatāras* appear? In some of the *Mahābhārata*'s *avatāra* accounts the *yuga* is not specified. I will mention now the ones where it is. Vaiśaṃpāyana says that Viṣṇu has had 'many thousands of manifestations in the past' (*prādurbhāvasahasrāṇi samatītāny anekaśaḥ* | Hv 31.10cd), but most of them are never described.

The man-lion *avatāra* comes in order to kill the demon Hiraṇyakaśipu, who became corrupted during a *kṛtayuga* (Hv 31.32). So this *avatāra* could potentially appear at a *kṛta–tretāyuga* transition (Biardeau 1976: 137 and n. 2; Soifer 1991: 101; Brockington 1992: 26). If so, then this could be the same trouble (*viparyāsa*) that the sages Ekata, Dvita, and Trita are told they will help the gods to dispel at the *kṛta–tretāyuga* transition (12.323.50–51).

The Rāma Dāśarathi *avatāra* occurs at a *tretā–dvāparayuga* transition (12.326.78), and also in the twenty-fourth *mahāyuga* (Hv 31.110, where *yuga* must mean *mahāyuga*). Thus the Rāma Dāśarathi *avatāra* occurs several *mahāyuga*s before the Kurukṣetra *avatāra*, which occurs in the twenty-eighth *mahāyuga* (Hv 13.39, quoted above, p. 50). Ekata and Dvita become apes in order to assist Rāma Dāśarathi at the *tretā–dvāparayuga* transition (12.326.79–81).

The Rāma Jāmadagnya *avatāra* appears in a *tretāyuga* (12.326.77), and his purge of the *kṣatriya*s, which is repeated twenty-one times (*triḥsapta*, 3 × 7; Dejenne 2009), occurs at a *tretā–dvāparayuga* transition (1.2.3; Biardeau 1976: 136; Thomas 1996: 84 n. 37; Fitzgerald 2002: 104). This is contradicted or supplemented by the presentation at 1.58, where Rāma Jāmadagnya's massacres are followed by a *kṛtayuga* (Fitzgerald 2002: 105 calls it a 'golden age'), and so Rāma Jāmadagnya would be in Kalkin's place, as it were, but in the past (Biardeau 1976: 141–142).

The numerical distinction between the *mahāyuga* of the Rāma Dāśarathi *avatāra* and the *mahāyuga* of the Kurukṣetra *avatāra*, coupled with the fact that there are a thousand *mahāyuga*s to get through, means that we do not necessarily have to envisage multiple *avatāra*s within the same *mahāyuga*.[34] This is an important point. There is no contradiction (and some nominal justice) in the fact that both Rāma Dāśarathi and Rāma Jāmadagnya are linked to a *tretā–dvāparayuga* transition, since there are many such transitions available. Perhaps also in principle there is no contradiction in Rāma Jāmadagnya perpetrating his massacres at one point in one *mahāyuga* and at a different point in another (or even, later in the same one); after all, his massacres are said to be repeated.

Some of the *avatāra*s seem to be cosmogonic in character (Brockington 1992: 24–25), as if rather than intervening to affect a world that is already in process, they would be making – or re-making – the world in the first place. In this sense they would implicitly be located at the beginning of the first *kṛtayuga* of a day of Brahmā, where a lot more has to happen than at the beginning of any of the 999 subsequent *kṛtayuga*s. This could arguably be the case for the tortoise *avatāra* (or Mohinī, 1.15–17), the fish *avatāra* (3.185, *avatāra* of Brahmā), the boar *avatāra* (12.326.71–72; Hv 31.21–30; Kātre 1934: 67–75), the dwarf *avatāra* (12.326.74–76; Hv 31.68–92; though Mbh 5.72.12 says that the *asura*

[34] By analogy with the principle of *kalpabheda* – whereby one might suggest that two particular events occurred in different *kalpa*s (González-Reimann 2009: 422; Minkowski 2004) – we might call this the principle of *mahāyugabheda*.

Bali was born the end of the *kṛtayuga*, *paryāyakāle dharmasya prāpte*), and the lotus *avatāra* (Hv 31.14–20). The plurality of myths perhaps matches the plurality of days of Brahmā.

Regarding the other *avatāras*, the details given above demonstrate the text's tendency to locate them at the transitions between *yugas* – that is, at *yugāntas* (Thomas 1988: 241; Koskikallio 1994: 259). Within this, they are mostly located at the transitions between descending *yugas*. There are more of such transitions. But **why** is there a tendency for *avatāras* to be located at such transitions? Of Viṣṇu's *avatāras*, only Kalkin (and Rāma Jāmadagnya where a *kṛtayuga* follows his massacres) is placed where an *avatāra* would make dharmic sense as per the *Bhagavadgītā* account.

A plurality of *avatāras* within a *mahāyuga* could be suggested by the various statements that the supreme god has different colours or qualities in successive *yugas* (white, red, yellow, black, 3.148.16–33; white, yellow, red, black, 3.187.31; *dharma*, *jñāna*, *bala*, *adharma*, 13.143.9). But these statements are cryptic, and may or may not refer to *avatāras*. Notable also is 7.28.23–26, where Kṛṣṇa tells Arjuna that he has four forms. One form does *tapas* on the earth, one witnesses good and bad deeds, one comes to the human world and performs deeds, and one lies sleeping for a thousand years and then grants boons upon waking. The *avatāra* aspect seems to be restricted to the third of these forms.[35]

The phrase *yuge yuge* ('in *yuga* after *yuga*') at Bhg 4.8 could indicate *yugas*, *mahāyugas*, or neither (González-Reimann 2002: 175, 193), and this is the case also at various other places where the phrase *yuge yuge* occurs. The sense of *yuga* in this phrase is sometimes hard to ascertain, and potentially deliberately so. Where it is possible to pin *yuge yuge* down, the sense is often **not** 'in each of the four *yugas*'.[36]

---

[35] According to the *Viṣṇupurāṇa* (3.2.56–59), Viṣṇu, in the role of preserver, takes form in each and every *yuga*: as Kapila in the *kṛta*, as a universal monarch in the *tretā*, as Veda-vyāsa in the *dvāpara*, and as Kalkin at the end of the *kaliyuga*. Twenty-nine Veda-vyāsas are named at *Viṣṇupurāṇa* 3.3.9–21, one from each of the 28 *mahāyugas* in this *manvantara* so far, plus the one to come in the next *mahāyuga*. In addition to these four forms per *mahāyuga*, Viṣṇu is also Kṛṣṇa and so on.

[36] Here is a full survey of the phrase *yuge yuge* in the *Mahābhārata*: 1.57.72 (complex variable decreases by a quarter); 3.148.7, 9 (complex variable decreases; the Hanūmat–Bhīma passage); 6.26.8 (*avatāra* appears; Bhg 4.8); 6.62.40 (Kṛṣṇa creates the cosmos); 7.172.81 (Nara and Nārāyaṇa are born), 86 (Aśvatthāman has worshipped Śiva); 8.65.18 (Arjuna has defeated the darkness missile, *rākṣasas*, and *asuras*); 12.64.25 (the ancient *dharmas* are rolled out); 12.220.41 (time brings down many thousands of Indras); 12.224.1 (complex variable decreases), 68 (*dharma* and *adharma* vary), 69 (*dharma* varies); 12.230.18 (the Vedas produce the Vedāṅgas); 12.327.53 (the *pravṛtti* seers perform sacrifices); 12.328.19 (Śiva is composed of Nārāyaṇa); Hv 2.54 (creatures from Dakṣa onwards are born); Hv 3.57 (the classes of gods arise); Hv 13.64 (Manu re-establishes the ancestral rites); Hv 30.15 (people speak of Viṣṇu); Hv 117.49, 50 (people receive the blessings they deserve). For *yuge yuge* in the *Ṛgveda*, see González-Reimann 1988: 56.

Soifer says:

> The ten avatāras are traditionally set to appear throughout the course of one Mahāyuga: the fish, tortoise, boar, and man-lion in the Kṛta; dwarf, Paraśurāma [i.e. Jāmadagnya], and Rāma Dāśarathi in the Tretā; Buddha and Kṛṣṇa in the Dvāpara; and Kalkin, yet to descend, in the Kali. (Soifer 1991: 146)

This tradition is not known in the *Mahābhārata*. It depends upon the idea of a standard group of ten *avatāras*, which also is not known in the reconstituted *Mahābhārata* (Bhandarkar 1965: 41–42), and is not standard in any case. In the tradition that Soifer cites, the distribution of *avatāras* to *yugas* follows the 4, 3, 2, 1 pattern, so that the shorter *yugas* have correspondingly fewer *avatāras*. Huntington wonders whether the shorter, less dharmic *yugas* should actually merit a higher rate of *avatāras*, given that solving dharmic problems is supposed to be the *avatāra*'s forte (Huntington 1960: 130–131; Huntington 1964: 34–35; Soifer 1991: 146–147). This is a version of our title problem.

Yudhiṣṭhira says that he knows, as Vyāsa and Nārada know, that Kṛṣṇa and Arjuna are 'the lotus-eyed duo of the three *yugas*' (*triyugau puṇḍarīkākṣau vāsudevadhanaṃjayau* ‖ 3.84.4ef), the seers Nara and Nārāyaṇa. He subsequently refers to Kṛṣṇa as *triyuga* (*triyugaṃ tvāṃ vadanty api*, 12.43.6d); and in between, Saṃjaya and then Dhṛtarāṣṭra have referred to Kṛṣṇa as 'Madhusūdana of the three *yugas*' (*triyugaṃ madhusūdanam*, 5.67.3b and 4d). These are the only occurrences of the compound *triyuga* in the *Mahābhārata*. This *triyuga* phrase is curious, as it seems to play on *triloka*, *triguṇa*, and so on, and also on the sets of three where there is a fourth (the Vedas with the *Atharvaveda*, the *varṇas* with the *śūdra*, and so on). In light of the triple ambiguity of the word *yuga* as discussed below – referring to one of the four *yugas*, or to a *mahāyuga*, or to a day of Brahmā – the word *triyuga* would not necessarily imply three of the four *yugas* in a *mahāyuga*; nor, if it did, would it indicate which three these would be. Thomas suggests 'the fourth presumably being omitted because of its adharmic nature' (Thomas 1988: 238 n. 20).

The situation whereby *avatāras* appear at *yugāntas* is complicated and poetically confected because the *yugānta*, the 'end of a *yuga*', involves three different senses of the word *yuga*, enumerated below – we could call them small *yuga*, *mahāyuga*, and mega-*yuga*. There is ambiguity because the same word, *yugānta*, has several senses. But there is also ambiguity because those three senses are similar concepts nested within and around one another, such that every end-of-day-of-Brahmā is also an end-of-*mahāyuga* and an end-of-*kaliyuga*, and every end-of-*mahāyuga* is also an end-of-*kaliyuga*. And there is also ambiguity because even without lexical parity, different lengths of cyclic time-unit are, in a sense, equivalent. Discussing Kuiper's interpretation of the Ṛgvedic hymns to Uṣas ('Dawn', Kuiper 1960), González-Reimann says that 'the hymns could refer not just to the diurnal cycle, to the succession of day and night, but to the annual regeneration of nature'[37] (González-Reimann 1988: 28, see also 78). In a similar vein, Gonda writes:

> All time passes in periods and a shorter period can easily be regarded as a partial manifestation of a longer one – 'there is in each single season (*ṛtu*) the form (*rūpam*) of all seasons' (ŚB. 8, 7, 1, 4; cf. 2, 2, 3, 7) – ; a succession of shorter periods that make up a longer one, each of them characterized by different events, may create the impression of being facets or different manifestations of the latter.
>
> (Gonda 1984: 27)

Time is the same cake however you cut it. As Bhīṣma says:

> *kalāṃśās tāta yujyante muhūrtāś ca dināni ca* |
> *ardhamāsāś ca māsāś ca nakṣatrāṇi grahās tathā* ‖ 4.47.1 ‖
> *ṛtavaś cāpi yujyante tathā saṃvatsarā api* |
> *evaṃ kālavibhāgena kālacakraṃ pravartate* ‖ 2 ‖
>
> The instants are joined together, and so are the hours, days, fortnights, months, lunar houses, planets, seasons, and years: thus the wheel of time revolves with the divisions of time.
>
> (4.47.1–2, trans. van Buitenen 1978: 97)

I take this to mean that all the instants joined together is the same as all the hours joined together, or all the days, or all the fortnights, and so on. On a clock face, the hour, minute, and second hands all trace the same circle, as would slower hands too, if they were there.

Three senses of *yugānta*

1. In the shortest sense of *yuga* – the *kṛta*, *tretā*, *dvāpara*, or *kali yuga* – there are four *yugānta*s in the cycle, one at the end of each *yuga*. Three are at descending transitions, and one, the *kaliyugānta*, is at an ascending transition. The *kaliyugānta* is in a special position because the *kaliyuga* is the last *yuga* in the *mahāyuga*.

2. In terms of *yuga* in the sense of *mahāyuga*, the *yugānta* would be the *kaliyuga* and/or its dusk, before the following *kṛtayuga*. Several Purāṇas apply a metaphor to the juncture between *mahāyuga*s, whereby 'the new Yuga grows out of the old one like grass after the forest fire' (Koskikallio 1994: 259; *Vāyupurāṇa*

[37] 'los himnos podrían referirse ya no solamente al ciclo diurno, a la sucesión día-noche, sino a la regeneración anual de la naturaleza'

58.109–110; *Brahmāṇḍapurāṇa* 1.2.31.110; *Matsyapurāṇa* 144.98–99). But this is a metaphor.

González-Reimann gives a misleading impression – at least as far as the *Mahābhārata* is concerned – when he suggests that the end of a *mahāyuga* would involve environmental destruction (González-Reimann 2002: 72, 140). He gives this impression partly because of the instances where *yuga* refers to a day of Brahmā, at the end of which there **is** environmental destruction (see below). Other scholars give the same misleading impression. Karve says that 'The earth with all the living beings is created at the beginning of Satya and is destroyed at the end of Kali, to be recreated at the start of a new Satya yuga' (Karve 1991: 183). Allen says that 'When in due course the *kali yuga* ends, the universe dissolves into the primal waters (undergoes *pralaya*), only to be recreated anew when the cycle restarts' (Allen 2006: 145). Hudson says that 'at the end of the Kali *yuga*, the world is destroyed and then recreated', and mentions 'Kṛṣṇa's role as creator and destroyer of the universe at the beginning of the Kṛta *yuga* and the end of the Kali *yuga*' (Hudson 2013: 149–150, 154). Taylor likewise says that according to the *Mahābhārata*, 'At the end of the Kali yuga, the age of decadence, the world is destroyed, then recreated, and the cycle begins again' (Taylor 2022: 77). These and other such accounts of the *mahāyugānta* should be received with scepticism;[38] they may perhaps accord with some Purāṇic accounts (Church 1971: 151–153; Dimmitt and van Buitenen 1978: 21–22), but they do not accord with the *Mahābhārata*. In Mārkaṇḍeya's account of the *mahāyugānta*, Kalkin kills some miscreants, but Vyāsa's *Harivaṃśa* account seems to be bloodless. The world is not destroyed and recreated at these junctures. As Fleet says, 'the Four Ages run on, in cycle after cycle, without any break; the "twilight" of one age gliding straight into the "dawn" of its successor' (1911: 482; see also *Viṣṇupurāṇa* 4.24.20–21).

In the *Mahābhārata* I have only found two verses that could suggest that the world would be destroyed at each *mahāyugānta*. At 3.187.32, Viṣṇu-Nārāyaṇa tells Mārkaṇḍeya:

> *trayo bhāgā hy adharmasya tasmin kāle bhavanty uta* |
> *antakāle ca saṃprāpte kālo bhūtvātidāruṇaḥ* |
> *trailokyaṃ nāśayāmy ekaḥ kṛtsnaṃ sthāvarajaṅgamam* ‖ 3.187.32 ‖
>
> At this time lawlessness reigns for three-fourths; and when the end-time has come, I become most terrifying Time and by myself destroy the entire universe with moving and standing creatures.
> (3.187.32, trans. van Buitenen 1975: 592, adapted)

[38] Compare Trautmann, who erroneously states that in the *Manusmṛti* account, 'at the end of the Kali, there is a general dissolution' (Trautmann 1995: 171). Taylor also gives this impression (2022: 77).

The first line of this verse (32ab) clearly refers to the *kaliyuga* as the portion of the *mahāyuga* in which *dharma* has been reduced by three-quarters. If this reference is carried through into the rest of the verse, then it will seem that the 'end-time' (*antakāla*) is the end of any *kaliyuga* and thus any *mahāyuga*. But if the last two lines are taken on their own, then the locative *antakāle* would be ambiguous, and we might most naturally take it to mean the end of the day of Brahmā, in keeping with other passages. Now, this verse is a three-line verse surrounded on either side by sequences of the more common two-line verses; and Hopkins says that 'Sometimes ... where one or three hemistichs make a stanza, it is merely a matter of editing' (Hopkins 1901: 194). If we were to group line 32ab with the previous verse – to which it refers back with the words *tasmin kāle*; that verse ended by mentioning the *kaliyuga* as the *yuga* in which Viṣṇu-Nārāyaṇa's colour is black – then this would facilitate our view of lines 32cd and 32ef as a separate statement, and of the *antakāla* as the end of a day of Brahmā.

The other possible suggestion that the world might be destroyed at the end of each *mahāyuga* is at Hv 32.17. Here, extreme meteorological events occurring during the war between the gods and the demons are apparently compared to those at the end of a *caturyuga* (*caturyugāntaparyāye lokānāṃ yad bhayaṃ bhavet* | Hv 32.17ab, no variants; Vaidya 1969: 235). This is the only time in the *Mahābhārata* that the word *caturyuga* is used to indicate the four-*yuga* cycle.[39] This suggestion of world-destruction at the end of the *mahāyuga* apparently conflicts with the much more detailed accounts of the same juncture given by Mārkaṇḍeya and Vyāsa; so one might reasonably interpret *caturyugānta* here as 'the end of the [one thousand] *caturyugas*' (i.e. the end of the day of Brahmā).

2½. I interject here some paragraphs about *manvantaras*. The *Mahābhārata* does not use the word *yuga* to refer to a *manvantara*, or the word *yugānta* to refer to the end of a *manvantara*. So this is a tangent.

The *manvantara* theory, which the *Mahābhārata* gives only in summary form, describes each day of Brahmā as being presided over, for equal periods of time, by fourteen successive Manus (Hv 7; González-Reimann 2009: 418 lists the other *Mahābhārata* references; see also Mankad 1942: 208–210; Gupta 1969: 311–317; Mitchiner 1978; Dimmitt and van Buitenen 1978: 23–24; Thomas 1988: 71–73). At the end of each *manvantara* there is a change not just of the Manu, but also of his sons, and the gods, and the cosmic sages; and in some texts the *manvantara* also has a dusk and a dawn, and in some texts there is destruction and re-creation of the universe at these points (Fleet 1911: 482 and n. 2; González-Reimann 1988: 139–140).

---

[39] As mentioned earlier (p. 15). The only other occurrence of *caturyuga*, at Hv 58.45c, is better interpreted as just 'the four *yugas*'; no cycle is necessarily implied. The full verse reads: 'Your coils are the four oceans, you know what separates the four social classes, you oversee the worlds' four ages, and when the four types of priests do a ritual, you get the benefit' (*catuḥsāgarabhogas tvaṃ cāturvarṇyavibhāgavit* | *caturyugeśo lokānāṃ cāturhotraphalāśanaḥ* ‖ Hv 58.45).

On one occasion the *Mahābhārata* may suggest such destruction and re-creation:

> *manvantareṣu saṃhārāḥ saṃhārānteṣu saṃbhavāḥ* | Hv 7.50ab ...
> *manvantareṣu saṃhāraḥ śrūyate bharatarṣabha* ‖ 51cd
> *saśeṣās tatra tiṣṭhanti devā brahmarṣibhiḥ saha* |
> *tapasā brahmacaryeṇa śrutena ca samanvitāḥ* |
> *pūrṇe yugasahasre tu kalpo niḥśeṣa ucyate* ‖ 52 ‖

Here are two translations:

> At the end of every Manu's era there's a destruction, and after every destruction there's a creation ... At the end of every Manu's era there's said to be a destruction, bull of the Bhāratas, and when that happens the gods and brahmin seers wait there with what remains, maintaining their austerities, their continence, and their knowledge. But when a thousand ages have elapsed, that's said to be the end of a cosmic cycle, and nothing remains.
>
> (*Harivaṃśa* 7.50ab, 51c–52, trans. Brodbeck 2019b: 24)

> When [all fourteen of] the Manu eras have finished there are destructions, and after the destructions there are creations ... We hear that when the Manu eras have finished there are destructions, bull of the Bhāratas; and then the gods and the brahmin seers, endowed with austerities, continence, and knowledge, subsist within what remains (*saśeṣa*), even though, since the thousand *yuga*s have elapsed, the *kalpa* is said to have nothing remaining (*niḥśeṣa*).
>
> (*Harivaṃśa* 7.50ab, 51c–52, new translation)

In the first of these two interpretations, the idea of different types of destruction (here *saṃhāra*) is similar to the idea of different types (or levels) of *pralaya* as described in various Purāṇas, with days of Brahmā adding up to lifetimes of Brahmās (see e.g. *Viṣṇupurāṇa* 6.3–4). Seven different births of Brahmā are described in Mbh 12.336: he is born from Nārāyaṇa's mouth, eyes, speech, ear, nose, egg, and lotus. But in the *Mahābhārata* Brahmā's multiple births are not linked to any cycle of time. To all intents and purposes, in the *Mahābhārata* there is no time-cycle longer than the days and nights of Brahmā, which proceed in an apparently infinite succession.

In the term 'day of Brahmā' in the *Mahābhārata*, Brahmā (or *brahman*) might as well stand for Viṣṇu-Nārāyaṇa. Nārāyaṇa is said to begin the process of creation by 'remembering' Brahmā (*sargasyādau smṛto brahmā prajāsargakaraḥ prabhuḥ* | 12.326.105ab). Vyāsa says of Viṣṇu: 'at the end of the *yuga* [i.e. day of Brahmā] he tucks the worlds away and goes to sleep, and at the start of the *yuga* he wakes up and erects the world' (*yugānte sa suptaḥ susaṃkṣipya lokān yugādau prabuddho jagad dhy utsasarja* ‖ 12.327.89cd).[40] González-Reimann says that 'Vaiṣṇavism appropriated Brahmā's role as creator by explaining that the god who wakes up and goes to sleep is Nārāyaṇa-Viṣṇu' (González-Reimann 2009: 415).

The second of the two translations above is more in keeping with the *Mahābhārata*'s overall cosmology. One might see this and other allegedly anomalous or rogue verses, which might seem to fit more straightforwardly in a Purāṇa context, as intrusions or influences from a parallel tradition; or one might imagine that parallel tradition (as we know it) as partially derivative, prompted by new interpretations (or misinterpretations) of particular *Mahābhārata* verses. This example, which turns on whether, in context, the word *manvantareṣu* means 'after every *manvantara*' or 'after all the *manvantaras*', is similar to the previous example, which turns on whether, in context, the compound *caturyugānta* means 'the end of every *caturyuga*' or 'the end of all the *caturyugas*'.

As stated above, the *Mahābhārata* does not use the word *yuga* in the sense of *manvantara*. And since we are in the twenty-eighth of the seventy-one *mahāyugas* in the current *manvantara* (Hv 13.39; González-Reimann 1988: 125, 127), from our point of view what happens in between one *manvantara* and another is a relatively distant issue.

3. In terms of *yuga* in the sense of a day of Brahmā (i.e. a *kalpa*, a thousand *mahāyugas*), the *yugānta* would involve the dissolution of the universe.

Biardeau says that 'When the epic speaks of a *yugānta*, all of the symbolism of the *pralaya* is found to be implemented'[41] (Biardeau 1976: 135). Scheuer writes of 'an ambiguity due to the fact that the *Mbh* does not clearly distinguish end-of-yuga and end-of-kalpa'[42] (Scheuer 1982: 156; see also 329–331, 350). Biardeau notes that 'Quite often a catastrophe is compared to the fire at the end of a *yuga*, when the end of a *kalpa* would be more appropriate since the end of a *yuga* is marked by a *saṃdhyā* in which no fire or wind is involved' (Biardeau 1997: 166).

As González-Reimann says, 'comparisons to the end of the yuga become a standard device for describing something deemed to be awe-inspiring, terrible and devastating' (González-Reimann 2002: 64). The reference tends to be to

[40] According to this idea, Viṣṇu would stay awake for a thousand *mahāyugas* at a time. This is a different sense of Viṣṇu's sleep from that which we find at Hv 40, where Viṣṇu wakes up (or is woken up) towards the end of the *dvāparayuga* in order to address the situation on Earth, and so he might be free to sleep except when engaging in an *avatāra* appearance. It is also a different sense of Viṣṇu's sleep from that which we find at Hv 40.23–25 in particular, where Viṣṇu sleeps every year for the duration of the rainy season, during which he is not worshipped and Indra does his job for him (on this González-Reimann refers to the fifth-century Gangdhar inscription of Viśvavarman; González-Reimann 2009: 415; Fleet 1888: 77).

[41] 'Quand l'épopée parle d'un *yugānta*, c'est tout le symbolisme du *pralaya* qui se trouve mis en œuvre'

[42] 'une ambiguïté due au fait que le *Mbh* ne distingue pas clairement fin-de-yuga et fin-de-kalpa'

the 'fire at the end of a *yuga*', with which any particularly ferocious warrior, for example, may be compared. There are also metaphorical references to the sun, wind, and clouds at the end of a *yuga*, playing upon the severity of the weather at that time (for references, see Biardeau 1976: 124; Koskikallio 1994: 260 n. 19; González-Reimann 2002: 65–71). In these metaphors the *yuga* must be a day of Brahmā, because the reference is to the events of the *pralaya*, the dissolution of the universe. This kind of *yugānta* is described by Mārkaṇḍeya at 3.186.56–76, with mention of severe drought, seven suns, the voracious doomsday fire, high winds, and terrible clouds which then rain until only ocean remains (Thomas 2007: 198). Thus although in the *Mahābhārata* the word *yuga* on its own (or in compounds other than *yugānta*) only rarely refers to a day of Brahmā, the compound *yugānta* very often refers to the end of a day of Brahmā. This *pralaya* event is distinct from the end of a *mahāyuga* (or the end of any of the four *yugas*) in terms of the sheer destruction involved, as is clear in Mārkaṇḍeya's accounts (of the end of a day of Brahmā in 3.186, and of the end of a *mahāyuga* in 3.188–189).

Because the word *yugānta* is repeatedly used in connection with the signs of the end of the world, Jacobi draws a historical conclusion:

> As the latter signs [i.e. of the end of the world] are frequently alluded to, in the form of similes in the Epics, etc., as occurring at the end of a yuga (instead of at the end of a kalpa), it is most probable that originally the yuga ended with the destruction, and consequently began with the creation of the world.
>
> (Jacobi 1908: 201 cols 1–2)

The hypothesised 'originally' here would accord with the view mentioned in connection with various scholars above, that the world is destroyed at every *mahāyugānta*. Thomas in similar fashion suggests that 'the basic cycle of creation and destruction [is] based around a single (*catur*)*yuga* unit, rather than 1000 repeating (*catur*)*yugas*' (Thomas 1988: 78). But Jacobi's 'most probable' conclusion is speculative, and does not further poetical appreciation. This kind of speculative historical conclusion, like Hopkins's scheme of the *Mahābhārata*'s development, is too easily repeated; when Gombrich says that the destruction of the world 'occurs at the end of the *kalpa*, but presumably was originally conceived as bringing the world to an end at the close of a *mahāyuga*', he is re-dispensing Jacobi's historicist meme (Gombrich 1975: 124; see also Mitchiner 1978: 24–27). The repetition of this meme within Indological discourse has led scholars to misrepresent the *Mahābhārata* as containing the allegedly 'original' idea as its typical presentation, whereas in fact, once one appreciates how common it is for the *Mahābhārata* to use the word *yuga* in the sense of day of Brahmā, the allegedly 'original' idea is hardly evident within the text. Hypothesising an earlier version of the text (or of an idea) can fuel misrepresentations and misinterpretations; and because such hypotheses are typically as unfalsifiable as they are unverifiable, once they start to do this, it is difficult to stop them.

In view of the destructive drama at the end of a day of Brahmā and the dharmic drama at the end of a *mahāyuga*, and in view of the multiple senses of the word *yuga* and the complexity of the temporal scheme that they embody, it is perhaps to be expected that the other types of *yugānta* – the ends of *kṛta*, *tretā*, and *dvāparayugas* – would also come to be linked with dramatic events, even if all that need actually happen at such junctures is that lifespan and *dharma* decline from one level to the next. Some such process of conceptual spillover could help to explain how most of the human (or semihuman) *avatāras* listed above could have been pegged to such junctures, even though **that** kind of *yugānta* (the end of a *yuga* in our shortest sense) should be much easier to negotiate than the *yugānta* that ends a *mahāyuga*, or the *yugānta* that dissolves the universe.

The notion of conceptual spillover is slightly clumsy in that it could suggest, along with Jacobi, that the poets did not differentiate successfully between the three senses of *yugānta*, and that they allowed images from one type of *yugānta* to interfere – inadvertently or accidentally, and thus unfortunately – with their presentation of another type of *yugānta*, as if by sheer collision of ideas. But I do not think they did.[43] Poets, by definition, are masters of meaning. If we are tempted to think of an *avatāra* appearance at a *tretāyugānta* or a *dvāparayugānta* as somehow misplaced, we must nonetheless acknowledge that much of the conceptual spillover from the second and third senses of *yugānta* is appropriate to the *avatāra* concept. The second sense of *yugānta* – the end of the *mahāyuga* – marks the place where *dharma* most needs rebooting. And the third sense of *yugānta* – the end of the day of Brahmā – carries an image of great destruction, which fits several of the *avatāra* myths, even though the total environmental destruction that occurs at the *pralaya* does not occur when Rāma Dāśarathi or Rāma Jāmadagnya or the Kurukṣetra *avatāra* team perform their respective culls. So although an *avatāra* appearance at a descending *yuga* transition might seem somehow misplaced, by co-opting images from the other two senses of *yugānta* the poets are able to present a passable composite image of the *avatāra* and locate it there.

The ambiguity of the word *yuga* enables the dramatic mythological presentation of an *avatāra* at multiple junction-points in time, and thus enables the difficult trick of presenting the business of divine action from a perspective within time. From our point of view in attempting to answer the title question, the ambiguity of the word *yuga* allows dramatic resonance to be transferred onto the end of the *dvāparayuga* from the end of the *mahāyuga* and from the end of the day of Brahmā. Additionally, because the *yugānta* can be the end of three different things, the text's three detailed descriptions

[43] The different senses of *yugānta* are not here viewed chronologically, as if one or more were already there when another (or others) arrived.

of the *yugānta* can work differently in their different contexts. As discussed in Chapter 2, Mārkaṇḍeya presents very similar descriptive passages twice in quick succession, first to describe the end of the day of Brahmā, and then to describe the end of the *mahāyuga*. As discussed in Chapter 6 below, Vyāsa presents a very similar descriptive passage in Hv 116–117, but the ambiguity of the word *yuga* allows this passage to describe the end of the *kaliyuga*, which is more to the point here because Vyāsa is speaking in the *kaliyuga*, several generations after Mārkaṇḍeya's descriptions. Since the three passages are very similar, one might imagine that they are descendant versions of one original passage, and that in the poetic environment of that imaginary original passage the word *yuga* was not multivalent. That may historically be so (who knows?), but in our terms of reference the image is out of place. When we see similar passages in three different textual contexts, we must understand them in those contexts.

The instability theory

We now move on from our consideration of the general ambiguity of the word *yuga*, to the specific question of what happens to *dharma* at the end of *kṛtayuga*s, *tretāyuga*s, and *dvāparayuga*s. And here we introduce an idea that is very important for this monograph, and that will be discussed in some detail. As an alternative to – or in addition to – the notion of conceptual spillover via the ambiguity inherent in the word *yugānta*, we could imagine that on the downward trajectory, the transition between *yuga*s is not a period of automatic and regular dharmic descent (as per Figures 7–9 above), but is a particularly unstable period during which an *avatāra* is required in order to supervise something which might otherwise go awry. Perhaps in a descending dusk we can imagine a drop in *dharma* beyond the basic level of the following *yuga*, with the *avatāra* then required in order to restore *dharma* up to that level. Thomas says that a *yugānta* 'is essentially a time between times that is seen as highly dangerous and unstable, fraught with the potential for destruction' (Thomas 1988: 245–246). Koskikallio too suggests that instability, impurity, and chaos would typically be found at the liminal juncture of two descending *yuga*s (Koskikallio 1994: 259–261). Thomas speaks of 'the trough of the *yugānta* period', saying that the *avatāra* 'overcomes the intensified *adharma* of the juncture, where the tendency to chaos is acute, but only rescues *dharma* from the trough of the *yugānta* period to re-establish it at the next stage of its chronic decline' (Thomas 1988: 268). This would be something like Figure 10 (the nadir at 0.5 is arbitrary).

Thomas thus argues that the *yugānta* of any of the four *yuga*s is a dangerous and unstable time (Thomas 1988: 245–265). There is ambiguity inherent at such places, which are neither one thing nor another: Thomas cites the man-lion *avatāra* story as a lesson in liminality (Thomas 1988: 246; see also Soifer 1991:

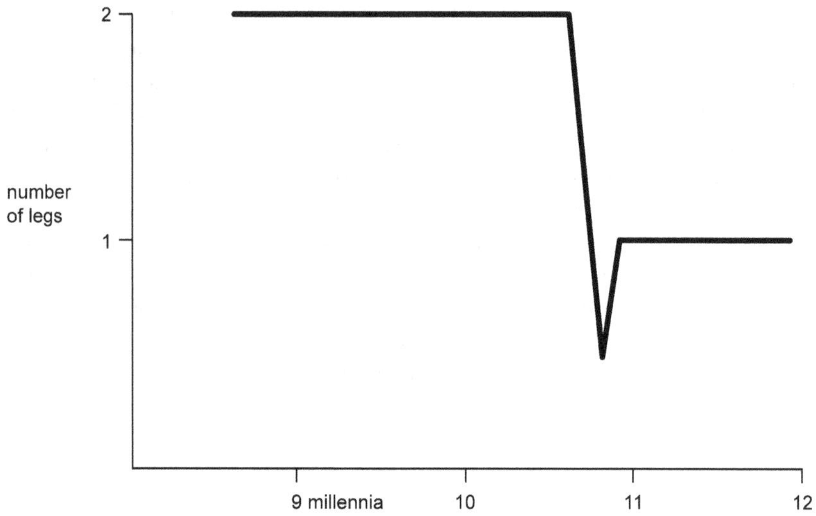

Figure 10: *Dvāpara* to *Kali* Transition (with Trough).

102–104), a perspective that can be supported by additional secondary literature (e.g. van Gennep 1960; Turner 1969).

In this idea there seems to be a sense in which the old *yuga* (whichever it may be) is worn out – is 'on its last legs'. Imagine you have and continuously use some kind of appliance, tool, or item. Imagine replacing it only if you have to. You repeatedly experience your item being unreliable towards the end of its time, and remind yourself to replace it. When you finally do, you are amazed at the full and smooth functioning of the new one, though it is not quite the same. Each one you have, in a way, has a dawn and a dusk. The *yugānta* is when it just breaks. The demon breaks it, and the *avatāra* defeats that demon by delivering the new one.

The scenario is very different with items of which you might have a new one supplied to you automatically every however so often – new uniform, computer, company car, or whatever, supplied for example by a reliable employer, parent, or spouse – even though the old one still works fine. Then you might never need to worry about it ever breaking. So which way does God do it with *yuga*s of time? Which scenario applies?[44] Years seem to come again and again

[44] If we imagine a *yuga* having to be replaced because it breaks, this implies that if it had been replaced before it broke, this would have to have happened earlier, and so the *yuga* would have to have been shorter. But what I am contrasting here are the two kinds of replacement: replacement because it is broken, and replacement in advance so that it never will be. In the latter idea, if the *dvāparayuga* had not been replaced by the *kaliyuga* after two thousand years because its time was up (even though it was not on its last legs), and if it had instead been allowed to run on, who knows how long it may have lasted before it broke?

automatically, like fresh sheets when one lives in a hotel. Would *yugas* not work in the same way?

Although no *Mahābhārata* passage gives a general *yugānta* theory that would apply to all four *yugas*, Thomas cites four passages that could conceivably suggest such a theory. In the first passage, Bhīma is said to be 'shaking the earth with his feet like the earthquake at the joints of time' (*kampayan medinīṃ padbhyāṃ nirghāta iva parvasu* ‖ 3.146.38ab, trans. van Buitenen 1975: 500). But here the reference is not necessarily to the ends of the four *yugas*.

In the second passage, the turning of the *yuga* is juxtaposed with other cosmic signs when Duryodhana says, in a message to Yudhiṣṭhira:

> *anilo vā vahen meruṃ dyaur vāpi nipaten mahīm* |
> *yugaṃ vā parivarteta yady evaṃ syād yathāttha mām* ‖ 5.158.16 ‖
>
> Or, indeed, the wind shall carry off Meru, the sky shall fall on earth, the *yuga* shall turn around, if what you said to me comes true [i.e. if the Pāṇḍavas prevail against the Kauravas]!
> (5.158.16, trans. van Buitenen 1978: 477, adapted)

As noted above, the arrival of the *kaliyuga* does approximately coincide with the Pāṇḍava victory. But Meru is not blown away, and the sky stays up. Here, too, *yuga* could mean *mahāyuga* or day of Brahmā. So these two passages are ambiguous.

In the third passage (5.72.11–18), Bhīma compares Duryodhana with a list of eighteen disgraceful kings who arose in various families at *yugāntas* (*yugānte kṛṣṇa saṃbhūtāḥ kuleṣu puruṣādhamāḥ* ‖ 5.72.17cd). Here it may seem that the word *yuga* must mean one or other of the four *yugas* in all eighteen cases, since Bali, the first of the listed kings, is explicitly linked with the *kṛtayugānta* (*paryāyakāle dharmasya prāpte*, v. 12).[45] But the intent of the list is that all these kings 'defiled their dynasties' (*kulapāṃsanāḥ*, v. 17); they 'extirpated their kinsmen, friends, and relations' (*ye samuccicchidur jñātīn suhṛdaś ca sabāndhavān* ‖ 5.72.11cd, trans. van Buitenen 1978: 349). So perhaps the sense of *yuga* here is that these kings, in contrast to their forefathers, brought to an end an era (a *yuga*) of prosperity and power for their people, just as Duryodhana threatens

[45] The full list is: 1. Bali of the *asuras*, 2. Udāvarta of the Haihayas, 3. Janamejaya of the Nīpas, 4. Bahula of the Tālajaṅghas, 5. Vasu of the Kṛmis, 6. Ajabindu of the Suvīras, 7. Kuśarddhika of the Surāṣṭras, 8. Arkaja of the Balīhas, 9. Dhautamūlaka of the Cīnas (Chinese), 10. Hayagrīva of the Videhas, 11. Varapra of the Mahaujases, 12. Bāhu of the Sundaravegas, 13. Purūravas of the Dīptākṣas, 14. Sahaja of the Cedis and Matsyas, 15. Bṛhadbala of the Pracetas, 16. Dhāraṇa of the Indravatsas, 17. Vigāhana of the Mukuṭas, and 18. Śama of the Nandivegas. In this connection we note also that 'The king who fails to serve as a refuge for his subjects is considered to be Kali' (*aśaraṇyaḥ prajānāṃ yaḥ sa rājā kalir ucyate* ‖ 12.12.27cd, trans. Fitzgerald 2004a: 191, adapted; Fitzgerald has 'the demon Kali', which is gratuitous).

to bring such an era to an end for the Kurus (and much as, according to the Islamophobic myth, Aurangzeb brought a great Mughal era to an end; Truschke 2017: 7–14, 103–107). If so, then the word *yugānta* would here be associated with these kings in a non-technical sense, even though the technical idea (but not the label) of the *kṛtayugānta* is additionally associated with Bali in particular, due to the famous dwarf-*avatāra* story (Hv 31.68–92; Macdonell 1895: 168–177; Macdonell 1897: 37–41; Soifer 1991).

In the fourth passage, a description is given of the *tretā–dvāparayuga* transition that includes, among other dismal signs, a twelve-year drought, the retrograde motion of Bṛhaspati (Jupiter), and the southward motion of the moon (12.139.13–23). This description being in a story of Viśvāmitra, it is notable that in other Viśvāmitra stories, the drought here is caused not by the waning of the *yuga* but by the absence of a king, since this is the period during which Satyavrata Triśaṅku was in exile and Vasiṣṭha, a brahmin, was ruling the kingdom of Ayodhyā (Hv 9.88–10.20; Brodbeck 2018a: 268–274). Thus the reference to the *tretā–dvāparayuga* transition at 12.139.13–14 may have been an attempt to provide a new explanation for the drought only when this story about Viśvāmitra was developed independently of the Satyavrata cycle and the previous explanation fell by the wayside. If some *Mahābhārata* poets imagined a general theory of instability at the end of each of the four *yuga*s, it may have been a recent, improvised theory, presumably involving the kind of conceptual spillover (from the end of the *mahāyuga* and the end of the day of Brahmā) discussed above. However, such a text-historical suggestion may not be helpful, since a minority report may not necessarily be either early or late.

At the same time as Thomas argues for instability at the end of each of the four *yuga*s, she seems also to accept something like what we have been calling conceptual spillover, since she notes that 'the events surrounding the *mahāyugānta* represent an echo of the greater turmoil and eventual destruction to come [at the end of the day of Brahmā]' (Thomas 1988: 261), and she gives details of how Mārkaṇḍeya's description of the *mahāyugānta* in 3.188 contains precise 'echoes' of his description of the end of the day of Brahmā in 3.186 (pp. 261–262).[46]

Given the ambiguity of the word *yuga*, it is not clear that Thomas can demonstrate a general theory of instability at the end of each of the four *yuga*s. But the fourth passage (at 12.139.13–23) is curious, and even if it does not establish that there was such a general theory, nonetheless there may have been. Such a theory would nicely accommodate the mythology whereby, at the end of some *yuga*s, a particular demon takes over but is then defeated by the *avatāra* at the transition. The demon would personify the *yugānta* crisis. In advanc-

[46] On the 3.188 description, Biardeau says that 'With signs proper to the Kali age are mixed elements that evoke the end of a *kalpa* ... that the sun is suddenly found accompanied by six others is very clearly a borrowing from the story of the *pralaya*' ('Aux signes propres à l'âge Kali se mêlent des éléments qui évoquent la fin d'un *kalpa* ... que le soleil se trouve soudain accompagné de six autres est très clairement un emprunt au récit de *pralaya*', Biardeau 1976: 133).

ing such a theory Thomas notes, in connection with Heesterman's work on the *rājasūya* (Heesterman 1957), that more generally in ancient India 'the junctures between units of time have been presented as dangerous and unstable' (Thomas 1988: 265), and that ritual action has traditionally been the means for negotiating such junctures.

> What the *avatāra* does ... is what the *yajamāna* did in the *rājasūya*; he re-establishes *dharma*, and specifically the boundaries of *dharma* – *dharmasetu*/*maryādā* – at the juncture between two periods of time, when they are most vulnerable to disintegration.
>
> (Thomas 1988: 267–268)

In this way, as per Figure 10, the *avatāra* would have a rationale for appearing 'whenever *dharma* declines and *adharma* is on the rise' (Bhg 4.7, quoted earlier). Despite the fact that the text's most graphic descriptions of dharmic decay are descriptions of the *kaliyuga* or its latter phases, the descending transitions at the ends of the first three *yuga*s are points at which, overall, *dharma* declines and *adharma* increases; and the *avatāra* would then come at these points to stabilise *dharma* to the required level.

We will have more to say about the ritual aspect – 'what the *yajamāna* did in the *rājasūya*' – in Chapter 5. But ritual at the junctures of time can evoke the idea that each ritual is somehow necessary to avert disaster; and in terms of very occasional divine rituals, Viṣṇu can be drawn into the modifications of his own universe for narrative effect.

Bearing in mind the triple sense of the word *yuga*, we can understand how the location of *avatāra*s at *yugānta*s could imply that any *yugānta* is an unstable period, as Thomas argues. But is this justified? When rituals for the full and new moon or the new year are pegged to specific junctures in time, they are not actually necessary in order to move time forward. The moon and sun will follow their own pattern regardless, whether or not the ritualists imagine that the ritual is there to correct, counteract, and forestall a chaos that would otherwise set in at that time (but that never actually does, perhaps because they make sure the ritual is always performed).[47] The ritual actions that human beings perform might conceivably not be performed if, for example, all human beings die. But the sun and moon would continue in their cycles regardless, and so whatever rituals Viṣṇu-Nārāyaṇa has to perform in order to keep time faithfully moving, they are not rituals such as human new-year rituals, which require a particular type of agent and might conceivably not occur in its absence. Rather, they are the kind of rituals that must be fully happening already in any case, and to say

[47] Here I introduce scientific knowledge. Even taking the modern and colonial spatialisation of time into account (Kaul 2022), how could it be kept out? If it is at odds with ancient Indian belief, the risk is that this would lead to under-estimation of the aspect of *dharma* that coincides with natural rhythms.

that Viṣṇu-Nārāyaṇa intervenes to do something in particular as a response to circumstances at this or that point in the cycle of time would be to speak overdramatically, and to under-estimate the subtlety and complexity of his continuous role.

With regard to the proposed instability of the *yugānta*, the textual evidence is severely limited. Perhaps the primary motivation for supposing that any *yugānta* is an unstable period would be in order to explain why the *avatāra*s should be located at such junctures. The problem of the unstable *yugānta* is not mentioned in the *Mahābhārata*'s various expositions of the *yuga* cycle; in relation to such general expositions, Biardeau says that 'The passage from one *yuga* to another can even remain implicit ... and still less is it a question of "dusks", or of crises that mark the steps of the degradation ... It is indeed a continuous process'[48] (Biardeau 1976: 122). I suspect that if none of the *avatāra*s were placed at descending *yuga* transitions, we would easily imagine such transitions to be unproblematic. Reduction of lifespan and *dharma* could occur automatically, with no need for an *avatāra*. But that is not how it works as far as telling stories about it is concerned. The *Mahābhārata* is a narrative text evoking diverse narrative genres, each of which would have pre-existing standard characters; it is not a specialised work of philosophy or theology. And if we were to accept Thomas's theory of instability at the end of every *yuga*, then we would have an answer to our title question, since the *avatāra* would be required at the *dvāparayugānta* in order to restabilise *dharma* at the *kaliyuga* level.

The particular kind of instability envisaged here is the kind that allows the level of *dharma* to fall below that of the incoming *yuga*, because this would allow the *avatāra* to be raising the level of *dharma* when it appears at the *dvāparayugānta*, as per Figure 10. This raising of the level is required in order to make sense of Kṛṣṇa's claim that he comes when *dharma* has fallen, in order to 'protect the virtuous, destroy the wicked, and reestablish *dharma*' (Bhg 4.8, trans. Cherniak 2008: 203, adapted). If the instability at the *dvāparayugānta* had instead caused the level of *dharma* to be higher than the level appropriate for the body of the *kaliyuga*, then the *avatāra* would be reducing the level of *dharma*, and Kṛṣṇa's description of the *avatāra*'s effect would not fit. Yet as we shall see in Chapter 5, when Brahmā gives his account of the problem that prompted this *avatāra*, he describes a situation whereby the level of *dharma* on earth is very high indeed, too high for the Earth's comfort (Hv 41). So instability, in and of itself, would not be enough to make sense of Kṛṣṇa's claim at Bhg 4.8. Nonetheless, it would address the title question, since every *yuga* would have to be inaugurated by an *avatāra*.

[48] 'Le passage d'un *yuga* à un autre peut même rester sous-entendu ... et il est encore moins question de « crépuscules », ou de crises qui marqueraient les étapes de la dégradation ... Il s'agit bien d'un processus continu'

In terms of the mythologised crisis at a descending *yuga* transition, Hiltebeitel sees the Kurukṣetra war as presenting a microcosm:

> In terms of time, all the epic's events occur at the end of a yuga (*yugānta*), a sort of 'liminal' period in which these four figures [i.e. Bhīṣma, Droṇa, Karṇa, and Śalya] and their *parvans* (literally 'knots, joints') seem to represent the sum of the yugas, as if all four yugas were potentially present at the point of transition.
>
> (Hiltebeitel 1976: 286)

Like the four *yugas*, the four leaders of the Kaurava army, namely Bhīṣma, Droṇa, Karṇa, and Śalya, lead it for progressively decreasing periods (ten days, five days, two days, one day), and the fifth such leader, namely Aśvatthāman (whose banishment inaugurates the *kaliyuga* at Hv 43.58–59), can represent the *kaliyuga*'s dusk (or, according to Katz, the *pralaya*, thus making this into a model of the last *mahāyuga* in a day of Brahmā; Katz 1985: 121 n. 20; Katz 1989: 255, 259 n. 11). Thomas says that 'the battle essentially charts the gradual breakdown of *dharma* from the well-maintained rules of conduct in the first days, to the chaotic bloodbath of the *sauptika*' (Thomas 1988: 265).

Hiltebeitel's analogy between the structure of the Kurukṣetra war and the structure of the *mahāyuga* is quite convincing (see also Hiltebeitel 1976: 283, linking the four Kaurava leaders with the four colours, and thus with the *mahāyuga* as a whole, as per 3.148.16–33 and 3.187.31). This kind of microcosmic representation might potentially be present also at the other *yuga* transitions, not just at the *dvāpara–kaliyuga* transition. It is as if the *yugānta* instability were represented by a miniature *mahāyuga*, containing, as a *mahāyuga* does, every level of *dharma*: 4, 3, 2, 1, and perhaps even less than 1.

The drama of the transition from one descending *yuga* to another is a result of those *yugas* being conceived as stable steps, rather than the *mahāyuga* deteriorating continuously throughout its duration. If the *mahāyuga* deteriorated continuously, perhaps there would only be one transition point: the junction with the next *mahāyuga*, where *dharma* must be rebooted. But the overall reduction of lifespan and *dharma* that occurs across the *mahāyuga* is represented jerkily and severally. Time is moved forward not just at the end of each *mahāyuga* but also at the end of each *yuga*. But does this always require an *avatāra*?

With regard to *avatāra*, the question of representation is crucial. Poet or not, how can one represent the action of God? We live within time, just as the *Mahābhārata*'s authors and our other and more distant ancestors did; and although it is one thing to imagine, however vaguely, that God would be the basic prompt and facilitator of the temporal system within which we live, God's specific action within time is subtle and mysterious, if indeed it exists at all. Divine action is divine: God does what people cannot and could not do. God does time. God's sphere of operations transcends time, and thus transcends action as we know it. God's action is a different kind of action because of God's total perspective. No moment within time is closer to God, or further away from God, than any other.

This concept may be theological, but its expression is also mythological, since it depends on the types of stories that can meaningfully be told. In the *Mahābhārata*, the *avatāra* stories seem often to be stories about helping sufferers. There is a complainant sufferer, then a powerful intervention providing remedy, and the socio-political function and birthright of the male *kṣatriya*-with-brahmin is standardly thus affirmed.

Thomas argues that there is a cosmic crisis at every *yugānta* that calls for *avatāra* treatment, as shown in Figure 10; and if we accept this, we can answer our title question. But can that be all there is to it? Can we see evidence in the *Mahābhārata* narrative of cosmic *dharma* levels dropping terribly low at the *dvāparayugānta*? Thomas draws on Hiltebeitel's analogy of the four-part Kurukṣetra war as a microcosm, suggesting that 'the battle essentially charts the gradual breakdown of *dharma*' (Thomas 1988: 265), but one could not chart the drop in *dharma* between the *Karṇaparvan* and the *Śalyaparvan* – the crucial juncture in this instance – let alone chart *dharma*'s drop below the level of the incoming *parvan* as per Figure 10. In real time the whole war is happening at the *dvāparayugānta*. In what sense is *dharma* troughing there?

Perhaps here one might zoom out, from the microcosm of the eighteen-day war, onto the section of the Bhārata genealogy between Pratīpa and Parikṣit (1.90.45–96), and identify this as a peculiar end-time mess that Kṛṣṇa, the *avatāra*, mends when he revives Parikṣit after the war (Mbh 14.65–69). Perhaps this section of genealogy could be seen as an adharmic wrinkle in the texture of time, indicating the collapse of the old *yuga* at this liminal point. As for the Kurukṣetra war, at first it is a squabble between two sides of a patriline, but so many armies get involved from so far afield that it becomes a monstrously massive event; its deaths – including all one hundred of Gāndhārī's sons and all five of Draupadī's – seem to indicate an aberrance, a knot or joint in time. We will explore the Kurukṣetra details at the end of Chapter 5.

In relation to Figure 10, although in this and the preceding graphs of the *dvāpara–kaliyuga* transition (Figures 7–9) the y axis is labelled 'legs of *dharma*', nonetheless according to the textual accounts *dharma* is not independent, but is part of a complex variable involving also lifespan, duration of *yuga*, and in some accounts also size and other factors. If size tracks *dharma* and *dharma* troughs (or is generally unstable) at the end of each *yuga*, then at *yuga* transitions there would be uncommonly small (and/or large) people. And duration of *yuga* is part of the same complex variable. How can duration of *yuga* be unstable at the end of each *yuga*? When exactly would that instability apply?

We must also ask again: even were Figure 10 to represent the transition between descending *yuga*s more accurately than any of Figures 7–9, would the Figure 10 transition require an *avatāra* to effect it any more than the transitions represented in Figures 7–9 would? In principle any of these transition scenarios might be effected with the aid of an *avatāra*, or without (i.e. automatically, by the sheer constant will of God). That the human king makes the new year in the Vedic *rājasūya* ritual might suggest that a new *yuga* would need an *avatāra* to make it. But at Hv 40.34–36 the *kṛta–tretāyuga* and *tretā–dvāparayuga* transitions occur while Nārāyaṇa is asleep. In any case, if an *avatāra* **is** involved, the Figure 10 transition is the only one that fits the *Bhagavadgītā* idea that the *avatāra* would cause the level of *dharma* to rise – which otherwise would happen only at the *mahāyugānta*.

The *yuga* machine

The various myths of the specific *avatāras* make it seem that some external intervention would be required to set time onto a new phase, to inaugurate a new *yuga* or *mahāyuga*. But need it be so? Consider Figure 11. It is the image of an actual machine that might be fashioned.

As long as this machine has not yet been fashioned, dear reader, you may join me in imagining that it would work as here described. Picture a circular disc on its edge, like a solid and spokeless wheel. It is mounted inside the machine, facing outwards. By causing a rotation geared to this disc (as if powered from a waterwheel, but steadier), God makes it rotate very very slowly, like a rotating face.

There is groove cut into the face of the disc, from the disc's rim, and then further in and around the disc, then out again onto the rim. This groove guides the route of a floating height-indicator. The indicator is a thick washer, with a bit of dowel jammed fast through it and protruding on either side. The far end of the dowel sits on the rim and then, as the face rotates, it falls into and tracks the groove in the disc's face. Parallel to the upper part of the rotating face, the fixed panel at the front of the machine is just more than the thickness of the washer away from the disc's face, and the near end of the dowel sits in a vertical slit in this panel, a slit just wider than the diameter of the dowel. As the face and the groove go round, the indicator tracks the rim or groove with the far end of the dowel, and with the near end it can track only down and up within the slit, if the groove happens to move the indicator towards or away from the centre of the rotating face. On the outside of the panel, the slit is marked 4 at its top end and 1 at its bottom end as per Figure 11, and position on that scale is what the indicator indicates.

Gravity keeps the dowel in contact with the rim, or with the floor of the groove. We can imagine the indicator moving down from 4 to 1, assisted by gravity, and it can cover the distance smoothly, or in steps, depending on the route of the groove. Here, since the indicator indicates the *yuga*, the groove is stepped as per Figure 12. The indicator stays at 4 on the disc rim for a while, and

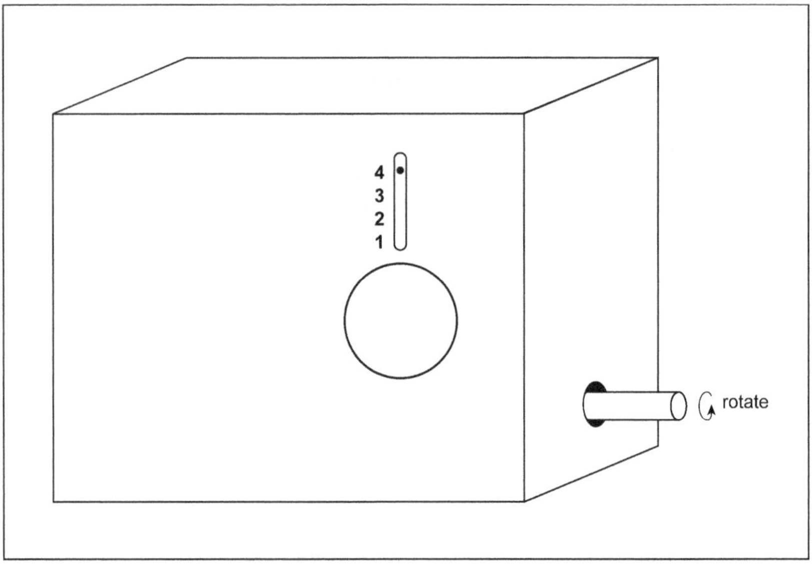

Figure 11: The *Yuga* Machine.

then when the groove opens up it falls to 3, and then, falling sooner each time, it falls to 2 and then to 1, its lowest position.

Then there is a twang and a whack, and the indicator is thrust up suddenly and precisely, out of the groove and back onto the rim. The indicator moves from 1 to 4 smoothly and quickly, and because of the precise thrust upwards the indicator follows the groove and does not jam the mechanism. And the disc continues rotating. Does it here begin its next rotation? Not from the point of view of the outside rotator.

How does the indicator get whacked back up, availing itself of the long vertical exit from the groove as it does so? Well, there is a peg protruding from the face of the disc, as shown in Figure 12. The peg is positioned at a specific point in relation to the route of the groove. But the peg is closer to the centre of rotation than the bottom end of the groove is, and so even when the peg comes up to its highest position, it never interferes with the indicator. The peg sticks out almost enough to meet the panel at the front of the cabinet (which has a circular glass section here, for viewing the mechanism through, as seen in Figure 11). There is a twangy bar sitting roughly horizontally, whose left-hand end is fixed securely somewhere beyond the edge of the rotating disc, whose right-hand portion extends across the front of the disc, and whose right-hand end whacks the indicator upwards. As the peg comes round, moving downwards and leftwards from its highest position, it engages the bar and pulls it down until the peg, moving now from left to right, releases the end of the bar. At that point, which is just the right point (such is the precise tuning of the mechanism), the stretched and released bar twangs up beyond its initial resting position, whacks the washer up along the obliging groove with some force, and

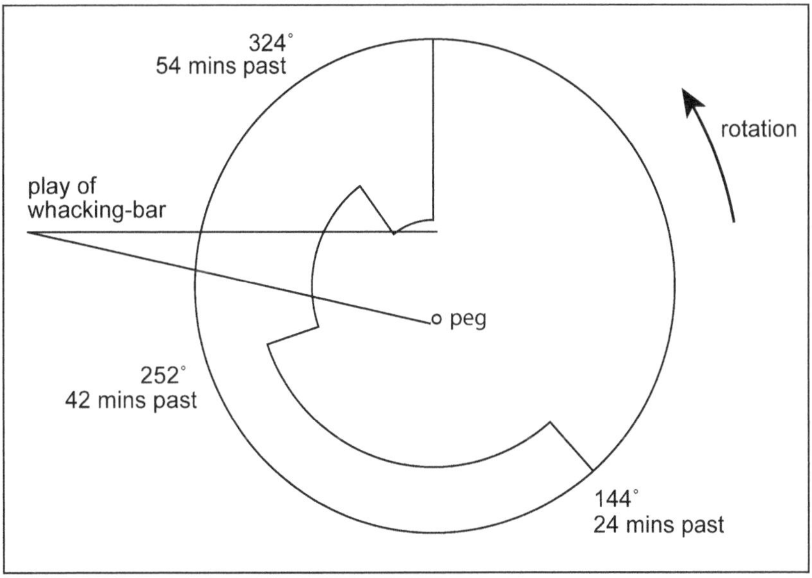

Figure 12: Rotating Disc and Groove.

comes to rest in its central position, where the peg will engage with it again on the next revolution. See Figure 13 for a side view of the mechanism.

Slotting the indicator back onto the rim of the disc at the start of the *kṛtayuga* would require the indicator to be whacked just right. I envisage something like a one-way trapdoor at the exit of the groove, to prevent re-entry. At the crack of the dawn of the *kṛtayuga*, the indicator should not be whacked too far away from the rim of the disc.

In Figure 12 the dawns and dusks have effectively been omitted, or envisaged somewhat as in Figure 9 (sudden transition; though in the machine it is not completely sudden, as it involves the acceleration or deceleration due to gravity). Were the dawns and dusks to be envisaged differently, some transition-period patterns would be impossible to engineer with this machine (e.g. that of Figure 10, which would imply the need for four twangs per cycle).

The point of this visualisation is that here, the apparent events in the course of time's rotation are just the vagaries of the indicator's route down and back up as it follows the rim and groove. For the movement down, gravity is constant. Given the twanginess of the bar and the route of the groove, if it appears that God is acting in particular at the *yuga* transitions, this is an illusion arising from the nature of the apparatus. It is *māyā*. And this is true of all the *yuga* transitions, even the *kali–kṛtayuga* transition. By manifesting simultaneously as the constant force of gravity and the constant rotation of the disc, God acts in the same manner throughout. This image is thus offered here as one way of thinking how the *yuga*s could work. In this analogy, *avatāra*s would be incidental to the movement of time. There might still be *avatāras*, but they

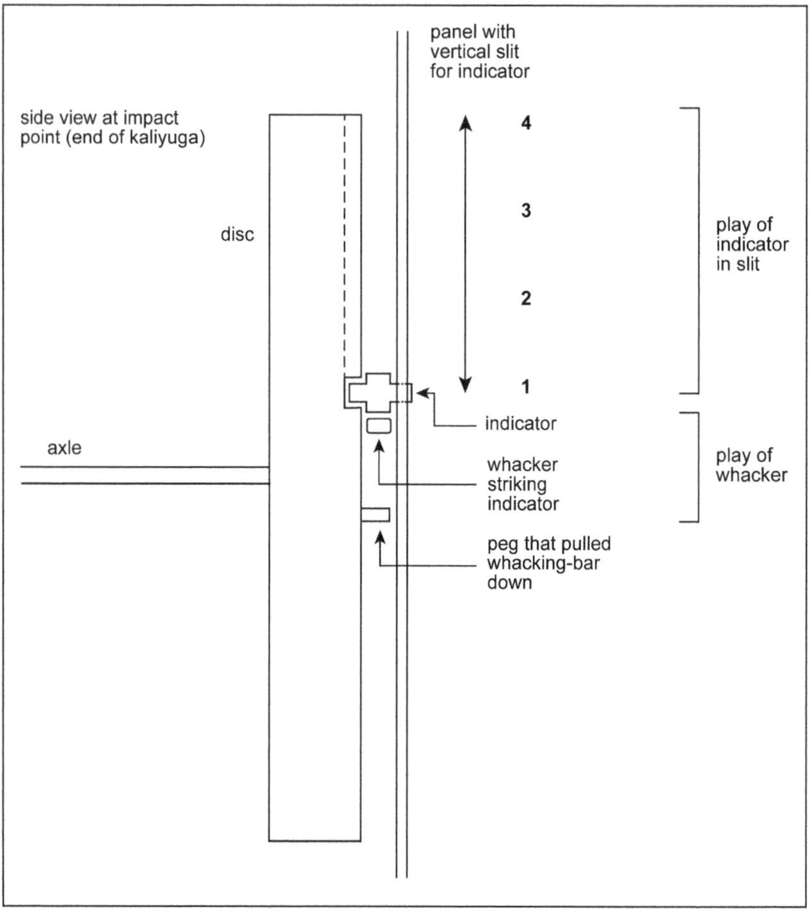

Figure 13: Side View of the Mechanism.

would not have the purpose of moving time across temporal junctures. The idea of any *avatāra* intervening for that purpose would be a mythological dramatisation of the route of the groove in the face of time.

To sum up the monograph so far. We began with a methodological discussion, orienting our view of the text. We then announced the *yuga* cycle via the *Manusmṛti*, and demonstrated it with a survey of *Mahābhārata* passages about the *yugas*. We paused over the complex variable that varies from *yuga* to *yuga*, and we paused over the structure of the cycle in light of the natural systems that it resembles and evokes. We discussed the dawns and dusks, and the Purāṇic system of multiplying the years by 360. We placed the Kurukṣetra war within the *yuga* cycle, at the transition from the *dvāparayuga* to the *kaliyuga*, where *dharma* decreases. We posed our basic research question, as per the monograph's title, in light of previous scholarship. We introduced the *avatāra* principle and the other *avatāras* of Viṣṇu in light of the *yuga* cycle as the

Mahābhārata presents it. In the *Mahābhārata* the focus is on the Kurukṣetra war, a particular site of divine activity within the world. We enumerated three senses of the word *yuga*, and introduced the interplay between three consequent senses of *yugānta*, the 'end of the *yuga*'. Because of this interplay, the ends of each of the four *yuga*s are imbued with aspects of the ends of the *mahāyuga* and the day of Brahmā. We explored Thomas's proposal that the end of each *yuga* is an unstable period requiring the *avatāra* to fix the *dharma* level appropriate for the next *yuga*. That proposal is allied to the notion that junctions in time require specific ritual action in order to be negotiated safely. And we used a mechanical analogy to illustrate how time might be imagined to move through the *yuga*s without any specific *avatāra* action at all.

I set the instability theory aside to some extent in Chapter 5. There I try to understand the text's presentations in terms of the larger *mahāyuga* cycle, whereby there is movement down from level 4 beyond level 2 and back up again. In terms of storytelling about the effecting of this cycle – which is apparently the *avatāra*'s special function – I think that the movement down and up is basic, and that the stories represent aspects of both extremities and apparently opposed impulses.

In Chapter 6 I focus on the latter extremity and ask more directly about the dharmic reboot at the end of the *kaliyuga* by tracking forward, from Janamejaya who hears the story of his ancestors, to the ancient audience who hear the story of Janamejaya, and who hear the *Bhagavadgītā* within it.

CHAPTER 5

The Kurukṣetra *Avatāra* and the Divine Plan

The two functions of the *avatāra*

The Kurukṣetra war happens because Viṣṇu-Nārāyaṇa manifests himself as Kṛṣṇa. This is encapsulated in the *Bhagavadgītā*, where Kṛṣṇa restores Arjuna's resolve to fight by demonstrating his own divine identity.

What is the principle of *avatāra*? Kātre says that the *avatāra* 'is supposed to descend to the earth for making some outstanding achievement' (Kātre 1934: 38). But outstanding in what way? In this section we will compare a series of statements of the *avatāra* principle (albeit not in their order of presentation). These statements are taken from the *Mahābhārata* itself; they may or may not also be aspects of the post-*Mahābhārata* tradition, but they are certainly not retrospective imports into our text. All of them are from the ascribed perspective of Viṣṇu-Nārāyaṇa himself, and together they constitute his view of his own behaviour. These are not explanations of any *avatāra* in particular; they are general explanations of why there is ever an *avatāra* at all. The question of whether the *avatāra* principle was extrapolated from pre-existing traditions about specific divine appearances, or whether, conversely, such traditions instantiated a pre-existing principle, is out of range according to our methodology. But the fact that the text does present a general principle is significant, and from our point of view extremely useful.

Our first statement is Kṛṣṇa's statement to Arjuna in the *Bhagavadgītā*, most of which was already quoted in Chapter 3. According to Kātre, this passage states 'The general rule as to the occasion and the purpose of an avatāra of God' (Kātre 1934: 48; see also e.g. Biardeau 1976: 117–118; Soifer 1991: 6; Matchett 2001: 162–163).

How to cite this book chapter:
Brodbeck, S. 2022. Divine Descent and the Four World-Ages in the *Mahābhārata* – or, Why Does the Kṛṣṇa *Avatāra* Inaugurate the Worst *Yuga*?. Pp. 89–140. Cardiff: Cardiff University Press. DOI: https://doi.org/10.18573/book9.e.

ajo 'pi sann avyayātmā bhūtānām īśvaro 'pi san |
prakṛtiṃ svām adhiṣṭhāya saṃbhavāmy ātmamāyayā ‖ Bhg 4.6 ‖
yadā yadā hi dharmasya glānir bhavati bhārata |
abhyutthānam adharmasya tadātmānaṃ sṛjāmy aham ‖ 7 ‖
paritrāṇāya sādhūnāṃ vināśāya ca duṣkṛtām |
dharmasaṃsthāpanārthāya saṃbhavāmi yuge yuge ‖ 8 ‖

Despite being unborn and essentially imperishable, despite being the lord of all beings, I resort to my phenomenal nature and come into being through my creative power. I send myself forth whenever *dharma* declines and *adharma* is on the rise, Bhārata; age after age I come into being to protect the virtuous, destroy the wicked, and reestablish *dharma*.
(*Bhagavadgītā* 4.6–8, trans. Cherniak 2008: 203, adapted)

As Hiltebeitel notes (2011b: 562), Arjuna's cognisance of this statement is reflected a few chapters later, when he says at Bhg 11.18 that Kṛṣṇa is *avyayaḥ śāśvatadharmagoptā*, 'the unchanging protector of the everlasting *dharma*' (trans. Hiltebeitel). In Kṛṣṇa's *Bhagavadgītā* statement, the *avatāra*'s function is to re-establish *dharma*. The 're' in Cherniak's translation is something of an interpretation; 'reestablish' could alternatively be 'make stand', 'fix', or 'settle'. But whatever it is, it alters the ratio between 'virtuous' and 'wicked' in the direction of the former. Thus one would expect the level of *dharma* to be higher after the *avatāra*'s appearance than before it.

Our second statement is similar to the first. After the Kurukṣetra war, the seer Uttaṅka is minded to curse Kṛṣṇa for having allowed the war to take place (Laine 1989: 217–224; Black 2021: 172–173). In the process of explaining himself to Uttaṅka, Kṛṣṇa says:

viddhi mahyaṃ sutaṃ dharmam agrajaṃ dvijasattama |
mānasaṃ dayitaṃ vipra sarvabhūtadayātmakam ‖ 14.53.11 ‖
tatrāhaṃ vartamānaiś ca nivṛttaiś caiva mānavaiḥ |
bahvīḥ saṃsaramāṇo vai yonīr hi dvijasattama ‖ 12 ‖
dharmasaṃrakṣaṇārthāya dharmasaṃsthāpanāya ca |
tais tair veṣaiś ca rūpaiś ca triṣu lokeṣu bhārgava ‖ 13 ‖
ahaṃ viṣṇur ahaṃ brahmā śakro 'tha prabhavāpyayaḥ |
bhūtagrāmasya sarvasya sraṣṭā saṃhāra eva ca ‖ 14 ‖
adharme vartamānānāṃ sarveṣām aham apy uta |
dharmasya setuṃ badhnāmi calite calite yuge |
tās tā yonīḥ praviśyāhaṃ prajānāṃ hitakāmyayā ‖ 15 ‖

O best of the twice-born, know that *dharma* is my first born son, beloved product of my mind, O brahmin, whose nature is compassion for all beings. O best of the twice-born, in order to protect and establish the *dharma* in the three worlds, (taking on) this or that dress or form, I go through cycles of many births, with men now living, and those departed,

O Bhārgava. I am Viṣṇu, I am Brahmā and Śakra, the origin and the passing away, the creator and destroyer of all beings. Seeking the welfare of creatures, for all those living in *adharma*, I have entered various wombs to set the boundary of *dharma*, when the *yuga* has wandered.

(14.53.11–15, trans. Laine 1989: 220–221, adjusted and reparagraphed)

This passage reiterates Viṣṇu's special relationship with, and effect upon, levels of *dharma*. But at this stage, since we do not know what sense of *yuga* is intended, it is not clear how regularly Viṣṇu would appear.

Our third statement overlaps significantly with the first two. It is from the child Nārāyaṇa's speech to Mārkaṇḍeya in Mbh 3:

yadā yadā ca dharmasya glānir bhavati sattama |
abhyutthānam adharmasya tadātmānaṃ sṛjāmy aham ‖ 3.187.26 ‖
daityā hiṃsānuraktāś ca avadhyāḥ surasattamaiḥ |
rākṣasāś cāpi loke 'smin yadotpatsyanti dāruṇāḥ ‖ 27 ‖
tadāhaṃ samprasūyāmi gṛheṣu śubhakarmaṇām |
praviṣṭo mānuṣaṃ dehaṃ sarvaṃ praśamayāmy aham ‖ 28 ‖

Whenever, sage, the *dharma* languishes and *adharma* rears up, I create myself. When Daityas bent on harm spring up in this world invincible to the chiefs of the Gods, and terrifying Rākṣasas, then I take on birth in the dwellings of the virtuous and, entering a human body, I appease it all.

(3.187.26–28, trans. van Buitenen 1975: 592, adapted)

This statement adds a new aspect: the function of re-establishing *dharma* is linked to Nārāyaṇa's defeat of demons on behalf of the gods (Matchett 2001: 167–169). This is broadly confirmed by the various stories of Viṣṇu-Nārāyaṇa's appearances, in which he typically kills demons in order to assist and rescue the gods (as at Hv 32–38, in the Tārakāmaya war). By implication, the gods represent *dharma* and the demons represent *adharma*, and these representations allow Viṣṇu's role to be encapsulated in stories of a familiar mythic type. If we think about the four *yugānta*s within the *mahāyuga* cycle, then stories of *asura*-slaying *avatāra*s, in order to have a beneficial dharmic effect, would have to be pegged to the *kaliyugānta*; or, according to Thomas's instability theory, they could equally be pegged to any of the three other *yugānta*s, if *dharma* has troughed there.

The integration of the gods and demons into the story of *dharma* is confirmed by Bhīṣma's statement (statement 3½):

sa pūrvadevo nijaghāna daityān sa pūrvadevaś ca babhūva samrāṭ |
sa bhūtānāṃ bhāvano bhūtabhavyaḥ sa viśvasyāsya jagataś cāpi goptā ‖ 13.143.10 ‖

yadā dharmo glāyati vai surāṇāṃ tadā kṛṣṇo jāyate mānuṣeṣu |
dharme sthitvā sa tu vai bhāvitātmā parāṃś ca lokān aparāṃś ca yāti ‖ 11 ‖
tyājyāṃs tyaktvāthāsurāṇāṃ vadhāya kāryākārye kāraṇaṃ caiva pārtha |

He is the original god who slew the Daityas,
He is the original god who became lord of all.
He is the creator of beings, his future is his past,
He is the guardian of this whole world.

When *dharma* declines for the gods
Then Kṛṣṇa is born among humans.
After standing by *dharma*, the self-created one
Attains the distant and the highest worlds.

To kill *asuras* he acts properly or improperly
But he spares those who should be spared, Pārtha.
(13.143.10–12b; see also 7.156.22)

González-Reimann says that 'demons ... can be converted very easily into those responsible for the loss of dharma'[49] (González-Reimann 1993: 18). But would this be a conversion? Since demons seem to be adharmic by definition, it is difficult to imagine what kind of demons they could have been before such a conversion. Rather, the activity of demons seems to be equivalent to the decline of *dharma*. Thus I do not think we can distinguish defeating demons as a second *avatāra* function over and above the boosting of *dharma*. The two ideas are combined as aspects of one function. One might think of the demonic aspect as a mythological dramatisation of the dharmic aspect.

Our final and fullest statement of the *avatāra* principle occurs in the *Nārāyaṇīya* section of Mbh 12. If the first three statements were from the horse's mouth, this one is from the horse's mind. After Brahmā has created creatures, Nārāyaṇa thinks to himself:

jātā hīyaṃ vasumatī bhārākrāntā tapasvinī ‖ 12.337.29ef
bahavo balinaḥ pṛthvyāṃ daityadānavarākṣasāḥ |
bhaviṣyanti tapoyuktā varān prāpsyanti cottamān ‖ 30 ‖
avaśyam eva taiḥ sarvair varadānena darpitaiḥ |
bādhitavyāḥ suragaṇā ṛṣayaś ca tapodhanāḥ |
tatra nyāyyam idaṃ kartuṃ bhārāvataraṇaṃ mayā ‖ 31 ‖
atha nānāsamudbhūtair vasudhāyāṃ yathākramam |
nigraheṇa ca pāpānāṃ sādhūnāṃ pragraheṇa ca ‖ 32 ‖
imāṃ tapasvinīṃ satyāṃ dhārayiṣyāmi medinīm |

[49] 'los demonios ... pueden ser convertidos muy fácilmente en responsables de la pérdida de dharma'

> *mayā hy eṣā hi dhriyate pātālasthena bhoginā* ‖ 33 ‖
> *mayā dhṛtā dhārayati jagad dhi sacarācaram* |
> *tasmāt pṛthvyāḥ paritrāṇaṃ kariṣye saṃbhavaṃ gataḥ* ‖ 34 ‖

> The poor Earth has been burdened with the weight [of creatures]. Many powerful Daityas, Dānavas, and *rākṣasa*s will come to be on earth. On the basis of their austerities, they will acquire excellent boons. Inevitably, made arrogant by the gift of boons, they have to oppress the groups of gods, and the seers whose wealth is in austerities. Then it is proper for the burden to be lifted, by me, using diverse forms on earth successively. By chastising the wicked and upholding the righteous, I will uphold the poor faithful Earth, for she is the one I uphold by means of the snake that rests upon the underworld. Upheld by me, she will uphold the world of the moving and motionless. And that is why, when I meet the occasion, I will rescue the Earth.
> (12.337.29e–34, trans. after Ganguli 1970: Santi Parva CCCL, 195)

Nārāyaṇa anticipates that the Earth will have a weight problem, caused by creatures pressing down on her. Also, the gods and seers will have problems caused by demons. Both problems are to be solved periodically by the *avatāra*. There is no mention of *dharma* or *adharma* here, but these are represented by the gods and demons, and also by the righteous and the wicked (*sādhu*s and *pāpa*s). Although the noun *dharma* in this quantitative sense is absent, the verb *dhṛ* (translated here as 'uphold') is used four times in connection with what Nārāyaṇa does to the Earth, and what the Earth thus does to the creatures.

In this *Nārāyaṇīya* statement, in contrast to the other statements reviewed above, the *avatāra* has two separate functions. It defeats demons, by implication re-establishing *dharma*, and it also reduces the weight of creatures upon the Earth (Kātre 1934: 49; Matchett 2001: 163–165). The two functions are mixed together in the extract, which keeps switching its focus from one to the other. But whenever it switches from one to the other, it does so at the end of a line. The material that mentions the function set out above – the function of re-establishing *dharma* (by defeating demons) – is contained in five lines: 30ab, 30cd, 31ab, 31cd (these four lines are consecutive), and 32cd. If we remove those lines, and remove the sentences that translate them, we get this:

> The poor Earth has been burdened with the weight [of creatures]. ... Then it is proper for the burden to be lifted, by me, using diverse forms on earth successively. ... I will uphold the poor faithful Earth, for she is the one I uphold by means of the snake that rests upon the underworld. Upheld by me, she will uphold the world of the moving and motionless. And that is why, when I meet the occasion, I will rescue the Earth.
> (12.337.29ef, 31e–32b, 33–34)

This is the second function. The removed lines on their own read as follows:

> ... Many powerful Daityas, Dānavas, and *rākṣasas* will come to be on earth. On the basis of their austerities, they will acquire excellent boons. Inevitably, made arrogant by the gift of boons, they have to oppress the groups of gods, and the seers whose wealth is in austerities. ... [I will act] By chastising the wicked and upholding the righteous ...
>
> (12.337.30a–31d, 32cd)

These lines do not make sense on their own in the way that the lines about the Earth do. The impression that the rescue of the Earth is primary is enhanced by its encompassing presence at the start, middle, and end of the passage.

It looks as if this is a composite passage, and that the two *avatāra* functions that it describes are not just conceptually distinct, but here are also textually distinct, insofar as they are gathered into different groups of lines. If we were to think about the passage being built up historically in stages, we might imagine redactors as agents within this process, inserting the lines about one *avatāra* function into a passage that was previously just about the other. But if we think about the passage as a representation of Nārāyaṇa's thoughts, then its seemingly composite form might rather be a way of showing that Nārāyaṇa is thinking two things at once. The experiment of removing those five lines serves to emphasise that the *avatāra* function of reducing the weight of creatures for the benefit of the Earth is a function separate from that of boosting *dharma*, even though both *avatāra* functions occur to Nārāyaṇa, apparently for the very first time, simultaneously integrated.

In the rest of this chapter, the difference between these two functions will be emphasised. In terms of the progress of a *mahāyuga*, I will suggest that the function of lightening the Earth's burden, which has been the 'second' function in this section, takes effect before, and separately from, the function of restoring *dharma*.

The earth and death

Referring to Frazer (1919: 45–77), Eliade says that 'in most traditional cultures ... Death was unknown to the mythic Ancestors and is the consequence of something that happened in primordial times' (Eliade 1977: 13). With regard to the *avatāra* function of rescuing the Earth, we will now focus on a story that explains the origin of Death (*mṛtyu*, feminine) in terms of the problem of overpopulation for the Earth. This story is in the *Mokṣadharmaparvan*, as taught by Bhīṣma to Yudhiṣṭhira (Mbh 12.248–250; for summary and discussion see Doniger O'Flaherty 1976: 228–230; Long 1977: 77–80).

> *prajāḥ sṛṣṭvā mahātejāḥ prajāsarge pitāmahaḥ* |
> *atīva vṛddhā bahulā nāmṛṣyata punaḥ prajāḥ* ‖ 12.248.13 ‖

> *na hy antaram abhūt kiṃ cit kva cij jantubhir acyuta* |
> *nirucchvāsam ivonnaddhaṃ trailokyam abhavan nṛpa* ‖ 14 ‖
>
> At the time of creation, the Grandfather, full of fiery energy, created living beings. These creatures increased in age and number to excess, but they did not die again. Then there was no space anywhere between creatures; there was no space to breathe, so congested was the triple universe.
>
> (12.248.13–14, trans. Doniger O'Flaherty 1994: 38)

Brahmā tried to work out what to do, but he could not, and he became frustrated and angry, and his anger burned the creatures and threatened their survival. Śiva came and told him not to be angry, because it is dangerous.

> *prajāpatir uvāca* |
> *na kupye na ca me kāmo na bhaveran prajā iti* |
> *lāghavārthaṃ dharaṇyās tu tataḥ saṃhāra iṣyate* ‖ 12.249.3 ‖
> *iyaṃ hi māṃ sadā devī bhārārtā samacodayat* |
> *saṃhārārthaṃ mahādeva bhāreṇāpsu nimajjati* ‖ 4 ‖
>
> I am not angry, said Prajāpati,[50] Nor is it my wish that living creatures should cease to exist. But in order to lighten the earth I have sought this destruction. This goddess Earth, oppressed by the burden, has kept urging me to destroy them, for she is sinking into the waters under the burden, great god.
>
> (12.249.3-4, trans. Doniger O'Flaherty 1994: 38–39, adapted)

Śiva told Brahmā that anger is not the way to solve the problem, and said: 'I beg that all creatures may be subject to repetitions of birth and death' (*yācāmy āvṛttijāḥ prajāḥ*, 12.249.12d, trans. Doniger). So Brahmā withdrew the fire of his anger, and 'fashioned periodic activity and quiescence' (*pravṛttiṃ ca nivṛttiṃ ca kalpayām āsa vai prabhuḥ* ‖ 12.249.14cd, trans. Doniger). These are suggestive terms. In the context of Brahmā's problem, they imply the invention of death. Sure enough, the dark woman Death appears, dressed in red, from the apertures of Brahmā's body, and Brahmā tells her to make it so that everyone will, at some point, die. She is horrified, objects on grounds of *dharma*, and goes off to perform *tapas*. Brahmā eventually confronts her again, telling her that she will incur no *adharma*, for this is her *dharma*. He tells her that her tears will become diseases, and that

---

[50] Long notes that 'Although Brahmā claims that he is not angry, in truth he is, and it is because he cannot devise a means of delimiting his expenditure of creative energies that the creation, paradoxically, is threatened with wholesale destruction' (Long 1977: 77).

> *sarveṣāṃ tvaṃ prāṇinām antakāle kāmakrodhau sahitau yojayethāḥ* ǀ
> 12.250.34ab ...
> *tasmāt kāmaṃ rocayābhyāgataṃ tvaṃ saṃyojyātho saṃharasveha jantūn* ‖ 35cd ...
> *atho prāṇān prāṇinām antakāle kāmakrodhau prāpya nirmohya hanti* ‖ 36cd

> When the time comes for the end of all creatures that breathe, you will employ desire and anger together ... Therefore welcome desire; join together [with desire] and destroy creatures here.
>
> ... Then she began to destroy the life's breath of creatures that breathe, at the time of their end, bewildering them with desire and anger.
>
> (12.250.34ab, 35cd, 36cd, trans. Doniger O'Flaherty 1994: 42–43, adjusted)

And that is the story.

Doniger differentiates the problem of overpopulation from the problem of demons:

> In the earlier layers of the mythology as it appears in the Brāhmaṇas, the earth simply sinks into the cosmic waters in the course of time, and it (or she) is rescued by a fish, a tortoise, or a boar. Later, these three animals become the first three avatars of Viṣṇu, and the boar is made to battle demons as well as to rescue the earth. The amoral motif of the earth sinking into the waters is then combined with the idea that a demon has carried her away to the demonic subterranean (or subaquatic) hell, and from here it is merely one additional step to say that she sinks into the waters because of the weight of the demons upon her.
>
> (Doniger O'Flaherty 1976: 258)

The differentiation of the 'amoral' earth-rescue myth from the gods-versus-demons myth is here done chronologically, but the important thing is the differentiation, which is effectively the same as the differentiation of the two *avatāra* functions as described above. The degree to which these two myths are 'combined' in the *Mahābhārata* is debatable; in some parts of the text they are simply juxtaposed. The Earth's weight problem is usually not connected with the action of a demon or demons. There is no special weight-demon; weight is not a matter of *adharma* such as a demon would typically supply.

After surveying Death in Hindu mythology, Long says:

> [A]ll the myths are in agreement that without the entry and continued operation of death in withdrawing from the temporal world those creatures whose terms of life have matured, and thereby providing space for

> new beings, the universe would soon suffocate under the weight of its own superfluous progeny ...
>
> The theists ... identify the event of death, regardless of its immediate cause, as the expression of the omniscient will of a gracious deity, who grants death as a boon to the world for the orderly progression of the parade of creatures ... Viewing the entire drama of the cosmic process *sub specie aeternatatis*, one discovers that creation and destruction, at all levels of the universe, are nothing more than two phases of a divine game that is being carried out on a playing field of cosmic proportions. (Long 1977: 92)

Although the story of the origin of Death would presumably be set near the beginning of the day of Brahmā, in terms of the *yuga* cycle and this monograph the crucial point for understanding the Earth's overpopulation problem is that it links to the diminishing of lifespan from *yuga* to descending *yuga*.

At 3.148.11 Hanūmat says, perhaps hyperbolically, that in the *kṛtayuga* there is no death (*na kṣīyante ca vai prajāḥ*). This would fit an end-of-*kṛtayuga* location for the story of the origin of Death. The story of the origin of Death fits the *Yugapurāṇa*'s description of the *kṛta–tretāyuga* transition, which is marked by the advent of Death (*kṛtānta*) and the Tārakāmaya war (*Yugapurāṇa* 12–13). By standard, lifespans are four, three, two, and one hundred years in the successive *yuga*s (Mbh 12.224.24–25; Ms 1.83), and lifespan matches length of dawn and dusk. But it is all relative.

Decreasing lifespan across the *mahāyuga* would mean decreasing population. Even if people were born at the same rate in every *yuga*,[51] the population would be higher in the earlier *yuga*s, because more generations would be alive at once, whether breeding or not. So, as the *mahāyuga* wears on through the *yuga*s, the weight on the Earth is lifted, by there being decreases in population, by there being shortening of lifespans. Thus, over the course of the *mahāyuga*, one general instance of the Earth's problem is solved, to recur in the next *kṛtayuga*. If we track the Earth's suffering onto human lifespan, then she should suffer most during the *kṛtayuga*, when *dharma* is at its highest, and her load should be lightest during the *kaliyuga*, when *dharma* is at its lowest. The lifting of the Earth's burden that occurs at the end of the *kṛtayuga* would be paradigmatic, because it is the first reduction in lifespan, the point at which death's encroachment begins.

The weight on the Earth could be diminished through reduction of size of unit upon her, as well as through reduction of numbers. According to several passages, it is not just *dharma* and lifespan that diminish through the *yuga*s,

---

[51] Mārkaṇḍeya mentions an increase in birth-rate at the *yugānta* (*bhavanti bahujantavaḥ* ... *bahuprajā* ... *striyo*, 3.186.34–35), but this does not imply rising birth-rate across the *mahāyuga* as whole. On the contrary, it seems likely that decreasing lifespan across the *mahāyuga* would result in each person having a shorter 'breeding window', and thus fewer children.

but also size. This is mentioned by Hanūmat and Bhīma (*varṣman*, 3.148.7, 9), and by Mārkaṇḍeya (*deha*, 3.186.32). Size is only one of a variety of additional parameters that are occasionally said to decline through the *yugas* (see above, p. 26), but in the *Harivaṃśa* we see reduction of size by the time of the Kurukṣetra generation at the *dvāpara–kaliyuga* transition, because Mucukunda, asleep since a previous *yuga* (compare the huge Hanūmat encountered by Bhīma), realises, after waking up like Rip van Winkle in Lilliput, that everyone else is small (Hv 85.55–56, 62).[52]

The *Mahābhārata* does not emphasise the size factor nearly as much as it emphasises the lifespan factor. But the inclusion of size as a descending factor alongside lifespan would cause the Earth's burden to be reduced in a compounded and accelerated fashion as the *yugas* wear on: not only would there be fewer people, but they would also be smaller, and thus lighter. Accordingly we might be puzzled by the implied recurrence of the Earth's problem. Why would lifespan (and perhaps also size) need to be reduced three times, and not just once? Perhaps the Earth's ability to support even diminished populations would be iteratively affected by the diminutions of *dharma*. We saw at 3.148.7 that the Earth is among those who 'adjust to time from *yuga* to *yuga*' (trans. van Buitenen 1975: 504, quoted earlier).

If we link the story of the origin of Death with the *avatāra* function of lightening the Earth's burden (as mentioned by Viṣṇu in the *Nārāyaṇīya* passage at 12.337.29–34), then insofar as the *avatāra* has two functions, the *avatāra* would seem to be a holistic symbol of the *mahāyuga* cycle: a symbol of the downward trend of lifespans and *dharma*, and a symbol of their rebooting. In the various statements of 'the *avatāra* principle' surveyed above, the function of rescuing the Earth (which is presented in the *Nārāyaṇīya* statement) is thus not only different from, but is also in the opposite direction to, and fundamentally opposed to, the function of rebooting *dharma* (which is presented in all of the statements). These two functions address two different problems described in the *Nārāyaṇīya* statement: the problem of overpopulation, and the problem of misbehaviour. If they were problems that were solved once per *mahāyuga*, these two problems would be solved in different ways, and at different points in the cycle: the problem of overpopulation would be solved (or at least paradigmatically addressed) at the *kṛtayugānta*, and the problem of misbehaviour would be solved at the *kaliyugānta*.[53] Given the spillage of the first solution into

[52] Change of general human size through time is not just a Hindu idea: speaking of the Jain system with its six descending and six ascending ages, Gombrich notes that 'In the sixth age, at the end of the descending era, human stature finally descends to about a foot, the human life span to sixteen years, and men live brutishly in caves, feeding on raw flesh' (Gombrich 1975: 132).

[53] Thus Biardeau expresses herself in a particularly unfortunate manner when she says that 'The Kaliyuga comes to a point where the Earth can no longer survive, overwhelmed as she is by the weight of *adharma*, and a new *mahāyuga* must recommence' ('Le Kaliyuga arrive à un point où la Terre ne peut plus vivre, accablée qu'elle est par le poids de l'*adharma*, et il faut

the further drops of level into the *dvāparayuga* and the *kaliyuga*, and given that the end of the *kṛtayuga* is forty per cent of the way through the *mahāyuga*, we might say that these two solutions are applied approximately at two opposing extremities of the cycle.

The bottom line is the invariable connection between length of lifespan and level of *dharma*. When *dharma* is turned up to 4 again for the start of the new *mahāyuga*, lifespan is too. But that longer lifespan is what makes it then necessary for lifespan to be reduced again. And that affects *dharma*: it is made explicit that the decrease of *dharma* is caused by the decrease in lifespan (*saṃrodhād āyusas*, 12.224.65; 12.230.14).

Yet if we are to have a general theory of what an *avatāra* does, then the *avatāra* must solve both problems, wherever that *avatāra* appears – for example, at the *dvāpara–kaliyuga* transition. Because a *mahāyuga* is divided into four *yuga*s, each of which is stable for *dharma* and lifespan, there are several transition-points within it where the dynamics of the whole cycle might be represented. If two transition-points, the *kṛtayugānta* and *kaliyugānta* transitions, each necessarily represent one *avatāra* function rather than the other, then perhaps the other two, the intermediate descending transitions, are peculiarly able to represent both functions at once.

The two functions of the *avatāra* align with switching points at either extremity of the *mahāyuga* cycle. And crucially, what is good for the Earth is not necessarily good for humans. Insofar as we want to live long and be dharmic, the appeasement of the Earth is not in our direct interest. We do not want to die, and it is because of the Earth that we must. God can presumably view the two *avatāra* functions – the two switching solutions at the two extremities of the cycle – without prejudice, but we cannot. There are obvious ways in which we are better off in the *kṛtayuga*.

Our view of the *mahāyuga* as an oscillation under the influence of two different forces has a precursor in the work of Huntington:

> [T]he very activity of restoration generates a counter-force which leads inexorably toward another crisis. The *avatāra*-legends are vivid examples of particularly critical events in this cyclical pattern described by the pendulum of cosmic power ...
>
> Every victory contains within itself the latent seed which, full-grown, becomes the next crisis ... As with a hypothetical pendulum which might oscillate continuously without any friction to slow its movement, the world-process is ever in a dynamic balance, in the sense that gross imbalances initiate auto-corrective processes. These in turn lead to an opposite imbalance ...

---

qu'un nouveau *mahāyuga* recommence', Biardeau 1976: 120). This is to conflate the two problems and place them both at the end of the *mahāyuga*.

> The growth of evil as the *yugas* succeed each other is due to an expanding realization or actualization of the inherent polarity in man and the universe.
>
> (Huntington 1964: 13, 32, 38)

We have refined Huntington's insight by distinguishing the two functions of the *avatāra*. In this section we have discussed the *Mahābhārata*'s story of the invention of Death, and we have aligned it with the *avatāra* function of lightening the Earth's burden, and with the *kṛtayugānta* opposite the *kaliyugānta*. One might imagine this basic bipolar scenario, moving repeatedly between the same two extremities, as one idea, one dynamic (Idea 1), and imagine the *tretāyugānta* and *dvāparayugānta* as another, perhaps logically subordinate idea (Idea 2). This kind of logical subordination is implied in the suggestion, made above, that the *avatāras* at the intermediate *yugāntas* could mediate and combine the opposing characteristics of both poles/problems/solutions.

Eltschinger has also recently separated these two ideas, arranging them chronologically (Eltschinger 2020). He notes that the *tretāyuga* and *dvāparayuga* are not mentioned in Aśvaghoṣa's writings, or in the parts of the *Rāmāyaṇa* and the *Yugapurāṇa* that he takes to be oldest, and he agrees with González-Reimann that the *yuga* scheme was a late addition to the *Mahābhārata*. He suggests a two-stage development of the *yuga* scheme. In the first stage there is just the idea of an ideal time degenerating towards a *yugānta* apocalypse, and in the second stage the (*mahā*)*yuga* is divided into four: 'original apocalyptic/prophetic accounts of the *yugānta* were provided with a new meaning by incorporating them into the alien and most probably more recent framework of the four *yugas*' (p. 47). Comparable is Thomas's suggestion that the identification of Śakuni as Dvāpara 'is perhaps a secondary identification, built onto an identification of Duryodhana as Kali which has its roots in the word's other associations: strife, discord and bad kings' (Thomas 1988: 302). But Thomas notes that

> I am essentially trying to establish the underlying logic of the connections, rather than make any statement about the chronology of the idea's development. ... I think it unlikely that the epic composition worked in this way; I think it is more a case of an awareness of connections that the composers use to enrich their themes by resonance, rather than a set of consequentially reasoned ideas.
>
> (Thomas 1988: 303 n. 65)

Regardless of whether one regards Eltschinger's speculative historical argument as convincing, our explorations of the *avatāra* functions have brought us to a similar subdivision of ideas, viewing the *Mahābhārata* data synchronically. Ideas may be subdivided for analysis without historical implications.

Three accounts of the earth's problem

The Kurukṣetra *avatāra* is collaborative, in that it involves the simultaneous manifestation of many other gods apart from Viṣṇu, for the same purpose. Kṛṣṇa acts like the ringmaster of a deadly circus in which many other descended gods play starring roles: Dharma as Vidura and Yudhiṣṭhira, Vāyu as Bhīma, Indra as Arjuna, Kali as Duryodhana, Sūrya as Karṇa, Bṛhaspati as Droṇa, and so on (Couture 2001).

The collaborative Kurukṣetra *avatāra* is repeatedly said to aid the Earth. Scheuer calls this the *Mahābhārata*'s central myth ('le mythe central du *Mbh*', Scheuer 1982: 156; see also 105 n. 47). In aiding the Earth, the Kurukṣetra *avatāra* fits the *Nārāyaṇīya* statement discussed above, and is something like the boar *avatāra*, where the boar descends to raise the submerged Earth, as depicted at Udayagiri (von Stietencron 2005a: 15; Willis 2009: 41).

The mythology of the Earth puts her in a special relationship with the king (Derrett 1959; Hara 1973). The king is the husband of the Earth: she represents the physical territory over which he rules, whose bounty he prompts for the good of his subjects. This is dramatically enacted in the story of Pṛthu, the first king. Thinking of his subjects, Pṛthu confronted the Earth aggressively, with weapons, but she fled from him (Hv 5.40–45). Finally, cornered, she reminded him that 'If you kill me, you will not be able to nourish your subjects, your majesty' (*hatvāpi māṃ na śaktas tvaṃ prajānāṃ poṣaṇe nṛpa* | Hv 5.51ab); and she became his daughter (*duhitṛtvaṃ ca me gaccha*, 6.6a). Since then she has provided her bounty in her various ways (Hv 6), and has passed from king to king. She narrates her own history to Viṣṇu at Hv 42.14–53, mentioning the boar *avatāra* (v. 34).

The Earth's teachings to Kṛṣṇa are narrated by Bhīṣma at Mbh 13.100. Kṛṣṇa asked the Earth what a good householder should do, and she detailed all the many offerings that a householder must regularly make, stressing his duty to host and feed guests – his basic duty to provide. The Earth is an appropriate teacher for this, as she is the paradigm of the patiently bountiful host and sponsor. In the story of the Earth sinking under her burden, we see the weight upon the householder (Bowles 2019).

When the Earth's bounty is detailed in Hv 6, it is bounty of grain for Pṛthu and his human beings, and separate specific bounty – through which each group is able to be what it is – for the seers, gods, ancestors, snakes, demons, *yakṣas*, *rākṣasas*, *gandharvas*, mountains, and trees. This milking of the Earth has to do with far more than the relationship between a king and his subjects, seeming also to be the very creation of the known world; and so it has to do not just with Pṛthu and his successors but with the God above the gods, who is set in a relationship of codependence with her. For Earth's link with Viṣṇu, see Gonda:

> Terrestrial divinities of female sex are again and again the partners of the god's [i.e. Viṣṇu's] avatāras: Sītā, Satyabhāmā, Kṛṣṇa's wife who was considered a partial embodiment (*aṃśa-*) of the goddess Earth. Viṣṇu's relations with the earth are, indeed, a very important element in the avatāra conception which in its classical form may be regarded as a more exalted development of the god's helpful and loving interest in our planet and its occupants.
>
> (Gonda 1954: 125–126)

In terms of the Kurukṣetra *avatāra* which is our immediate concern, a poetic allusion to this *avatāra* for the Earth is made by the story at Hv 71.22–35. Here, as Couture has argued, the hunchbacked woman – the king's maidservant – whom Kṛṣṇa miraculously alters into bodily perfection represents the Earth being restored by the Kurukṣetra *avatāra* (Couture 2011). Accepting Couture's interpretation, the Earth's problem would here be, metaphorically, her being misshapen, and consequently (sexually frustrated and) unable to fulfil her proper function with respect to the king. As soon as she is restored she propositions Kṛṣṇa directly, but in keeping with his non-royal role he turns her down, and she repairs to the king

In all accounts of the Kurukṣetra *avatāra*, the result of the *avatāra* is the same: more than a billion men die (11.26.9). But in the *Mahābhārata* there are three divergent accounts of Earth's initial problem: two accounts in the *Ādiparvan* (Mbh 1), and one in the *Harivaṃśa*. In this section we will look at each of them in turn. There are various other allusions to the deed of the gods for the Earth (Hiltebeitel 2011b: 571–575; Hiltebeitel 2018: 258–259), but I pass over those allusions here, because they do not describe the initial problem.

Bhīṣma's account. Before discussing the accounts of the Earth's problem, we briefly look at Bhīṣma's account of the reason for the Kurukṣetra *avatāra*, which hardly mentions the Earth. In this passage (Mbh 6.61–62, in the *Viśvopākhyāna*), Bhīṣma is explaining to Duryodhana why the Kaurava side is losing, and will lose, the war. Bhīṣma recounts what he heard from cultured sages (*yat tu me kathitaṃ tāta munibhir bhāvitātmabhiḥ* | 6.61.36ab). The celestials once saw Brahmā report to, worship, and petition Viṣṇu-Nārāyaṇa. After praising Viṣṇu, Brahmā said:

> *tvaṃ gatiḥ sarvabhūtānāṃ tvaṃ netā tvaṃ jaganmukham* |
> *tvatprasādena deveśa sukhino vibudhāḥ sadā* ‖ 6.61.61 ‖
> *pṛthivī nirbhayā deva tvatprasādāt sadābhavat* |
> *tasmād bhava viśālākṣa yaduvaṃśavivardhanaḥ* ‖ 62 ‖
> *dharmasaṃsthāpanārthāya daiteyānāṃ vadhāya ca* |
> *jagato dhāraṇārthāya vijñāpyaṃ kuru me prabho* ‖ 63 ‖ ...
> *vibhajya bhāgaśo "tmānaṃ vraja mānuṣatāṃ vibho* ‖ 67cd
> *tatrāsuravadhaṃ kṛtvā sarvalokasukhāya vai* |
> *dharmaṃ sthāpya yaśaḥ prāpya yogaṃ prāpsyasi tattvataḥ* ‖ 68 ‖

Thou art the Refuge of all creatures, and thou art their Guide. Thou hast the Universe for thy mouth. Through thy grace, O Lord of the gods, the gods are ever happy. Through thy grace the Earth hath always been freed from terrors. Therefore, O thou of large eyes, take birth in the race of Yadu. For the sake of establishing righteousness, for slaying the sons of Diti, and for upholding the universe, do what I have said, O Lord ... Dividing Thyself into portions, take birth, O Lord, among human beings. And slaughtering the *Asuras* there for happiness of all the worlds, and establishing righteousness, and winning renown, Thou wilt again truly attain to *Yoga*.

(6.61.61–63, 67c–68, trans. Ganguli 1970: Bhishma Parva LXV, 171)

After Brahmā's audience with Viṣṇu ended, he reported back to the celestial onlookers:

tenāsmi kṛtasaṃvādaḥ prasannena surarṣabhāḥ ǀ
jagato 'nugrahārthāya yācito me jagatpatiḥ ǁ 6.62.7 ǁ
mānuṣaṃ lokam ātiṣṭha vāsudeva iti śrutaḥ ǀ
asurāṇāṃ vadhārthāya saṃbhavasva mahītale ǁ 8 ǁ
saṃgrāme nihatā ye te daityadānavarākṣasāḥ ǀ
ta ime nṛṣu saṃbhūtā ghorarūpā mahābalāḥ ǁ 9 ǁ
teṣāṃ vadhārthaṃ bhagavān nareṇa sahito vaśī ǀ
mānuṣīṃ yonim āsthāya cariṣyati mahītale ǁ 10 ǁ

I was talking even with His cheerful self, ye bulls among gods. The Lord of the Universe was solicited by me, for the good of the Universe, to take his birth among mankind in the family of Vasudeva. I said unto him, – For the slaughter of the *Asuras* take thy birth on the Earth! – Those *Daityas*, *Dānavas* and *Rakshasas*, of fierce form and great strength, that were slain in battle, have been born among men. The illustrious and mighty Lord, taking birth in the human womb, will live on the Earth, accompanied by Nara, for their slaughter.

(6.62.7–10, trans. Ganguli 1970: Bhishma Parva LXVI, 172, adapted after Cherniak 2009: 19)

Bhīṣma closes his account to Duryodhana by underlining his source:

etac chrutaṃ mayā tāta ṛṣīṇāṃ bhāvitātmanām ǀ
vāsudevaṃ kathayatāṃ samavāye purātanam ǁ 6.62.26 ǁ
jāmadagnyasya rāmasya mārkaṇḍeyasya dhīmataḥ ǀ
vyāsanāradayoś cāpi śrutaṃ śrutaviśārada ǁ 27 ǁ

Even this was heard by me, O sire, from *Rishis* of cultured soul talking in their assembly, of Vasudeva, that ancient one. And O thou that art

> well-versed in scriptures, I heard this from Rama, the son of Jamadagni, and Markandeya of great wisdom, and Vyasa and Narada also.
> (6.62.26–27, trans. Ganguli 1970: Bhishma Parva LXVI, 173)

Bhīṣma's account is a presentation of the reason for the Kṛṣṇa *avatāra*, or the *avatāra* of 'the two Kṛṣṇas' (Nara and Nārāyaṇa; Hiltebeitel 1984; see also 5.48.21). Unlike the three passages discussed below, it is not a presentation of the reason for the collective Kurukṣetra *avatāra*. Bhīṣma mentions the Earth early in his account, when Brahmā says 'Through thy grace the Earth hath always been freed from terrors' (6.61.62ab); but this is vague. Thereafter the Earth is not mentioned except as the location for Viṣṇu's birth, which is 'for the good of the Universe' (*jagato 'nugrahārthāya*, 6.62.7c) because Viṣṇu will thereby defeat demons and raise *dharma*. All Bhīṣma's references are to the best-known function of the *avatāra*. This function is bolstered by the fact that the demons born on earth are those that were previously killed in battle (perhaps in the Tārakāmaya war, narrated at Hv 32–38).

Bhīṣma's account, focusing exclusively upon the dharmic function, would fit the *kaliyugānta* and a Kalkin type of intervention. If we accept the instability theory detailed in Chapter 4, then it would also fit at any other transition too, but in a different way. That is why, for the purposes of this chapter, I effectively set aside the instability theory. But when the request for intervention comes from the Earth it is a different request, because it involves the depopulation function, and because the response is more collaborative; as we shall now see, in presenting and discussing the three accounts of the Earth's problem, which Bhīṣma did not mention.

1.58. In the first *Ādiparvan* account (Matchett 2001: 34–35), Vaiśaṃpāyana describes to Janamejaya how, after Rāma Jāmadagnya's massacres, the *kṣatriya* class was replenished with brahmin assistance (1.58.4–7).

> *evaṃ tad brāhmaṇaiḥ kṣatraṃ kṣatriyāsu tapasvibhiḥ* |
> *jātam ṛdhyata dharmeṇa sudīrgheṇāyuṣānvitam* |
> *catvāro 'pi tadā varṇā babhūvur brāhmaṇottarāḥ* ‖ 1.58.8 ‖

> Thus the Kṣatriya order was fathered on Kṣatriya women by ascetic Brahmins, and it flourished according to *dharma*, possessed of a very long lifespan; so once again four classes existed, with the Brahmins at their head.
> (1.58.8, trans. Smith 2009: 17–18, adjusted)

Here the four classes seem to stand in for the four legs of the bull of *dharma*. A *kṛtayuga* followed (vv. 9–24). Then demons, defeated elsewhere by the gods, began to be born on earth as humans and animals, and with the rise in numbers 'the earth herself could not support herself' (*mahī* | *na śaśākātmanātmānam iyaṃ dhārayituṃ dharā* ‖ v. 29, trans. Smith, as are other imminent translations from this passage). The demons who were kings behaved badly 'in their hundreds and thousands' (*śatasahasraśaḥ*, v. 33d), and conditions deteriorated. Since Earth was 'oppressed in this way by those mighty demons, arrogant in their valour and strength' (*evaṃ vīryabalotsiktair bhūr iyaṃ tair mahāsuraiḥ* ǀ v. 35ab), since she was 'overwhelmed by demons' (*ākrāntāṃ dānavair balāt*, v. 36d) and 'afflicted by the burden she bore and troubled for her safety' (*bhārārtā bhayapīḍitā*, v. 37b), she repaired to Brahmā.

tat pradhānātmanas tasya bhūmeḥ kṛtyaṃ svayaṃbhuvaḥ ǀ
pūrvam evābhavad rājan viditaṃ parameṣṭhinaḥ ǁ 1.58.41 ǁ
sraṣṭā hi jagataḥ kasmān na saṃbudhyeta bhārata ǀ
surāsurāṇāṃ lokānām aśeṣeṇa manogatam ǁ 42 ǁ
tām[54] *uvāca mahārāja bhūmiṃ bhūmipatir vibhuḥ* ǀ
prabhavaḥ sarvabhūtānām īśaḥ śaṃbhuḥ prajāpatiḥ ǁ 43 ǁ
yadartham asi saṃprāptā matsakāśaṃ vasuṃdhare ǀ
tadarthaṃ saṃniyokṣyāmi sarvān eva divaukasaḥ ǁ 44 ǁ
ity uktvā sa mahīṃ devo brahmā rājan visṛjya ca ǀ
ādideśa tadā sarvān vibudhān bhūtakṛt svayam ǁ 45 ǁ
asyā bhūmer nirasituṃ bhāraṃ bhāgaiḥ pṛthak pṛthak ǀ
asyām eva prasūyadhvaṃ virodhāyeti cābravīt ǁ 46 ǁ
tathaiva ca samānīya gandharvāpsarasāṃ gaṇān ǀ
uvāca bhagavān sarvān idaṃ vacanam uttamam ǀ
svair aṃśaiḥ saṃprasūyadhvaṃ yatheṣṭaṃ mānuṣeṣv iti ǁ 47 ǁ

But Earth's purpose was already known to the self-born supreme lord, O king; how could the creator of the universe not know all the thoughts of those who inhabit the realms of the gods and demons, heir of Bharata?

Then, great king, Lord Brahmā Prajāpati, the benevolent, the mighty, origin of all beings, the lord of Earth, replied to Earth: 'The problem that has brought you to my presence, Lady Earth, is one on which I shall employ all those who live in heaven!' With these words, O king, the god Brahmā gave Earth leave to depart. Then the creator of creatures himself addressed all the gods; and he said to them, 'To cast off this burden from Earth, all of you must use portions of yourselves to take birth separately on earth to counteract it!' And in just the same way the blessed one convened the hosts of Gandharvas and Apsarases, and spoke these excellent words to all of them: 'Use portions of yourselves to take birth as you please among mortals!'

(1.58.41–47, trans. Smith 2009: 19–20)

---

[54] The critically reconstituted text has *tam* 'him, it' at 1.58.43a (Sukthankar 1933: 258; Dandekar 1971–1976, vol. 1: 84), but this is a misprint. Kinjawadekar's edition of the vulgate has *tām* 'her' (at 1.64.45a; Kinjawadekar 1929: 121), but the only variants listed for this *pāda* in the critical edition are for the vocative *mahārāja*, 'O great king'. See also Smith 2009: 793.

The gods agreed, and together approached Nārāyaṇa to ensure his participation (vv. 48–51).

This account has been interpreted by de Jong primarily in terms of overpopulation (de Jong 1985; see also Vielle 1986: 116–117). But it also facilitates the presentation of the Kurukṣetra war as a version of the battle between gods and demons, since the excess population seems to be caused by demons. Their bad behaviour exacerbates the problem as Vaiśaṃpāyana describes it, but Earth's complaint seems primarily to be about numbers. Reading this account in relation to levels of *dharma*, one might imagine that the *avatāra* would effect the transition from a *kaliyuga* to the next *kṛtayuga* by getting rid of the demons. In the presentation at 1.58, Rāma Jāmadagnya's purge of *kṣatriyas* led to a *kṛtayuga*;[55] and the situation that the Kurukṣetra *avatāra* will resolve looks like a *kaliyuga* (intervening *yugas* elided) that will again be addressed by a purge of (demonic) *kṣatriyas*. But this does not fit with the location of the latter purge at a *dvāpara-kaliyuga* transition.

1.189. In the second *Ādiparvan* account, the *Pañcendropākhyāna* ('Story of the Five Indras'), Vyāsa is speaking to Drupada, to convince him to marry his daughter Draupadī to all five Pāṇḍava brothers. Vyāsa tells Drupada:

vyāsa uvāca ǀ
purā vai naimiṣāraṇye devāḥ satram upāsate ǀ
tatra vaivasvato rājañ śāmitram akarot tadā ǁ 1.189.1 ǁ
tato yamo dīkṣitas tatra rājan nāmārayat kiṃ cid api prajābhyaḥ ǀ
tataḥ prajās tā bahulā babhūvuḥ kālātipātān maraṇāt prahīṇāḥ ǁ 2 ǁ
tatas tu śakro varuṇaḥ kuberaḥ sādhyā rudrā vasavaś cāśvinau ca ǀ
praṇetāraṃ bhuvanasya prajāpatiṃ samājagmus tatra devās tathānye ǁ 3 ǁ
tato 'bruvaṃl lokaguruṃ sametā bhayaṃ nas tīvraṃ mānuṣāṇāṃ vivṛddhyā ǀ
tasmād bhayād udvijantaḥ sukhepsavaḥ prayāma sarve śaraṇaṃ bhavantam ǁ 4 ǁ
brahmovāca ǀ
kiṃ vo bhayaṃ mānuṣebhyo yūyaṃ sarve yadāmarāḥ ǀ
mā vo martyasakāśād vai bhayaṃ bhavatu karhi cit ǁ 5 ǁ
devā ūcuḥ ǀ
martyā hy amartyāḥ saṃvṛttā na viśeṣo 'sti kaś cana ǀ
aviśeṣād udvijanto viśeṣārtham ihāgatāḥ ǁ 6 ǁ
brahmovāca ǀ
vaivasvato vyāpṛtaḥ satrahetos tena tv ime na mriyante manuṣyāḥ ǀ
tasminn ekāgre kṛtasarvakārye tata eṣāṃ bhavitaivāntakālaḥ ǁ 7 ǁ
vaivasvatasyāpi tanur vibhūtā vīryeṇa yuṣmākam uta prayuktā ǀ
saiṣām anto bhavitā hy antakāle tanur hi vīryaṃ bhavitā nareṣu ǁ 8 ǁ

[55] Elsewhere, as mentioned in Chapter 4, Rāma Jāmadagnya is pegged to the *tretā-dvāparayuga* transition (1.2.3; 12.326.77).

Vyāsa said:
In the olden days the Gods sat at a session in the Naimiṣa Forest, O king. Yama Vaivasvata held the office of the butcher priest.

Then Yama, when consecrated, O king,
No longer killed any one of the creatures;
And thus the creatures grew numerous,
Being freed from death and the onslaught of Time.

Then Śakra, Kubera, and Varuṇa,
The Sādhyas, the Rudras, the Vasus, and Aśvins
Repaired to Prajāpati, guide of the world –
These Gods, and still others, foregathered there.

And, assembled, they spoke to the sovereign teacher:
'Our fear is severe from this waxing of men.
And atremble with fear, and our joys to pursue,
We have all come seeking shelter with you.'

Brahmā said:
Why should you stand in fear of man, when you are all immortal? Let there never be fear in you from mortals.

The Gods said:
Since the mortals have become immortal, there is no difference anymore. And, upset by this equality, we have come here to seek difference!

Brahmā said:
The session keeps Yama occupied,
And that is the reason that men do not die.
When he's done with the rite with his single mind,
The time of death will return for them.

Vaivasvata's body will strengthen thereby,
And employed with the vigor of you yourselves,
It will spell their end at the time of death –
And might it will mean over humankind!
(1.189.1–8, trans. van Buitenen 1973: 370–371, adapted)

So the gods have complained to Brahmā, and he has said that there is a solution in store. They have to wait, then help.

Then Indra, following a trail of floating lotuses, found a woman standing weeping in the water at the source of the Gaṅgā, and in response to his enquiries she led him away.

tāṃ gacchantīm anvagacchat tadānīṃ so 'paśyad ārāt taruṇaṃ darśanīyam |
siṃhāsanasthaṃ yuvatīsahāyaṃ krīḍantam akṣair girirājamūrdhni ‖
1.189.14 ‖

He followed her while she led the way,
And he saw nearby a handsome youth,
On a lion-throne seated, a young woman with him,
Playing at dice on a Himālayan peak.
(1.189.14, trans. van Buitenen 1973: 371, adapted)[56]

This was Śiva. Indra slighted him and was thus imprisoned in a cave, along with 'four others who matched his splendor' (*tulyadyutīṃś caturo 'nyān*, v. 20b). Śiva said:

... *yoniṃ sarve mānuṣīm āviśadhvam* |
tatra yūyaṃ karma kṛtvāviṣahyaṃ bahūn anyān nidhanaṃ prāpayitvā ‖
1.189.25bcd
āgantāraḥ punar evendralokaṃ ...

You shall all enter a human womb.
Having wrought great feats of violence there
And sped many others to their deaths,
You shall go again to the world of Indra ...
(1.189.25b–26a, trans. van Buitenen 1973: 372–373)

Śiva then said they would be sired by gods, and married to Śrī in human form (vv. 27–29). Then he took them to see Nārāyaṇa, who plucked two hairs that would become Baladeva and Kṛṣṇa (vv. 30–31). Vyāsa now tells Drupada that the Pāṇḍavas are those five Indras and Draupadī is Śrī-Lakṣmī, and he gives Drupada divine sight so he can see this for himself (vv. 32–40). Vyāsa concludes, stressing that Śiva decrees five husbands for Draupadī (vv. 41–49), and Drupada goes along with it (Black 2021: 73–78).

In this story, the weeping woman tells Indra that he will find out who she is and why she is weeping (1.189.13), but this is never explicitly narrated. Van Buitenen says 'it does not become clear who she is' (van Buitenen 1973: 465). Hiltebeitel has consistently maintained that she is Śrī (Hiltebeitel 1976: 170–173; Hiltebeitel 2001: 120, 186; Hiltebeitel 2018: 120–128). Reich follows Hiltebeitel in this, to the extent that she calls this 'the myth of the Five Indras in the Cave and Śrī' (Reich 2011: 30–33). But since this story explains the Kurukṣetra

[56] I adjust van Buitenen's translation of *yuvatīsahāyaṃ* from the plural ('young women') to the singular, since this is a reference to Pārvatī, as Hiltebeitel has noted (Hiltebeitel 1976: 94–97, 171; Hiltebeitel 2018: 123–124). Smith's summary has 'a youth playing dice with some young women' (Smith 2009: 74).

avatāra, the weeping woman would rather be the suffering Earth. Scheuer says we are told she is Śrī at 1.189.29 and 33 (Scheuer 1982: 106), but we are not: there the reference is to the woman who will marry the Pāṇḍavas, with no indication that this would be the same woman as the one who was weeping. Scheuer is then in a bind, because he sees that the weeping woman **should** be the Earth:

> She represents, if not the earth herself, at least the 'śrī' of the earth, the sacrificial splendour (born of sacrifice) which cannot be separated from the earth. Doesn't this weeping woman who has descended into the water (plunged: vyavagāhya) symbolise the situation of the earth in distress, in danger of being submerged by the waters?[57]
>
> (Scheuer 1982: 106)

Previously I have suggested, as Scheuer effectively does, that the weeping woman is somehow both Śrī **and** the Earth (Brodbeck 2006: 105; Brodbeck 2009a: 35–36). But in the current context it is not desirable to continue fudging the matter.

Hiltebeitel's argument to the effect that the weeping woman is Śrī has several aspects. Hiltebeitel points out that the meeting between Indra and Śrī at Mbh 12.221 occurred at the same source-of-the-Gaṅgā location (Hiltebeitel 1976: 170, referring back to 160–162); but this argument is circumstantial at best. Hiltebeitel refers to the weeping woman's promise that Indra will recognise her in due course as evidence that she is Śrī, and points especially to her use of the word *iha* ('here') at 1.189.13a (*tvaṃ vetsyase mām iha yāsmi śakra*; p. 170 n. 78); but this argument is obscure. Hiltebeitel's most convincing argument is his reference to 'the mythological convergences' (ibid.); but mythological convergences can be cited in favour of either identification. In his 1976 monograph Hiltebeitel was following Dumézil in focusing on Śrī and sovereignty in a comparative Indo-European context, and thus the identification of the weeping woman as Śrī served his overall argument; but if one takes one's lead from the text, then in view of the Earth's clear role in the scene at Mbh 1.58, the mythological convergences are more saliently in favour of identifying the weeping woman as Earth, along the lines of the Scheuer quotation above.

Having convinced himself of her identification as Śrī, Hiltebeitel overtranslates the *tāṃ* at 1.189.29c. The line reads: *tāṃ cāpy eṣāṃ yoṣitaṃ lokakāntāṃ śriyaṃ bhāryāṃ vyadadhān mānuṣeṣu* ‖ 29cd. Since Hiltebeitel thinks that Śrī is present, he translates this as: 'he [i.e. Śiva] also appointed that young woman, desired by the world, Śrī herself, to be their wife among men' (Hiltebeitel 1976:

[57] 'Elle répresente, sinon la terre elle-même, du moins la « śrī » de la terre, la splendeur sacrificielle (née du sacrifice) qui ne devrait pas être séparée de la terre. Cette femme en pleurs qui est descendue dans l'eau (plongée: vyavagāhya) ne symbolise-t-elle pas la situation de la terre en détresse, en danger d'être submergée par les eaux?'

173). But it would perhaps rather be: 'he also appointed Śrī – [who is] the young woman desired by the world – to be their wife among humans'.

In his later work, Hiltebeitel proceeds as if the identification of the weeping woman as Śrī is unproblematic (Hiltebeitel 2001: 120, 186; Hiltebeitel 2018: 120–128). As far as I know, he never acknowledges the possibility that she could be the Earth, asserting instead that 'the *upākhyāna* of the five former Indras never mentions the goddess Earth ... Vyāsa leaves the Earth goddess out' (Hiltebeitel 2018: 127, 128). But this means that even while linking 'this *upākhyāna* and the main story', Hiltebeitel tends to see the Kurukṣetra war as having been fought 'for the sovereignty of Yudhiṣṭhira', rather than for the rescue of the Earth (Hiltebeitel 2018: 122). In contrast, while I would admit that the matter is not completely unambiguous (hence, for example, 1.app100.115–116), I take the weeping woman to be the Earth.

In the 1.189 account of the reason for the Kurukṣetra *avatāra*, the problem is overpopulation and the lack of distinction between humans and gods. But here it is not the Earth who complains to Brahmā, but the gods. Their complaint is lodged before she is mentioned, and is of a different nature from hers. Her complaint, such as it is in this account (she never says why she is weeping), is presented as if it is a subordinate means that enables the gods' problem to be represented in a different form, in such a way that it can be solved. But the solution to the gods' problem is also an indignity to them, and thus a fitting punishment for the pride of the various Indras, since it requires them to take form as disgusting human beings and do disgusting things. When the gods complain, they are made to get their hands dirty by sorting the problem out themselves. By implication, when in the 1.58 account the Earth herself complains and the same gods have to sort the problem out, it is the same problem. In the 1.58 account all the Earth has to do is complain to Brahmā, and he makes the gods sort the problem out for her, even though they themselves have not complained.

<u>Hv 40–45</u>. In Hv 40, where the *Harivaṃśa* account begins, the *kṛtayuga* and *tretāyuga* pass by while Nārāyaṇa is asleep, but towards the end of the *dvāparayuga* the seers wake him up (40.35–41). Brahmā describes the situation to him (Hv 41). Human kings are behaving impeccably; they are 'capable of making it the *kṛtayuga* again' (*bhūyaḥ kṛtayugaṃ kartum utsahante narādhipāḥ* ‖ 41.12cd).[58] But because of this, death has no dominion, and the Earth is suffering.

[58] This high level of *dharma* seems out of keeping with the *dvāparayuga* or the *kaliyuga*. In light of this, we might refer to the aforementioned idea that the end of any of the four *yuga*s would be a period of instability (Thomas 1988: 245–246, 268; Koskikallio 1994: 259–261), in the sense that at the *yugānta* the level of *dharma* could go lower than the level of the next *yuga* (the trough as per Figure 10) – or, potentially, higher (a spike, unpictured).

seyaṃ bhārapariśrāntā pīḍyamānā narādhipaiḥ |
pṛthivī samanuprāptā naur ivāsannaviplavā ‖ Hv 41.18 ‖
yugāntasadṛśaṃ rūpaṃ śailoccalitabandhanam |
jalotpīḍākulā svedaṃ darśayantī muhur muhuḥ ‖ 19 ‖
kṣatriyāṇāṃ vapurbhiś ca tejasā ca balena ca |
nṛṇāṃ ca rāṣṭrair vistīrṇaiḥ śrāmyatīva vasuṃdharā ‖ 20 ‖

While being trampled by the kings, this broad earth has been worn out by their weight, and she has come to me like a ship on the verge of capsizing. Sweating, and welling up with tears again and again, she looks like she does at the end of the age, when the mountains that hold her down have been unfastened. The jewel-bearing earth is quite worn out by the bodies and brilliance and power of the *kṣatriya*s, and by the numerous nations of people.

(*Harivaṃśa* 41.18–20)

There is a surfeit of settlements, and 'the Earth has no space left' (*bhūmir nirvivarīkṛtā*, v. 22d); hence she and the emaciated god Death (*kāla*) have come to Brahmā for help (v. 23). Brahmā says that 'Regarding the removal of the Earth's burden, the task is to kill just the kings' (*rājñāṃ caiva vadhaḥ kāryo dharaṇyā bhāranirṇaye* ‖ 41.31cd).

This is Earth's suggestion also. When, in the company of the gods, she meets with Nārāyaṇa himself in the gods' assembly-hall, she says to him:

etad yuṣmatpravṛttena daivena pariṇāmitā |
jagaddhitārthaṃ kuruta rājñāṃ hetuṃ raṇakṣaye ‖ Hv 42.51 ‖

Now I have become bowed down because of the sacred business that is in progress for all of your sakes, and so, for the good of the world, you must create a pretext for destroying the kings in battle.

(*Harivaṃśa* 42.51)

This will relieve her of her burden (vv. 52–53).

The gods are keen to descend to earth to arrange this. Brahmā explains that by already sending the ocean, and Gaṅgā, and the Vasu gods to earth in human form, he has laid foundations for a rift in the Bhārata royal line (Hv 43). So the gods now descend to engineer the war by exploiting that rift:

tato 'ṃśān avaniṃ devāḥ sarva evāvatārayan |
yathā te kathitaṃ pūrvam aṃśāvataraṇaṃ mayā ‖ Hv 43.69 ‖

Then every single one of those gods sent a portion of themselves down to earth, as per the descent into characters that I described for you earlier.

(*Harivaṃśa* 43.69)

Since the *Harivaṃśa* account is Vaiśaṃpāyana's second direct account to Janamejaya of the reasons for this *avatāra*, this verse appears to refer to the list of divine identities that Vaiśaṃpāyana presented at Mbh 1.61, just after the first account.

After the gods have descended, at Nārada's prompting Nārāyaṇa descends too, not just for the success of this plan to rescue the Earth, but also to kill Kaṃsa, who is the archdemon Kālanemi reborn, and to kill various other demons who have similarly been reborn on earth (Hv 44–45; see also 12.326.82, quoted on p. 49 above, naming Kaṃsa).

The *Harivaṃśa* account thus provides two reasons for Viṣṇu-Nārāyaṇa's descent. Only one of them is the necessity for the *kṣatriya* purge, and only the other one involves killing demons.[59] These two reasons for Viṣṇu's descent correspond to the two functions of the *avatāra* that we identified and disentangled in the *Nārāyaṇīya* passage at 12.337. The differentiation of these two prompts for the *avatāra* – overpopulation and problems with demons – has been noted before in connection with the *Harivaṃśa* account (Brinkhaus 2001: 28; Viethsen 2009). The two causes are combined in the 1.58 account, just as the two functions are combined at 12.337. In the *Harivaṃśa* account the two causes are juxtaposed, but not really combined (compare González-Reimann 1993). The main task is accomplished by the gods en masse, but the additional task of killing demons is mentioned in connection with Viṣṇu alone.[60]

In the *Harivaṃśa* account, unlike the 1.58 account, the *kṣatriya* purge is explicitly located at the *dvāpara–kaliyuga* transition. But whereas in the 1.58 account the *kṣatriya* purge is to occur following explicitly demonic *kṣatriya* behaviour, in the *Harivaṃśa* account there is very good *kṣatriya* behaviour. Kātre says that 'Overburdening of the earth due to the numerousness even of righteous races and not at all involving Adharma and wickedness seems also to have occasioned some avatāras', adding a footnote referring only to this *Harivaṃśa* passage (Kātre 1934: 49). Kātre writes as if this would be a different *avatāra*, but it is the same Kṛṣṇa *avatāra* whose reason for descending was described at 1.58 and who told Arjuna that he incarnates because of *adharma*. In the *Harivaṃśa* account the *kṣatriya*s are behaving impeccably, and the descent of demons to earth (and the gods-against-demons dynamic) is invoked only through Nārāyaṇa's extra task of killing Kaṃsa and company in Mathurā.[61]

---

[59] Matchett conflates the two reasons when she has Nārada tell Viṣṇu 'that Earth's present trouble [i.e. the trouble that the other gods have already descended in order to solve] is caused by the Daityas [Kaṃsa et al.]' (Matchett 2001: 33–34). In fact Nārada presents the demonic problem as a separate issue.

[60] Elsewhere in the *Mahābhārata*, Kṛṣṇa explains why he killed Kaṃsa in terms of the benefit to his relatives (González-Reimann 1993: 15, with references).

[61] The addition of the Mathurā task might be understood partly in terms of the *Harivaṃśa* account's location, since by this point in the *Mahābhārata* the story of the war has effectively been completed, and Vaiśaṃpāyana is responding to Janamejaya's additional questions about

All three *Mahābhārata* accounts of the Earth's problem have in common that the problem remedied by the *avatāra* involves overpopulation. The 1.189 account, presented by Vyāsa, differs from both of the other accounts in that it does not mention demons. Demons are involved in the other two accounts in different ways. In the 1.58 account, the overpopulation seems to be caused by the descent of demons, and by implication it is the demons who must be culled. But in the *Harivaṃśa* account, the only demons mentioned are the ones who are to be dealt with by Nārāyaṇa's extra, Mathurā mission (mentioned only in this account). The Earth's problem in the *Harivaṃśa* account is really the absence of death, though here death's absence (which in 1.189 is caused by his duties at the *satra*) is enforced by the *kṣatriyas*' exemplary behaviour (Hv 41.16), and so when Earth comes to complain to Brahmā she does so 'Placing the god Death, emaciated and helpless, before her' (*seyaṃ nirāmiṣaṃ kṛtvā niśceṣṭaṃ kālam agrataḥ* | Hv 41.23ab). Death is there too when she speaks to Viṣṇu in the assembly-hall on Mount Meru: Earth and Death leave together at Hv 43.66 and 44.1. In the *Harivaṃśa* account Death (*kāla*) is masculine, as he was in 1.189 in the person of Yama.

As far as dharmic effect is concerned, in the 1.58 account the *avatāra* must increase *dharma*, because the purge is of demonic *kṣatriyas*. In the 1.189 account the purge is of excess mortals (the backlog from when Yama was out of action), without any specified dharmic character. The problem is simply death's absence.[62] By implication Yama should be on duty, and in facilitating his return there might be a basic sense in which the *avatāra* restores *dharma*. But the *avatāra* does not affect how dharmic mortals are. In the *Harivaṃśa* account the purge is explicitly of good *kṣatriyas*; but there is no immediate need to have them behave worse, just to have fewer of them. As Brahmā presents it in the *Harivaṃśa*, the overpopulation is caused by exemplary *kṣatriya* behaviour; but apart from that, the Earth's problem would be the same as it is in the 1.189 account – no death. If we ask the *Harivaṃśa* account whether the *avatāra* increases *dharma*, we would like to say that it increases *dharma* in a basic sense by restoring death (*kāla* should not starve), without wishing to reduce dharmic behaviour to that end. Since in the *Harivaṃśa* the *avatāra* has the additional mission to kill Kaṃsa and company, who are adharmic qua demons, *dharma* will also, to that extent, be increased. This latter dharmic increase is similar to the way in which *dharma* would be increased in the 1.58 account where, unlike here, the overpopulation is demonic.

As far as the *yuga* cycle is concerned, the 1.58 account is not explicitly pegged to the *dvāpara-kaliyuga* transition, but it does not appear to fit there, because the solution is to cull demonic *kṣatriyas*, which will cause *dharma* to

Kṛṣṇa and his family. Compare Hv 91.21, which identifies killing Naraka as the reason for Kṛṣṇa's birth.

[62] Here we might infer a high level of *dharma*, because *dharma* and lifespan are part of the same complex variable; but this is not made explicit.

increase, and because the purge that the *avatāra* must effect is juxtaposed with Rāma Jāmadagnya's purges, which led to a *kṛtayuga*. The 1.189 account also is not pegged to the *dvāpara–kaliyuga* transition, and it could only fit there if the overpopulation problem were independent of the *yuga*. The *Harivaṃśa* account **is** pegged to the *dvāpara–kaliyuga* transition, in keeping with the location of the Kurukṣetra war there during the central narration; but at first glance it does not fit there, because the initial situation, as Brahmā presents it, is one of all-but-perfect *dharma*, notwithstanding the recent presence of Kaṃsa and company. Indeed, given the temporal location of the events (Viṣṇu awakes and/or is woken 'towards the end of the *dvāpara*', *dvāparaparyante*, Hv 40.36), when Brahmā tells Nārāyaṇa that the Earth's problem is caused by the impeccable behaviour of the *kṣatriyas* (Hv 41), how does he expect this to be received? Brahmā would know, and Nārāyaṇa too as soon as he realises how long he has slept for, that at this juncture the *dharma* level will move from 2 to 1. Nārāyaṇa, knowing the laws of the cosmic average, would have a view that transcends the local descriptions of *kṛtayuga* life under Bhīṣma (or any recent kings),[63] a perspectival difference permitting the important idea that the king can and does make the *yuga* (Thomas 2007). But could Bhīṣma's or anyone's excellent rule during the *dvāparayuga* really cause such overpopulation as the Earth complains of towards its end? As mentioned earlier, it might seem that the Earth gets more sensitive as the *mahāyuga* wears on.

In the 1.189 account the problem that the *avatāra* solves is presented to Brahmā in the first instance by the gods, and it is presented as a problem of excessive similarity between gods and humans. In this account, the problem for the Earth is not specified. Nonetheless, since we know from 1.58 that the Earth suffered from overpopulation prior to the *avatāra*, as soon as we hear that Yama was not doing his job, we anticipate that overpopulation would be a problem for her here too. Indeed, when the gods' complaint to Brahmā is voiced in terms of excessive similarity (1.189.6), these terms of reference are slightly unexpected, since in the preceding verses we have been told that 'the creatures grew numerous, / Being freed from death and the onslaught of Time', and that the gods' first comment to Brahmā was that 'Our fear is severe from this waxing of men' (1.189.2, 4, trans. van Buitenen 1973: 370, quoted earlier). It is only after Brahmā asks the gods to specify precisely why this would trouble them that they mention the excessive similarity between humans and themselves. Up to that point, their complaint seems to represent the Earth's complaint of overpopulation, just as Brahmā represented it to Nārāyaṇa in Hv 41.

Thus in the 1.189 account, where the problem is not to do with demons or with a dearth of *dharma* (and where in these respects it matches the *Harivaṃśa*

---

[63] For the *kṛtayuga* under Bhīṣma, see 1.102.5; compare 1.62.7–10 (Duḥṣanta); 1.69.45–48 (Bharata); 1.94.1–17 (Śaṃtanu); Hv 68.30 and 79.35 (Kṛṣṇa).

account's main reason for the *avatāra*), the problem is nonetheless presented in two different forms, depending on whether it is the explicit problem for the gods, or the implicit problem for the Earth.

To revert to Bhīṣma's account of the reason for the Kṛṣṇa *avatāra*: Bhīṣma's account is more akin to Nārada's Hv 44 add-on, and to the unhappy mix of demons into the overpopulation problem at 1.58, than it is to the various accounts of the overpopulation problem on its own (1.58 imagined without the demons; 1.189; Hv 40–43). But by encompassing just Kṛṣṇa and Arjuna, Bhīṣma's account can refer, in its context, to the defeat of Duryodhana in the Kurukṣetra war (where Kṛṣṇa himself does not fight). By implication, the Kaurava forces (perhaps even Bhīṣma himself) are flush with demonic energy that the Pāṇḍavas guided by Kṛṣṇa are sure to destroy. The Kurukṣetra war is thus represented in terms of just one function of the *avatāra*. The elision of what is typically the Earth's side of the story is perhaps in keeping with Bhīṣma's vow to neglect the feminine (1.94.88, etc.; Black 2021: 23–56). If Bhīṣma is indeed relating exactly what he heard, then it seems to be a version of the encounter between Brahmā and Viṣṇu rather different to the one Vaiśaṃpāyana presents at Hv 40–43, where Brahmā represents the Earth's problem, after which the Earth herself reports to Viṣṇu in the assembly-hall atop Mount Meru. In Vaiśaṃpāyana's earlier version at Mbh 1.58 the Earth does not report directly to Viṣṇu, but nor does Brahmā; here it is Indra who speaks to Viṣṇu to ensure his involvement for the Earth's benefit (1.58.51–59.2).

In light of the myth of the origin of Death (12.248–250) as discussed above, whereby Death is the treatment for the problem of the Earth's burden, we wish to relate to the Kurukṣetra *avatāra* in terms of the dynamics of the *yuga* cycle. As explored above through the accounts at 1.58, 1.189, and Hv 40–45, the situation and cause of the *avatāra*'s Kurukṣetra appearance does not immediately allow a clear view of the relation between the *yuga* cycle and the *avatāra*. But overpopulation is the common factor in all the Earth stories, and the crucial point for understanding the Earth's overpopulation problem, as mentioned earlier, is that it is linked to the diminishing of lifespan from *yuga* to *yuga*. The story of the origin of Death fits the 1.189 story of Death's neglect and promised rectification of his duty; and it fits the *Harivaṃśa* story where, when Earth goes to see Brahmā and then Nārāyaṇa, Death (*kāla*) comes along too, all poorly (Hv 41.23; 43.66; 44.1).

Insofar as it is a story of overpopulation being remedied, the story of the Earth being rescued by the Kurukṣetra *avatāra* seems to be a story of the diminishing of lifespan, which would happen in its first and paradigmatic form at the *kṛtayugānta*. But insofar as it is a story of *dharma* being re-established, the story of the Kurukṣetra *avatāra* would most naturally be placed at the *kaliyugānta*.

The view from the gods

In the previous section, the reasons for the Kurukṣetra *avatāra*, as the *Mahābhārata* presents them, were described and compared in terms of the problem affecting the Earth. In this respect the problem was seen to be, primarily, overpopulation. In the *Harivaṃśa* account the *avatāra* task of killing demons is, as it were, tacked on at the end, without reference to the Earth or her sufferings.

Jāmi and *pṛthak*. We return now to the problem for the gods early in the *mahāyuga*, as articulated, out of time, at Mbh 1.189. Here *dharma* is not the problem. Prompted by Brahmā, the gods say that 'mortals have become immortal, there is no difference (*viśeṣa*) anymore ... upset by this equality (*aviśeṣa*), we have come here to seek difference (*viśeṣa*)!' (1.189.6, trans. van Buitenen 1973: 370, quoted above).

This speech by the gods prompts us to interpret the *Mahābhārata*'s mythological narrative presentations in terms used in the Brāhmaṇa literature of the Vedic schools. In respect of genre there is a gulf between these two bodies of literature, and this has sometimes made it difficult to see continuities between them. It has been easier for scholars to see continuities between the Upaniṣadic texts and the soteriological portions of the *Mahābhārata* (see e.g. Edgerton 1965; Brodbeck 2018b). But the problems that the creator Prajāpati has with the cosmos in the Brāhmaṇas are akin to the problems that Viṣṇu-Nārāyaṇa has with the cosmos in the *Mahābhārata*. Kātre says that 'Prajāpati ranks as the highest god in the Brāhmanical literature and is nearer to Viṣṇu than to Brahman [i.e. Brahmā] of the Epics and the Purāṇas' (Kātre 1934: 67).

The importance of the Brāhmaṇa material to our project is suggested by Thomas, who proposes 'a more detailed investigation of the relationship between Vedic, and especially Brāhmaṇa theories of time, and those of the classical texts ... there seem to be considerable and well-founded connections between the epic and earlier ideas' (Thomas 1988: 310–311). The importance of the Brāhmaṇa material to our project is also suggested by Hegarty, even as he encapsulates our title problem:

> There is a tension between the idea of restitution of order (perhaps best expressed by the role of the *avatāra*, or incarnation, of Viṣṇu as Kṛṣṇa) and the inevitability of decline (best expressed by the idea of successive, declining *yugas*). However, the tendency towards dysfunction and the necessity of either restitutive or ameliorative action resonates with the Brāhmaṇas' problematic primary creation and is, in the Mahābhārata, a *leitmotif* at both the levels of divine and human action (though the, imperfectly and patchily reflected, *yuga* doctrine in the Mahābhārata throws up some paradoxes with regard to the inevitability of cosmic decline).
>
> (Hegarty 2012: 90 n. 34)

Hegarty's mention of 'the necessity of either restitutive or ameliorative action' resonates with the two functions of the *avatāra* as identified earlier in this chapter. Patnaik, Chatterjee, and Suar sum up the situation as follows (2009: 5): 'the disjointed time of the Vedas and the Āraṇyakas which constantly needs repair (provided by rituals) or which would lead to entropy later gets reflected in the entropic tendency of the *yuga*s (aeons) which move from purity to impurity'.

Smith gives a bibliography on Prajāpati (Smith 1989: 54–55 n. 12) and sets out Prajāpati's basic features as the Brāhmaṇa texts present them. He is the totality of time and space, and he also transcends that totality as its creator. But time after time, in the accounts of his creation, the creatures (*prajā*) of which he is lord (*pati*) are problematic.

> Many of these myths of Prajāpati's failed cosmogonic efforts can be divided into two types: the cosmic emanation is either insufficiently differentiated or intemperately scattered into a chaos of unconnected fragments ... When the story of Prajāpati's emission has the emitted creatures indistinct or overly similar, the principle of *jāmi* or excessive resemblance is recalled. When, on the other hand, the creatures are said to be dispersed or overly distinct from one another, the equally dangerous metaphysical excess of extreme differentiation, *pṛthak*, is represented. In either case, Prajāpati's procreative act results not in a cosmos but in a metaphysical mess.
>
> (Smith 1989: 58–59)

In the *jāmi* category, Smith mentions the creation accounts at *Taittirīya Brāhmaṇa* 2.2.7.1 and 3.10.9.1 (Dumont 1951: 640), *Pañcaviṃśa Brāhmaṇa* 24.11.2, and *Jaiminīya Brāhmaṇa* 1.117. The creatures are 'chaotically indistinguishable, being too much alike', and hence there is 'discord, rivalry, and cannibalism' (Smith 1989: 59). In the *pṛthak* category, which Smith says is more common, are accounts where Prajāpati's creatures resist him and flee from him, fearing that he will devour them. On *jāmi* and *pṛthak* as 'two symmetrical excesses' ('deux excès symétriques'), see also Verpoorten 1977: 84. Hegarty calls *jāmi* and *pṛthak* 'under-differentiation' and 'over-distinction' (Hegarty 2006a: 59 n. 20; Hegarty 2006b: 89 n. 38; Hegarty 2012: 89 n. 23), which would fit, one way or another, 'the necessity of either restitutive or ameliorative action' (Hegarty 2012: 90 n. 34, quoted above).

In creating, Prajāpati also, because he is now extended, becomes disjointed.

> *prajāpater ha vai prajāḥ sasṛjān asya* । *parvāṇi visasraṃsuḥ sa vai saṃvatsara eva prajāpatis tasyaitāni parvāṇy ahorātrayoḥ saṃdhī paurṇamāsī cāmāvāsyā ca rtumukhāni* ‖ *Śatapatha Brāhmaṇa* 1.6.3.35 ‖
>
> When Prajāpati had emitted the creatures, his joints became disjointed. Now Prajāpati is the year, and his joints are the two junctures of day and

> night, of the waxing and waning half-months, and the beginnings of the seasons.
>
> (*Śatapatha Brāhmaṇa* 1.6.3.35, trans. Smith 1989: 61, adapted)

No mention is made here of *yugas*. As far as we can tell from the Brāhmaṇa evidence, at this point the *yuga* scheme was either not known to these Vedic schools, or was not yet invented. But the *yuga* scheme divides time into sections with junctions between them, just as the days and the half-months and the seasons do, but on a larger scale. Prajāpati is the year by virtue of being the totality of time (Gonda 1984: 14–15, 78–91), so he would be the *mahāyuga* too, and the day of Brahmā.

In the case of Prajāpati, the aforementioned problem of *jāmi* or *pṛthak* is remedied by a secondary, ritual act, which effects 'Cosmogony, the production of an ordered universe out of a generated potential' (Smith 1989: 62). The problem of *jāmi* or *pṛthak* is corrected, and then the universe functions more stably. The correction is by way of counteracting, of boosting the other pole, so that if the initial problem was one of *jāmi*, then the ritual applies difference (pp. 63–64), and if the initial problem was one of *pṛthak*, then the ritual applies similarity (p. 64). Either way, the ritual establishes a productive balance between the two extremes: 'The sacrifice is a cosmogonic instrument, for the ritual process completes all the stages necessary for making an ontologically viable universe' (p. 63). Whichever polar problem the ritual restoration of Prajāpati was necessary in order to correct – whichever type of 'defectiveness of the merely natural' (Smith 1989: 68) – the two extremes are held in productive balance by the ritual calendar, which concentrates the ritual solution upon the joints between the sections of Prajāpati-as-time, and which was instituted in that first cosmogonic sacrifice.

In *Śatapatha Brāhmaṇa* 10.4.3, the gods are doing their sacrifice wrong in two different ways, and Prajāpati intervenes:

> ... *tān ha prajāpatir uvāca na vai me sarvāṇi rūpāṇy upadhatthāti vaiva recayatha na vābhyāpayatha tasmān nāmṛtā bhavatheti* ‖ *Śatapatha Brāhmaṇa* 10.4.3.6
>
> Prajāpati then spake unto them, 'Ye do not lay down (put on me) all my forms; but ye either make (me) too large or leave (me) defective: therefore ye do not become immortal.'
>
> (*Śatapatha Brāhmaṇa* 10.4.3.6, trans. Eggeling 1978: 357)

Here we see the two problems, of *jāmi* and *pṛthak*. But Prajāpati's ritual restoration is presented as a single and general solution to the problem of extension that he caused for himself when he first created, and it is in this general aspect that the gods facilitate Prajāpati's repair on an ongoing basis, by instituting the ritual that maintains the cosmos.

> ... [*devā*] *abhiṣajyann agnihotreṇaivāhorātrayoḥ saṃdhī tatparvābhiṣajyaṃs tat samadadhuḥ paurṇamāsena caivāmāvāsyena ca paurṇamāsīṃ cāmāvāsyāṃ ca tatparvābhiṣajyaṃs tat samadadhuś cāturmāsyair eva rtumukhāni tatparvābhiṣajyaṃs tat samadadhuḥ* ‖
>
> *Śatapatha Brāhmaṇa* 1.6.3.36

> With the *agnihotra* (the twice-daily sacrifice) they healed that joint (which is) the two junctures of day and night, and joined it together. With the new and full moon sacrifices, they healed that joint (which is) between the waxing and waning lunar half-months, and joined it together. And with the *cāturmāsyas* (quarterly sacrifices) they healed that joint (which is) the beginning of the seasons, and joined it together.
>
> (*Śatapatha Brāhmaṇa* 1.6.3.36, trans. Smith 1989: 65–66)

The ongoing role of healing Prajāpati through ritual, following the secondary creation of the ritual, is a role shared, among human beings in particular, by the brahmins (*Śatapatha Brāhmaṇa* 13.1.1.4; Smith 1989: 67; see also Parpola 1979: 145). In Gonda's analysis, the *agnicayana* ritual plays an important role in the repairing of the exhausted Prajāpati (Gonda 1984: 83–87). In terms of our *Mahābhārata* discussions, what is notable here is that two different cosmic problems, which are related to each other as opposites, are solved simultaneously, and also repeatedly, at the junctures of time.

In the *Mahābhārata*'s cosmic scheme, the days of Brahmā are marked out and ritually concretised by what are effectively the *agnihotra*s of Brahmā: the creation (via Dakṣa's daughters and so on) at the start of the day, and the *pralaya* at the end of the day. Within that day of Brahmā, as superintended by fourteen Manus, the regulation is at and through the junctions of *mahāyuga*s (the *yuga*s of the gods), and the junctions of *yuga*s, and the junctions of our years, months, and days. The junctions of years, months, and days are marked by human ritual, but the junctions of *yuga*s and *mahāyuga*s are beyond our scope, and would have to be marked out, if they are marked out, by rituals of the gods, such as we might see taking place in the Kurukṣetra war at the *dvāpara–kaliyuga* transition.

We will return to this question below. But insofar as a *mahāyuga* is an extended cycle with junctions in time, it involves simultaneously the two opposite problems of *jāmi* and *pṛthak*. As with the sacrifice, both problems are remedied by the same act, whenever it takes place. Marking out one extremity of a time-period makes no sense without marking out the other and implicitly scaling the range in between, implying a desirable midpoint that is then accentuated by repetition. In terms of the days of Brahmā, the midpoint is effectively the whole day of Brahmā, once things are stable after the creation, and before they are destabilised by the *pralaya*. In terms of the *mahāyuga*, we can imagine a midpoint between the problems of *jāmi* and *pṛthak*.

In the 1.189 account of the reason for the *avatāra*, the gods complain to Brahmā that 'mortals have become immortal, there is no difference (*viśeṣa*) anymore ... upset by this equality (*aviśeṣa*), we have come here to seek difference (*viśeṣa*)!' (1.189.6, trans. van Buitenen 1973: 370; compare Herrmann 1977: 165–167). This is the problem of *jāmi*. It is reported shortly before Yama resumes his operations with the assistance of the gods. This has been characterised above in terms of the problem for the Earth at the front end of the *mahāyuga* cycle, represented also in the overpopulation aspect of the 1.58 and Hv 40–45 accounts.

The problem at the back end of the *mahāyuga* is that of excessive difference (*pṛthak*): effectively, the world is in danger because human beings are too unlike the gods, departing from *dharma* to the greatest extent. Once they are differentiated by Death, gods and humans should stand in a relationship of ritual codependence. This is the 'wheel of sacrifice' described at Bhg 3.9–20. Sacrifice is 'supreme' (*paraṃ*) in the *dvāparayuga* (Ms 1.86; Mbh 12.224.27), but in the *kaliyuga* the centre does not hold, and humans neglect their duties to the gods and go too far in the other direction, which is intolerable.

The balance is a fine one. The balance, such as it is, is set by the first regulating act of Death that ends the *kṛtayuga*. After this, the Earth should be happy. But the act repeats; and as the *mahāyuga* wears on and their lifespan keeps decreasing, the people become less and less dharmic, and this continues past the midpoint. The bull is struggling, and the only way back is through a regulating act in the opposite direction. In the *yuga* scheme, rather than lifting the bull back up onto its legs one by one, the action in the opposite direction lifts the bull back onto all fours all at once; the upstroke is elided.

In Smith's discussions of the Prajāpati cosmogonies in the Brāhmaṇas, it was as if once a problem (e.g. of *jāmi*) has occurred and a secondary solution – the ritual – has been applied, then provided that solution can continue to be applied, creation should proceed well indefinitely. They are cosmogonies, after all. But according to the *yuga* scheme, after the solution has been applied at the first extreme, things go towards the other extreme, and so a solution needs to be applied repeatedly, at both extremes.

If this were all there was to it, we could have two rituals per cycle, as with the morning and evening *agnihotra*s and the full-moon and new-moon rituals. But within a *mahāyuga* there are four junction-points, not just two; and so, at least in regard to the intermediate points on the downstroke (*tretāyugānta* and *dvāparayugānta*), an alternative and paradoxical conception is required, whereby because each extreme anticipates and responds to the other, the solution encompasses the whole and is the same total solution wherever it is applied, and thus the world is correctly bounded.

Thus, when it comes to the *avatāra* and the *yuga*s,

> A character is required who can destroy what is bad to restore what is good, which implies, from an Indian point of view, two antinomic

> aspects that find their unity in the welfare of this triple world: it is sometimes the gods and sometimes the personified Earth who symbolise it ... And we will see these gods and this Earth sometimes inconvenienced by, sometimes rescued by the same character, depending on whether the accent is put upon the deed of destruction or upon the restoration of order ...[64]
>
> (Biardeau 1976: 183)

Biardeau's choice of the word antinomic ('deux aspects antinomiques') is significant. But where Biardeau's two antinomic aspects are destruction and restoration, which happen paradigmatically at the end of the day of Brahmā and, after a suitable pause, at the beginning of the next (Biardeau goes on to represent these aspects as 'rudraïque' and 'viṣṇuïque', respectively; compare Hesse 2000: 299), for us the two antinomic aspects are represented to some extent, for the *mahāyuga*, by *jāmi* (overpopulation) on the one hand and *pṛthak* (*adharma*) on the other. Biardeau sees the Earth and the gods as functionally equivalent (as Bhīṣma effectively does in the Mbh 6 passage discussed above, and as they arguably are in the 1.189 passage), and hence the placement of 'the accent' seems slightly whimsical. But by separating them we have connected 'the deed of destruction' with the solution to the *jāmi* problem and 'the restoration of order' with the solution to the *pṛthak* problem, and hence we have seen Biardeau's antinomic aspects operating complementarily across the *mahāyuga*, the accent falling differently at different points in the *mahāyuga*, moving repeatedly from one extreme to the other in steps, and then back again suddenly.

Kātre envisages the two extremes as *sattva* and *tamas*, within the Sāṃkhya triad:

> God is said to possess ... a mysterious power called Māyā by means of which he becomes what he really is not and does what he is not expected to do. Thus by means of his Māyā He puts on a definite personality and also assumes the three qualities which are, in fact, foreign to His primary character ...
>
> ... The simple results of his assumption of the three originally foreign qualities, *viz.*, Rajas, Sattva and Tamas are respectively the production, the nourishment and the destruction of the universe. When, however, he makes a mixture of the three qualities in different degrees, several complexities occur, *e.g.*, some of the numerous types of beings ... undergo excessive production or nourishment while others undergo

[64] 'Il faut un personnage qui puisse détruire ce qui est mauvais pour restaurer ce qui est bon, ce qui implique, du point de vue indien, deux aspects antinomiques qui trouvent leur unité dans le bien de ce triple monde: tantôt ce sont les dieux, tantôt c'est la Terre personifiée qui le symbolise ... Et nous verrons ces dieux et cette Terre, tantôt malmenés, tantôt tirés d'affaire par le même personnage, suivant que l'accent sera mis sur l'oeuvre de destruction ou sur la restauration de l'ordre ...'

> excessive decay or destruction at the same time. Thus an excess of Tamas in God results in the excessive production, flourishment, etc., of demons, increase of evil, consequent overburdening of the earth,[65] etc., and in the corresponding decay, destruction, etc., of gods. When God wants to change this state of affairs, he has to decrease his Tamas and to correspondingly increase his Sattva, the result being the flourishment, etc., of the pious races, the growth of Dharma and righteousness, etc., and correspondingly the destruction of evil races, the fall of wickedness and evil, etc. The ways in which God effects this change are so many, that of his incarnating himself on the earth being one of them.
> (Kātre 1934: 40–42)

The *Mahābhārata* does not present the two extremities of the *mahāyuga* in terms of *sattva* and *tamas*, and when the three *guṇas* are discussed they are usually all qualitatively distinct, as three different axes; but otherwise Kātre's idea of one scale and two extremities fits the *yuga* cycle. Superimposing Smith's terms upon Kātre's, *sattva* = *jāmi*, *tamas* = *pṛthak*.

In the 1.189 account, the gods prompt the movement away from *jāmi*, which is the movement away from *kṛtayuga*. So lifespan is reduced. But by reducing lifespan, *dharma* is reduced, eventually to the gods' detriment, at the pole of *pṛthak*, the nadir of *dharma*; so there is a reboot. The character of the Earth allows the gods off the hook – otherwise they would produce their next problem for themselves. Levels of lifespan and *dharma* are intimately correlated, and this affects the gods at both extremes. At one extreme people are too much like gods, and at the other extreme too unlike them.

Cosmic gender. In the Brāhmaṇa texts as Smith presents them, the problems of *jāmi* and *pṛthak* would be problems equally for the gods. And in the 1.189 account the problem of *jāmi* is voiced by the gods. But in this and the other *Mahābhārata* accounts of the reason for the collective Kurukṣetra *avatāra*, the problem of *jāmi* involves the Earth insofar as it is the overpopulation problem, and the gods' problem is more typically the problem of *pṛthak* and *adharma* – at the other pole of the *mahāyuga*, as it were. By introducing the Earth to take on the front-end complaint against *jāmi*, the *Mahābhārata* thus brings a gendered aspect into the *mahāyuga* oscillation. How seriously are we to take this gendering? Are we to take it theologically, in terms of the theology of Viṣṇu-Nārāyaṇa?

The Earth thus constructed is operationally uninterested in the matter of *dharma*, and despite the admixture of demons in the 1.58 account, she only has a problem if the population is too heavy. Indeed, in the Hv 40–45 account her

[65] Kātre, in common with Biardeau, other previous commentators, and the 1.58 account, conflates the dharmic problem for the gods with the population problem for the Earth. When the Earth's complaint is presented through the gods at 1.189, it is a problem of *jāmi*, not of *adharma* (*pṛthak*). They bring that latter problem upon themselves by speaking up in the first place.

interest seems to be inversely related to *dharma*, since it is the dharmicness of the *kṣatriyas* that causes the problem for Death and thus for her.

The gods are overwhelmingly male. When the celestial team descends to earth to solve the Earth's problem by making the Kurukṣetra war happen, the only goddesses mentioned are Śrī, Siddhi, Dhṛti, Mati, and Gaṅgā – incarnated as Draupadī, Kuntī, Mādrī, Gāndhārī, and Gaṅgā herself, respectively (1.61.95–98; Hv 43; Hv 13.25–40 mentions that Acchodā was born as Satyavatī). So if we ignore the woolly edges, the *mahāyuga*'s passage from one pole or extremity to another and then back again can seem to involve a mythological gendering of the poles. If the scenario is like a ball being passed repeatedly between two people, they would be two different people, and here they would be of different genders. To the extent that that was true (which here it is not quite), one might even say that those genders were opposite genders.[66]

It is extraordinary to gender the cosmos, and time, in this way. One might have thought that male and female were just types within the reproductive mechanism of some recent species or other. But here they are part of the explanation of our universe!

In a way, the universe so imagined is nicely balanced between the two genders. In principle, despite any masculine pronoun or grammatical gender, God, as the entirety and also the outside of the temporal universe, could and should be beyond these two gendered extremities, which would be subordinate aspects of the greater divinity. This is what Kṛṣṇa says in the *Bhagavadgītā* of his nature in respect of the two uncreated gendered entities in the Sāṃkhya philosophy, *prakṛti* and *puruṣa*, which between them constitute the world: he incorporates them and he is beyond them both (Bhg 7.4–5; 15.7–8, 16–20; see also *Śvetāśvatara Upaniṣad* 1.10). But it is **Kṛṣṇa** saying it, of his **masculine** highest self.

With respect to the gendering of the cosmogony, there is rich material in the early Sanskrit tradition (Brodbeck 2007: 146–149). It is often as if creation requires an in principle ungendered godhead – something like *tad ekam* or *brahman* – to polarise into two aspects, which then differ from each other enough to

66 The sense of opposition here (albeit collaborative opposition) between two genders is perhaps visible in the male gendering of those who are killed at Kurukṣetra for the good of the female Earth. Population reduction through a cull of *kṣatriya* (or *rākṣasa*) males is a gendered operation: women are not killed. And although culling all those males would certainly reduce the population, it would not reduce the size of the next generation in the way that culling females would. After Rāma Jāmadagnya's massacres, the *kṣatriya* widows soon have nouveau-*kṣatriya* sons sired by brahmins (1.58.4–8; Fitzgerald 2002: 94–95, 105). Culling females would decrease the number of babies born. So perhaps, the better to reduce her burden, the Earth should have called for a cull of women. But that would not have been as straightforward to organise. Diminishing population (i.e., in *yuga* terms, diminishing lifespan) might have been equally dramatically represented by the action of, for example, a virulent new disease; but lots of men assembling to attack each other with weapons must have been a long-known phenomenon, and a poetic phenomenon. On the singling out of *kṣatriyas* for destruction, see also Feller 2004: 283–286.

interact productively in a more or less gendered fashion. But still the godhead itself can be presented as masculine. Thus, in the *Manusmṛti*, God makes the world by making the waters and then ejaculating into them (Ms 1.8–9; see also Bhg 9.8–10; 14.3). The tendency of the masculine to colonise the feminine is evident particularly in origin myths (Hawthorne 2017); and it is also a tendency to colonise, as if pre-emptively, what should be beyond either gender.

This is not the place to explore the eventual theology of the *Mahābhārata* in full gendered detail. On the goddess in the *Harivaṃśa*, see Couture 1999; Yokochi 2001; Couture 2017: 5–8, 111–214; in the *Mahābhārata*, see Hiltebeitel 2018: 79–131. In the *Mahābhārata* we might glimpse the goddess in the person of:

- Śrī, who incarnates as Draupadī, of whom it is said at her birth that she 'shall lead the baronage to its doom ... shall in time accomplish the purpose of the Gods' (*kṣayaṃ kṣatraṃ ninīṣati* ‖ *surakāryam iyaṃ kāle kariṣyati*, Mbh 1.155.44–45, trans. van Buitenen 1973: 318).
- Earth (though her fundamentally terrestrial nature limits this role for her).
- Gaṅgā, who, for the good of the Earth, is involved in the Kurukṣetra *avatāra* some time before most of the gods are (Hv 43.15–55; Hiltebeitel 2012: 108–113). Gaṅgā descends in order to give birth, most notably to Bhīṣma, *avatāra* of a god, whose vow precipitates the Bhārata dynastic crisis into which other gods are born (as the Pāṇḍavas, etc.). In this list of goddesses, the foregoing are partnered with terrestrial kings, but the following are not.
- Umā-Pārvatī, Śiva's partner, who is a part of him, accompanies him in many scenes, and also acts apart from him.
- Kālī, who is seen by those killed in the night massacre shortly before they die, and had been dreamed of by them previously (10.8.64–67; Johnson 1998: 115–116; Hiltebeitel 2012: 119–121). Kālī also appears at Hv 32.19a, during the gods' darkest moment in the Tārakāmaya war, just before Viṣṇu appears.
- Nidrā (Sleep), 'the dark lady with the dark body and the eyes, who knows when the worlds will end' (*lokānām antakālajñā kālī nayanaśālinī* | *upatasthe mahātmānaṃ nidrā taṃ kālarūpiṇī* ‖ Hv 40.8). In some ways Nidrā resembles the goddess Rātrī, Night, in *Ṛgveda* 10.127; see also Jerome 1889: 160–163. For Nidrā as sleep and death see Hv 40.26–33; compare Mbh 12.248–250 where Death is female; see Hv 47–48 where Nidrā does Viṣṇu's bidding in the matter of Kṛṣṇa's birth and thus becomes the great goddess worshipped in all the world's wilds; see also Ekānaṃśā at Hv 96.11–19; Srinivasan 1981; Matchett 2001: 63–64, 218 nn. 55–56;[67] Couture and Schmid 2001; Schmid 2010: 165–194.

[67] Matchett suggests that Nidrā is Viṣṇu's daughter or sister (Matchett 2001: 46, 215 n. 5), but this could be to overinterpret *viṣṇuśarīrajā* at Hv 40.31, *viṣṇoḥ śarīrajāṃ* at Hv 48.10, and *sahajāṃ* at Hv 40.37.

If the Viṣṇu-Nidrā duo is outside time and sets the limits of time, it is (or they are) a duo as – and perhaps only as – viewed from within time.

This is also not the place to devise some kind of theoretical theology inspired by the *Mahābhārata* and acceptably applicable by ourselves in the present day. Here there would be a selection effect whereby aspects of the human reproductive scenario, and the consequent gender-complex within human culture, would be projected upon God, insofar as God relates to a universe within which there are humans, and is related to by humans. Perhaps we can imagine a space beyond this universe, beyond that God, and beyond any of the universes, within a greater godhead that has no outside, and that is neither masculine, feminine, nor neuter. But that would be a different project. And so we draw back from gendering the two forces that hold the *mahāyuga* in play – the force that rotates the handle on the side of the machine's cabinet, as it were, and the force of gravity. But still, the extremes of *jāmi* and *pṛthak* are highly suggestive in connection with the *Mahābhārata*'s *avatāra* principle, and in connection with the *Mahābhārata*'s stories of the reason for the Kurukṣetra *avatāra.*

From *rājasūya* to *mahāyuga*. Our perspective on the *mahāyuga* has been possible, to a large extent, because we were able to set aside the instability theory for the intermediate *yugānta*s, and think about the *mahāyuga* as a whole. But part of the instability theory is the idea that at junctions in time, there would be a ritual necessity to heal the joint, to recompose Prajāpati. We focus on that necessity now in terms of the king's performance of the *rājasūya* ritual.

On the *rājasūya* in the Brāhmaṇa texts, we defer to Heesterman. I quote him here at length. From the introduction to Heesterman's book:

> To the Vedic thinker the whole universe was constantly moving between the two poles – of birth and death, integration and disintegration, ascension and descent – which by their interaction occasion the cyclical rhythms of the cosmos. ... On the place of sacrifice the cosmic drama of death and rebirth, integration and disintegration, ascension and descent, is enacted and, reversely, [is] through the same code of connections brought to bear upon the macrocosmos. In the centre of this sacrificial world stands the sacrificer for whose benefit the cosmic processes are set in motion by the ritualists, who know the connections. Thus the whole world is centred upon the sacrificer, who 'becomes all this' and represents in his person the cosmic drama.
>
> ... [T]he sacrificer, realizing through the ritual symbols his identity with the universe, performs through the sacrifice the cyclical rhythm of the universe in a series of deaths and births. ... The rājasūya seems to have been originally a yearly repeated rite of cosmic regeneration and rebirth ...
>
> ... [T]he central rājasūya ceremonies cluster round the period of the turning of the year ... Viewed in this light the rājasūya seems to be an

> abridgement of what originally must have been an unremitting series of yearly ceremonies with the object of regenerating the universe. The king took a central place in it.
>
> (Heesterman 1957: 6–7, 10)

From the conclusion:

> [T]he rājasūya is not a royal consecration in the sense of a ceremony performed once and for all, to bestow royal power on a king. Its character can best be understood when compared with the yearly festivals known as *utsava* ... by means of which the powers active in the universe are regenerated. ... As has been seen they cluster round the turning of the year and are all in some way or other concerned with the regeneration of the year, which is conceived of both as an actual time unit and as a cosmological entity. ...
>
> In this light the rājasūya can be viewed as an abridged representation of the unending cyclical process of decay and regeneration. ... [It] points to an original pattern of yearly repeated unction and regeneration ceremonies.
>
> ... The king is ... not only the centre and pivot of the universe, he is the universe itself; he has been seen to encompass, like the cosmic man Prajāpati, the universe in respect both to space and to time. He is not conceived of as a static image of the cosmic structure, he impersonates the cosmic tide of regeneration and decay.
>
> ... Ascension and descent, disintegration and reintegration, chaotic dispersion and re-articulated structure, such are the terms of the cosmic rhythm as represented in the different phases of the rājasūya. ... [T]he unction exemplifies the cosmic role of the king: on the joint between two subsequent time cycles, having encompassed and articulated the universe during the course of the preceding time cycle, he emerges ... to be born; but at the same time he dies and disintegrates, to ripen ... towards a new birth at the end of the next time cycle when the same process starts all over again. In other words the king, as represented in the rājasūya, is the incorporation of the universe's moving forces: 'boom to bust, and boom again.'
>
> (Heesterman 1957: 222–224)

The king makes time here; he keeps it going on in its annual iteration (Inden 1998: 81–82). This is about the year: the year bounded by the peregrinations of the sun (moving apparently northwards towards the longest day, then southwards towards the shortest). Proferes emphasises the king's identity as the sun:

> The cosmic powers of the Vedic king were, in fact, precisely correlated to the properties and functions of the sun. ... [T]he officiants performing

> the unction ceremony [i.e. the central rite of the *rājasūya*] integrated the dispersed splendor of the cosmos and transformed the human king into the sun himself. ... The underlying motif of the royal unction was the (re-)birth of the king as the sun.
>
> (Proferes 2007: 2)

Proferes also discusses the *agnicayana* ritual in this connection. Proferes does not emphasise the year as Heesterman does; he is more interested in how the people are ritually embodied as the king through many fires combining, or many waters combining, into a totality. But that totality is also for all time insofar as it is for the whole year. Similar also is the *gavām ayana*, which Keith calls 'the model of the year rite' (Keith 1920: 56, 496–497; González-Reimann 2009: 413).

What happens at the junctions in the larger cycles of time, the cycles which human kings would not observe, but only perhaps hear about? We know about Brahmā's day starting and ending with creation and destruction respectively. But in what sense is there comparable ritual activity performed by the gods, or by Viṣṇu-Nārāyaṇa, at the junctures of *mahāyuga*s and/or *yuga*s? Only in the sense described by the *Mahābhārata* in its accounts of the *avatāra* principle and of the various *avatāra*s of Viṣṇu-Nārāyaṇa and other gods, particularly at Kurukṣetra.

In the case of the gods, the war that, directed by Brahmā, they facilitate and effect, as detailed in Mbh 6–10, is sometimes said to be a ritual of battle (Feller 2004: 253–293). But their impression of their own activity in so doing is heavily disguised, because in the text we see them predominantly as human characters who are incarnations of gods but do not know it. When the necessity for the collective *avatāra* appears, the gods do not seem to have anticipated it. The sense in which they would be ritual actors regenerating time (like the king in the Vedic *rājasūya*) is rather oblique. They do not seem to think they are descending onto the world-stage in order to move time from the *dvāpara* to the *kaliyuga* (against their own best interests). And we do not hear them talking among themselves about why this particular *avatāra* is a collective one. Although when the gods descend en masse in 1.58 and Hv 43 they seem quite keen to do so, elsewhere celestials are sent on their terrestrial errands as punishments for minor transgressions: see the cases of Mahābhiṣa and the Vasus (1.91), Dharma (1.101), the five Indras (1.189), Acchodā (Hv 13.25–40), and Gaṅgā and the Ocean (Hv 43). By implication, from the point of view of these latter gods, the timing of their descent is set by the timing of their transgression, not by the timing of some necessary ritual. And when *Mahābhārata* characters describe the Kurukṣetra war, in advance, as a ritual of battle, homologising it to the Vedic ritual (e.g. Bhīma at 3.242.14–15; Duryodhana at 5.57.12–13; Karṇa at 5.139.29–51; Janamejaya at 5.154.4), this seems to be a standard idiom in *kṣatriya* discourse about war, rather than indicating the ritual nature of the divine project that lies behind this particular *kṣatriya* conflict. There is a fit between that divine project, which is instigated by the Earth, and the role that the Earth seems to play as recipient of this war-sacrifice (Feller 2004: 268–277); but that latter role can largely be explained by the mythologisation of kingship as husbandry of the Earth.

In the case of Viṣṇu-Nārāyaṇa, he encourages and directs the Kurukṣetra theatre of war – he is, after all, one of the gods. But the sense in which his behaviour would be ritual activity to regenerate time is similarly and surpassingly moot. Saṃjaya says to Dhṛtarāṣṭra:

> *kālacakraṃ jagaccakraṃ yugacakraṃ ca keśavaḥ* ।
> *ātmayogena bhagavān parivartayate 'niśam* ‖ 5.66.12 ‖
> *kālasya ca hi mṛtyoś ca jaṅgamasthāvarasya ca* ।
> *īśate bhagavān ekaḥ satyam etad bravīmi te* ‖ 13 ‖

> The blessed Keśava makes the Wheel of Time, the Wheel of the World, and the Wheel of the *Yuga*s go around and around, ceaselessly, by his own Yoga. In truth I tell you: the blessed Lord alone governs time and death, and the standing and moving creatures.
> (5.66.12–13, trans. van Buitenen 1978: 336, adapted)

This is God's *yoga* rather than God's ritual. It is in a different register. God does *yoga* ceaselessly. What Kṛṣṇa (Viṣṇu) does is always more than what Arjuna (Indra) could do through *karmayoga* in his *kṣatriya* occupation on the Kurukṣetra battlefield.

To us it must seem that when a Vedic king performs a ritual to regenerate the year, it is a year that would have regenerated anyway, with or without his rite. So while there are suggestions that according to Vedic belief the king's rite causes the year, we would rather say that it represents the year. And just as we can think of years as uncaused by ritual, we can think of *yuga*s and *mahāyuga*s similarly. We can imagine that just as Nārāyaṇa makes years happen merely by being-doing what he is, irrespective of human royal performances, and without doing any particular ritual himself to effect them, so also he can make *yuga*s and *mahāyuga*s happen. Why would he have to come onto the stage to make *yuga*s or *mahāyuga*s happen, when he makes years happen just by being-doing what he is? Would *mahāyuga*s not be part of the same package as years? After all, 'The year was the epitome of time, and its basic cycle' (González-Reimann 2009: 413). As the Upaniṣad says:

> *dve vāva brahmaṇo rūpe kālaś cākālaś ca* । *atha yaḥ prāg ādityāt so 'kālo 'kalaḥ* । *atha ya ādityādyaḥ sa kālaḥ sakalaḥ* । *sakalasya vā etad rūpaṃ yat saṃvatsaram* । *saṃvatsarāt khalv evemāḥ prajāḥ prajāyante* । *saṃvatsareneha vai jātā vivardhante* । *saṃvatsare pratyastaṃ yanti* । *tasmāt saṃvatsaro vai prajāpatiḥ kālaḥ* । *annaṃ brahmaṇīḍam ātmā ca* । ... ‖ *Maitrī Upaniṣad* 6.15 ‖

> There are two forms of *brahman*: time (*kāla*) and the timeless (*akāla*). That which was before the sun is timeless, without parts (*akala*). That which began with the sun is time, with parts (*sakala*). The form of that with parts is the year, for all creatures are born from the year; once born here, they live by the year; in the year they meet their end. So the year is Prajāpati, time, food, the nest of *brahman*, and the self. ...
> (*Maitrī Upaniṣad* 6.15, trans. Roebuck 2003: 370)

Here time is one whole thing. And so we can see that the stories of specific *avatāra* acts could be metaphors, dramatisations of what was going to happen anyway, because Nārāyaṇa is what he is. The repeating cycle of the four successive *yuga*s (Figure 5) and the *Nārāyaṇīya* statement of the double *avatāra*-function (12.337.29–34) are in different registers, but they describe the same thing. They do so because the *yuga* cycle is oscillation between two poles, a double force keeping the level between 4 and 1, *mahāyuga* after *mahāyuga*, day of Brahmā after day of Brahmā, just as the year is kept within its prescribed limits, never being too hot for too long in the summer, or too dark for too long in the winter. In both cases, the cycle is faithfully protected at both extremities.

The stories of specific *avatāra* acts can only be metaphors in any case, because although we can imagine population (and thus the weight upon the Earth) being reduced, causally, by an *avatāra* acting within the world, that population reduction can only explain one aspect of a descending *yuga*-transition. At such a transition we need to have the complex variable reduced in its entirety (encoding, as it does, even the very duration of the new *yuga*), not just in its lifespan aspect. And the lifespan aspect has already been simplified into the population/weight aspect in order to facilitate the illustrative causal metaphor. Similarly, although we might be able to imagine *dharma* being increased, causally, by an *avatāra* acting within the world, that dharmic increase can only explain one aspect of an ascending (or trough-ending) *yuga*-transition, where the complex variable needs to increase in its entirety. The complexity of the variable means that any account of its being causally adjusted from within the world is seriously and necessarily incomplete.

We are caught between causation on the one hand and representation on the other. If we set aside the instability theory, then the best sense in which the *avatāra* could restore *dharma* at the *dvāpara–kaliyuga* transition would be in that restoring *dharma* is part of 'what Viṣṇu-Nārāyaṇa does' over the *mahāyuga* cycle as a whole. The *dvāpara–kaliyuga* transition is part of that cycle and thus synecdochically represents, through story, the whole cycle, facilitated in this by being an intermediate point between the two basic transition points at either extremity. The *dvāpara–kaliyuga* transition mimics the two previous transitions in serving up a decrement of the level as per the Earth's repeated demands, but the narrative representation at this transition exceeds that function, and includes also the dharmic boost, because that is part of the fuller story of the cycle.

The two *avatāra* functions in the Kurukṣetra story

The *avatāra* has two functions, pushing in one direction and then in the other, or pushing in one direction and simultaneously in the other. These two functions are prompted by excess population and lifespan at what we now think of as one extremity, and by excess venality at the other. As seen above in the accounts of the Earth's problem, these two *avatāra* functions are separable with regard to the Kurukṣetra *avatāra*. The 1.189 account does not mention the problem of waning *dharma*, and the Hv 40–45 account removes it summarily to Mathurā. But in the 1.58 account – the basic account for Janamejaya as he is hearing the story – the overpopulation problem and the dharmic problem are superimposed within the Kurukṣetra story.

Perhaps this is what we might expect of a story set at this point in the *mahāyuga*, during the downstroke between the two extremities. In the *tretā* and *dvāpara yuga*s, both problems are there, the overpopulation problem decreasing as the demonic or dharmic problem increases. The *tretā–dvāparayuga* and *dvāpara–kaliyuga* transitions, marking specific points along this range, could embody different ratios of one problem to the other. Perhaps on this basis we would expect that in a story set at the *dvāpara–kaliyuga* transition, the dharmic problem would be more evident than the overpopulation problem. All the same, what is actually going to happen at this transition point is that *dharma* and lifespan are going to be halved – that is, the overpopulation problem will be addressed (again), but the dharmic problem will not. Nonetheless, the *avatāra* that appears at this point is prompted by a combination of both problems. So how does this play out? During the narration, is the collective *avatāra* focused on ensuring the war so that masses of men can die (thus addressing the overpopulation problem), or is it focused on the good side winning and the bad side losing (thus addressing the dharmic problem)?

As we proceed to try to answer this experimental question, we must recall that although the Kurukṣetra war is placed at the *dvāpara–kaliyuga* transition, in *yuga* terms there are also various metaphors operating in the narrative. As per Hiltebeitel's analogy, the war itself is a microcosmic representation of an entire *mahāyuga* (Hiltebeitel 1976: 283, 286; p. 81 above); and as per Biardeau's analogy, the dicing match represents the *dvāpara–kaliyuga* transition and the war represents the *kali–kṛtayuga* transition (Biardeau 1976: 151–154; pp. 59–60 above). Biardeau's analogy in particular might be anticipated to interfere with the narrative's account of what the *avatāra* does; and it would do so by emphasising the solution of the dharmic problem by the war (and by Yudhiṣṭhira's reign after it).

The *Mahābhārata* narrative of the Kurukṣetra *avatāra* maintains ambiguity between the massacre-to-save-the-Earth purpose and the conquer-the-demons purpose. Crucial here is that on the Kaurava (losing) side, those who are traditionally held to be principal instigators of the war – the 'axis of evil', as it were – are Duryodhana, Śakuni, and Karṇa, who are seemingly all *avatāras* of gods (Kali, Dvāpara, and the Sun, respectively). Biardeau calls Kali and Dvāpara demons (see e.g. Hiltebeitel 1976: 94), but they are not characterised as demons in the story of Nala, or in any of the accounts of the Kurukṣetra *avatāra*, where they are presented alongside the other gods who descend to solve the Earth's problem (for Dvāpara see 1.61.72; for Kali see 1.61.80–81; Hv 43.5, 63; 44.4). The idea of Duryodhana being an incarnated god is certainly a difficult one, because his characterisation is often extremely negative: he is the 'evil-spirited, evil-minded disgracer of the Kurus ... a creature of discord, hated by all the world ... meanest of men' (*durbuddhir durmatiś caiva kurūṇām ayaśaskaraḥ* ‖ *jagato yaḥ sa sarvasya vidviṣṭaḥ kalipūruṣaḥ* | ... *puruṣādhamaḥ*, 1.61.80–81, trans. van Buitenen 1973: 153–154). But the point here is not what type of supernatural entity Duryodhana might or might not incarnate. The point is that insofar as Duryodhana and these other characters are presented as part of the solution to a problem that was reported before they were born, they cannot simultaneously be part of that problem.

In 11.8 Vyāsa emphasises Duryodhana's crucial role in the divine plan for the benefit of the Earth (Dumézil 1995: 196–197 [vol. 1: 168–169]). At the end of the war, after Dhṛtarāṣṭra's sons have all been killed, Vyāsa says to Dhṛtarāṣṭra:

jānatā ca mahābāho vidureṇa mahātmanā |
yatitaṃ sarvayatnena śamaṃ prati janeśvara ‖ 11.8.17 ‖
na ca daivakṛto mārgaḥ śakyo bhūtena kena cit |
ghaṭatāpi ciraṃ kālaṃ niyantum iti me matiḥ ‖ 18 ‖
devatānāṃ hi yat kāryaṃ mayā pratyakṣataḥ śrutam |
tat te 'haṃ saṃpravakṣyāmi
kathaṃ sthairyaṃ bhavet tava ‖ 19 ‖
purāhaṃ tvarito yātaḥ sabhām aindrīṃ jitaklamaḥ |
apaśyaṃ tatra ca tadā samavetān divaukasaḥ |
nāradapramukhāṃś cāpi sarvān devarṣīṃs tathā ‖ 20 ‖
tatra cāpi mayā dṛṣṭā pṛthivī pṛthivīpate |
kāryārtham upasaṃprāptā devatānāṃ samīpataḥ ‖ 21 ‖
upagamya tadā dhātrī devān āha samāgatān |
yat kāryaṃ mama yuṣmābhir brahmaṇaḥ sadane tadā |
pratijñātaṃ mahābhāgās tac chīghraṃ saṃvidhīyatām ‖ 22 ‖
tasyās tad vacanaṃ śrutvā viṣṇur lokanamaskṛtaḥ |
uvāca prahasan vākyaṃ pṛthivīṃ devasaṃsadi ‖ 23 ‖
dhṛtarāṣṭrasya putrāṇāṃ yas tu jyeṣṭhaḥ śatasya vai |

duryodhana iti khyātaḥ sa te kāryaṃ kariṣyati |
taṃ ca prāpya mahīpālaṃ kṛtakṛtyā bhaviṣyasi || 24 ||
tasyārthe pṛthivīpālāḥ kurukṣetre samāgatāḥ |
anyonyaṃ ghātayiṣyanti dṛḍhaiḥ śastraiḥ prahāriṇaḥ || 25 ||
tatas te bhavitā devi bhārasya yudhi nāśanam |
gaccha śīghraṃ svakaṃ sthānaṃ lokān dhāraya śobhane || 26 ||
sa eṣa te suto rājaṃl lokasaṃhārakāraṇāt |
kaler aṃśaḥ samutpanno gāndhāryā jaṭhare nṛpa || 27 ||
amarṣī capalaś cāpi krodhano duṣprasādhanaḥ |
daivayogāt samutpannā bhrātaraś cāsya tādṛśāḥ || 28 ||
śakunir mātulaś caiva karṇaś ca paramaḥ sakhā |
samutpannā vināśārthaṃ pṛthivyāṃ sahitā nṛpāḥ |
etam arthaṃ mahābāho nārado veda tattvataḥ || 29 ||
ātmāparādhāt putrās te vinaṣṭāḥ pṛthivīpate |
mā tāñ śocasva rājendra na hi śoke 'sti kāraṇam || 30 ||
na hi te pāṇḍavāḥ svalpam aparādhyanti bhārata |
putrās tava durātmāno yair iyaṃ ghātitā mahī || 31 ||

O strong-armed lord of peoples, the exalted Vidura understood it all, and he worked for peace with all his might. But it is my opinion that no being, even if he works at it for a long time, is able to thwart a course of events that is driven by fate [*daiva*]. I heard with my own ears what the Gods wanted to be done, and I shall now declare it to you.

Are you going to settle down?

Once in the past I hurried to Indra's hall of assembly. I felt refreshed when I got there. I saw the Gods gathered there and all the divine seers, with Nārada at their head. And, O lord of earth, I saw that Earth had come before the gods because she needed something done. Earth went up to the assembled Gods and said to them:

'Illustrious ones, quickly take care of that job you promised you would do for me in the house of Brahmā.'

When he heard what she said, Viṣṇu, who is adored by the whole world, smiled and said to Earth in that assembly of the Gods:

'The eldest of Dhṛtarāṣṭra's one hundred sons, Duryodhana he is called, will take care of that job of yours. Once you get him as a lord of earth, the job you need done will be done. Because of him the lords of the earth will gather together on Kurukṣetra, and attacking each other with sharp weapons, they will kill each other. And so, Goddess, your burden will be eliminated in a war. Go quickly to your own place and support the worlds, beautiful lady.'

King [Dhṛtarāṣṭra], your son was a piece of Kali born in Gāndhārī's belly to effect the destruction of the worlds. He was unforgiving, fickle, irritable, incorrigible. His brothers sprang up through the operation

> of fate [*daiva*], and they were like him. Śakuni, his mother's brother, and Karṇa, his very best friend, and the princes who joined with him sprang up on the earth for the sake of destruction. O strong-armed prince, Nārada understood the truth of this matter. O lord of earth, your sons perished through their own fault. Do not grieve for them, O Indra among kings, there is no reason for grieving. Really, the sons of Pāṇḍu have not done the least wrong, Bhārata. Your sons were vile, and they harmed the earth.
>
> (11.8.17–31, trans. Fitzgerald 2004a: 41, adapted)

The reference to Nārada's understanding the truth of the matter is a reference to what Nārada thought to himself on the occasion of Yudhiṣṭhira's *rājasūya*, to the effect that as per the divine plan, the kings assembled there were doomed later to kill each other in a massive war (2.33.11–20; compare Hv 81.1–13, illustrated on the cover). The propriety of Vyāsa's final charge ('Your sons ... harmed the earth') is unclear, since it could be argued that Duryodhana and his brothers did not harm the earth any more than the Pāṇḍavas did, and that in both cases, because they made and fought that war together, the effect was not harm to the earth, but good. There would then be no evil in this picture, only interplay in order to manufacture a necessary destruction.

Each set of cousins is as bad as the other. In the race to be the villain, Duryodhana takes the lead early, attempting to drown Bhīma and then burn the Pāṇḍavas, and then he and his brothers abuse Draupadī in the dicing hall, and he is not willing to give the Pāṇḍavas even five villages at the end of the exile. But the Pāṇḍavas' *rājasūya* ritual is provocative (as Janamejaya realises, Hv 115.14–23), and the Pāṇḍavas probably did not live out the final year of exile unidentified (Brodbeck 2021b; see also 7.11.17–18), and their tactics during the war, as advised by Kṛṣṇa, are diabolical. Childhood bygones be bygones, the only person on the Kaurava side who behaves worse than the Pāṇḍavas is Aśvatthāman. All the same, Aśvatthāman's deeds are very much to the point in terms of numerical destruction, and it could seem that both 'sides' are cooperating to make the massacre as thorough as possible, and thus to rescue the Earth. This fits with one of the *Mahābhārata*'s most conspicuous virtues as a work of literature: the characters are not simply separable into good and bad ones, and this lends a realism and depth to their portrayal (Satyamurti 2015: xxxi). The Earth's role is emphasised during the war by the poetic descriptions of the Earth/battlefield beautified by wreckage and gore (Feller 2004: 272–276; see also Brodbeck 2009a: 42–43).

Nonetheless, many of the characters are said in 1.61 to be demons in human form. In 1.58, after the description of the *kṛtayuga* following Rāma Jāmadagnya's massacres (the *kṛtayuga* for which the *kṣatriya* class was sired by brahmins), the demons make their entrance (1.58.25). Some are born as humans, some as animals.

atha jātā mahīpālāḥ ke cid balasamanvitāḥ ǀ
diteḥ putrā danoś caiva tasmāl lokād iha cyutāḥ ǁ 1.58.30 ǁ
vīryavanto 'valiptās te nānārūpadharā mahīm ǀ
imāṃ sāgaraparyantāṃ parīyur arimardanāḥ ǁ 31 ǁ
brāhmaṇān kṣatriyān vaiśyāñ śūdrāṃś caivāpy apīḍayan ǀ
anyāni caiva bhūtāni pīḍayām āsur ojasā ǁ 32 ǁ
trāsayanto vinighnantas tāṃs tān bhūtagaṇāṃś ca te ǀ
viceruḥ sarvato rājan mahīṃ śatasahasraśaḥ ǁ 33 ǁ
āśramasthān maharṣīṃś ca dharṣayantas tatas tataḥ ǀ
abrahmaṇyā vīryamadā mattā madabalena ca ǁ 34 ǁ

> Now some of them were born kings, filled with great strength, sons of Diti and Danu who had now fallen from their world to earth. Powerful, insolent, bearing many shapes, they swarmed over this sea-girt earth, crushing their enemies. They oppressed the brahmins, the barons, the farmers, and even the serfs, and other creatures they oppressed with their power. Sowing fear and slaughtering all the races of creation, they roamed all over earth, O king, by the hundreds of thousands, menacing everywhere the great seers in their hermitages, impious, drunk with power, insensate with drink.
>
> (1.58.30–34, trans. van Buitenen 1973: 137)

This is the 'demonic *kṣatra*' discussed by Fitzgerald (2004b: 57–59). According to Hegarty, 'the Mahābhārata tells of an intervention by the gods to rid the earth of a fractious warrior society' (Hegarty 2012: 58). Reich says that 'Rulers who ignore Brāhmaṇ guidance are seen as demonic, and when they do so, the gods and the Brāhmaṇs must violently intervene' (Reich 2011: 26–27). In this inflection, the descent of the deities would be to destroy the demons, whose earthly takeover must thus precede the Earth's complaint: 'the celestials in succession descended from heaven to earth, for the destruction of the enemies of the Gods' (*te 'marārivināśāya ...* ǀ *avateruḥ krameṇemāṃ mahīṃ svargād divaukasaḥ* ǁ 1.59.3, trans. van Buitenen 1973: 138). But despite these verses, there is not much evidence of great *adharma* before the birth of the Kurukṣetra *avatāras*. The departures from *dharma* that allow Vyāsa to sire the two regally compromised brothers Dhṛtarāṣṭra and Pāṇḍu (and thus set up the conditions for the war) are part of the gods' solution to the problem, not part of the problem itself. With the odd hiccup, the Bhārata line has been fairly proper up to this point; it is not clear that things have gone terribly wrong.

At 1.61.1–2 Janamejaya asks which gods, Dānavas, *yakṣas*, *rākṣasas*, and other beings took birth as which humans. One might think that Vaiśaṃpāyana would now list the demons who caused the problem, and the gods who solved it. But in fact, many of the men he lists as *avatāras* of demons are contemporary with the *avatāras* of the gods (and so are too late to cause the problem), many are obscure, and some are seemingly not very bad.

Vaiśaṃpāyana lists the following *avatāras* of demons (the word *avatāra* is not used): Jarāsaṃdha, Śiśupāla, Śalya, Dhṛṣṭaketu, Druma, Bhagadatta, the five Kekayas, Amitaujas, Ugrasena, Aśoka, Hārdikya, Dīrghaprajña, Malla, Rocamāna, Bṛhanta, Senābindu, Pāpajit, Prativindhya, Citravarman, Suvastu, Bāhlīka, Muñjakeśa, Devādhipa, Paurava, Prahrāda, Ṛṣika, Paścimānūpaka, Drumasena, Viśva, Kālakīrti, Śunaka, Jānaki, Kāśirāja, Krātha, Vikṣara, the king of Pāṃsu, Pauṇḍramatsyaka, Maṇimat, Daṇḍa, Daṇḍadhara, Jayatsena, Aparājita, the king of the *niṣādas*, Śreṇimat, Mahaujas, Abhīru, Samudrasena 'who knew the principles of Law and Profit' (*dharmārthatattvavit*, 1.61.52d, trans. van Buitenen 1973: 152), some other 'law-abiding king, devoted to the well-being of creatures' (*dharmātmā sarvabhūtahite ratah*, v. 53cd, trans. van Buitenen), Nandika, Karṇaveṣṭa, Siddhārtha, Kīṭika, Suvīra, Subāhu, Mahāvīra, Bāhlīka, Krodha, Vicitya, Surasa, Nīla, Vīradhāman, Bhūmipāla, Dantavaktra, Durjaya, Rukmin, Janamejaya, Āṣāḍha, Vāyuvega, Bhūritejas, Ekalavya, Sumitra, Vātadhāna, Gomukha, the kings of the Kārūṣas, Kṣemadhūrti, Śrutāyus, Uddhava, Bṛhatsena, Kṣema, Ugratīrtha, Kuhara, the king of the Kaliṅgas, Matimat, and Īśvara.

After listing these (including Aśoka, Siddhārtha, and Mahāvīra), Vaiśaṃpāyana moves on to list *avatāras* of gods and *gandharvas*.[68] Having named Duryodhana as the *avatāra* of (god) Kali, Vaiśaṃpāyana notes that Duryodhana's ninety-nine brothers were Paulastyas (1.61.82a, 83d) – that is, (*avatāras* of) *rākṣasas*, descendants of Pulastya (the ancestor of *rākṣasas*, 1.60.7). Śikhaṇḍin too is the *avatāra* of a *rākṣasa* (1.61.87cd).

Most of the recognisable characters in these lists of demonic kings are recognisable from the generations at and around the Kurukṣetra war. Potentially some of the unrecognisable ones were born earlier, and had constituted the demonic problem about which the Earth complained. But despite the brief passage at 1.58.30–34 quoted above, there are no stories of these named kings being wicked and oppressive in the old days, and they might just as well be minor characters contemporary with the Kurukṣetra war. So the demonic element of the 1.58 account of the Earth's problem is unsupported by the lists of demonic *avatāras*. Those lists only support the idea that there were demonic *avatāras* at the same time as the Earth's problem was being solved.

The *Harivaṃśa* account of the Earth's problem separates the overpopulation problem from the problem of demons, which is added in Hv 44 with mention of Kaṃsa, Keśin, Ariṣṭa, Kuvalayāpīḍa, Pralamba, Dhenuka, Cāṇūra, Muṣṭika, and two of Naraka Bhauma's cronies (Hv 44.66–74). These demons are killed by Kṛṣṇa and Baladeva, quite apart from the Kurukṣetra war, but in the same generation. This kind of swift-response unit – there are some demons causing trouble on earth, so Viṣṇu appears in person to neutralise them – is very different from the solution to the Earth's problem: the Earth's complaint was antici-

[68] Vaiśaṃpāyana omits to mention that Dhṛtarāṣṭra is the *avatāra* of a *gandharva* king. Vyāsa mentions this to Gāndhārī at 15.39.8 when listing the supernatural identities of the main characters.

pated by Brahmā, who sowed the seeds of its solution some time before Earth even voiced it (Hv 43.14–55). Other demon *avatāras* mentioned in 1.61.4–60 and killed by Kṛṣṇa and Baladeva include Jarāsaṃdha, Śiśupāla, Dantavaktra, and Rukmin.

The two *avatāra* functions are separate at Hv 40–45, but combined at Mbh 1.58. Combining them at 1.58 means overlaying demons, at an earlier point, onto (so that they become part of) the overpopulation problem. But this is not very successful, since elsewhere the named demons cannot have been active on Earth before Earth's complaint was made, and/or are largely incidental to the war that solves her problem.

But whether or not the overlaying of demons onto the overpopulation problem at 1.58 is theoretically successful, if gods are going to take birth en masse to rescue the Earth then they are surely going to conquer demons, for that is what gods do.

In Mbh 3, Duryodhana is so disheartened that he resolves upon suicide.

> *atha taṃ niścayaṃ tasya buddhvā daiteyadānavāḥ* |
> *pātālavāsino raudrāḥ pūrvaṃ devair vinirjitāḥ* ‖ 3.239.18 ‖
> *te svapakṣakṣayaṃ taṃ tu jñātvā duryodhanasya vai* |
> *āhvānāya tadā cakruḥ karma vaitānasaṃbhavam* ‖ 19 ‖
>
> Thereupon the Daityas and Dānavas, the gruesome denizens of the nether world who had been defeated by the Gods, now, hearing of his decision, in the knowledge that Duryodhana would wreck their party, performed a sacrificial rite in order to summon him.
> (3.239.18–19, trans. van Buitenen 1975: 691, adjusted)

The demons give him a pep-talk (3.240.1–24; Scheuer 1982: 265–274). They tell him not to die. They tell him he is theirs, and that they got him from Śiva and the goddess as a result of their austerities. They tell him that his top half is made out of diamonds, his bottom half out of flowers, and that he must press on with his campaign against the Pāṇḍavas.

> *tad alaṃ te viṣādena bhayaṃ tava na vidyate* |
> *sāhyārthaṃ ca hi te vīrāḥ saṃbhūtā bhuvi dānavāḥ* ‖ 3.240.10 ‖
> *bhīṣmadroṇakṛpādīṃś ca pravekṣyanty apare 'surāḥ* |
> *yair āviṣṭā ghṛṇāṃ tyaktvā yotsyante tava vairibhiḥ* ‖ 11 ‖
> *naiva putrān na ca bhrātṝn na pitṝn na ca bāndhavān* |
> *naiva śiṣyān na ca jñātīn na bālān sthavirān na ca* ‖ 12 ‖
> *yudhi saṃprahariṣyanto mokṣyanti kurusattama* |
> *niḥsnehā dānavāviṣṭāḥ samākrānte 'ntarātmani* ‖ 13 ‖
> *prahariṣyanti bandhubhyaḥ sneham utsṛjya dūrataḥ* | 14ab ...
> *daityarakṣogaṇāś cāpi saṃbhūtāḥ kṣatrayoniṣu* | 17ab
> *yotsyanti yudhi vikramya śatrubhis tava pārthiva* | 17cd ...

> You are in no danger, for the Dānavas have become heroes on earth in order to assist you. Other Asuras will take possession of Bhīṣma, Droṇa, Kṛpa, and the others; and possessed by them they will fight your enemies ruthlessly. When they engage in battle, best of the Kurus, they will give no quarter to either sons or brothers, parents or relatives, students or kinsmen, the young or the old. Pitiless, possessed by the Dānavas, their inner souls overwhelmed, they will battle their relations and cast all love far off. ... Bands of Daityas and Rākṣasas will take on lives in the wombs of the baronage and fight mightily with your enemies, O king ...
> (3.240.10–14b, 17a–d, trans. van Buitenen 1975: 692)

Naraka, for example, has taken possession of Karṇa (vv. 18–20, 32), who will kill Arjuna. Hence, say the Dānavas, the Pāṇḍavas will be beaten. In closing, they tell Duryodhana: 'you are always our recourse, as the Pāṇḍavas are of the Gods' (*tvam asmākaṃ gatir nityaṃ devatānāṃ ca pāṇḍavāḥ* ‖ 3.240.24cd, trans. van Buitenen).

Who are the demons kidding? Duryodhana (Kali) is part of the same collective *avatāra* as the Pāṇḍavas (Dharma, Vāyu, Indra, and the Aśvins). Śiva and the goddess have sold the demons a dummy. In this respect it looks as if this pep-talk, and the wider involvement of the demons against the gods at Kurukṣetra, far from frustrating the gods' purpose, will in fact aid it, thanks to the gullibility of the demons in opposing the gods in any possible context. If Duryodhana had killed himself in Mbh 3, the Pāṇḍavas would probably have regained their kingdom fairly easily, so there would have been no war and no depopulation. In any case, the alleged demonic influx occurs at a late point – when it is announced, the war is just a few years in the future – and so, despite the mention here of 'the wombs of the baronage', what is announced to Duryodhana is not demonic *avatāra*, which would apply from birth (Karṇa is the *avatāra* of the Sun), but demonic possession, which would come on later (as Karṇa is possessed by Naraka; on possession see Smith 2006: 245–283). As such, this announcement to Duryodhana has no apparent connection with the Earth's earlier problem, unless the demons who are now colonising some of the characters whom the gods created in order to help the Earth are the same demons whose activity within the world was a partial cause of the Earth's complaint in the first place.

We are finding it hard to make good theoretical sense of the demonic component in the 1.58 presentation of the Earth's initial problem. Perhaps this difficulty is, in part, a spillover from Biardeau's analogy, where the Kurukṣetra war cleanses the world of *adharma* and the *kṛtayuga* follows. The accounts of the Earth's problem at 1.189 and at Hv 40–45 have no demonic component, and the demonic component, such as it is, fits with the *avatāra* function of rebooting *dharma*, rather than with the function of reducing population. The adharmic spillage into the cull function is as if to explain and justify the deaths that must occur to reduce the population. It looks ethically neater to say that the warriors culled at Kurukṣetra were the demonic *kṣatra* (who thus deserved it) than to say – along with Hv 40–43 – that they were the paradigmatically dharmic *kṣatra*. This is so not least because a paradigmatically dharmic *kṣatra* would fit a point much earlier in the *mahāyuga*: by the time of the *dvāparayuga*, the *kṣatra* is fifty per cent demonic by definition.

Within the *Mahābhārata* account of the Kurukṣetra business as it unfolds, the demonic component in the Earth's initial problem is dramatised, out of time, as the Kaurava abuse of Draupadī at the dicing match, the Kurukṣetra war then being fought at least partly as restitution for Draupadī, to avenge the adharmic treatment that she suffered (Bowles 2008: xxv–xl; Brodbeck 2017a: 18; Hiltebeitel 2018: 252–263). Draupadī here stands for the kingdom and sovereignty over which the Pāṇḍavas and Kauravas are clashing and gambling – Earth and Śrī here combined as one. In terms of Draupadī and the Earth, the *Yugapurāṇa* seems to equate them. Describing the Kurukṣetra war that will take place at the end of the *dvāparayuga*, Śiva says:

> *eteṣām api vīrāṇāṃ rājñāṃ hetur bhaviṣyati* ǀ
> *drupadasya sutā kṛṣṇā dehāṃtaragatā mahī* ǁ *Yugapurāṇa* 36 ǁ
>
> The cause (of strife) of these royal heroes will be Drupada's daughter Kṛṣṇā, the Earth in another body.
>
> (*Yugapurāṇa* 36)[69]

If Draupadī represents the partisan Bhārata kingdom, fought over by two parties, suffering when the Kauravas have the kingdom and satisfied when the Pāṇḍavas have it back, then Draupadī's experience can be projected onto the Earth as initial complainant, as if Earth's complaint to Brahmā and Nārāyaṇa is, like Draupadī's complaint to her husbands during the dicing match, a complaint that the wrong party is in control of her, and that accordingly she is being badly treated. This dynamic fits with the otherwise rogue intrusion of the demonic trope into the 1.58 account of the Earth's problem. By implication, if the Earth has a problem at all, it is a problem that will be solved by the gods, and that is thus, almost by definition, a problem caused by demons. At this point in the Pāṇḍava story there is no equivalent to the overcrowding of the Earth in the meta-story, unless it were the complaint that Draupadī has five husbands, not one. Nonetheless, Draupadī is **not** satisfied after the Kurukṣetra war, because she loses her sons and her natal family (in the night massacre), and perhaps this fits with the fact that the Earth's problem, though solved in the short term

[69] Compare Mitchiner 2002: 102. I adopt Mitchiner's parenthesis but diverge from him in the interpretation of the last *pāda*. Mitchiner has: 'The cause (of strife) of these mighty kings will be Kṛṣṇā, the daughter of Drupada: (and) the earth will go to (her) destruction.' Eltschinger 2020: 49 quotes Mitchiner.

by a depopulation operation at the *kṛta–tretāyuga* transition, recurs also at the *tretā–dvāparayuga* and *dvāpara–kaliyuga* transitions.

Draupadī's abuse means that the Kaurava–Pāṇḍava conflict is more than just a succession conflict: it is a conflict between abusers and defenders. And so in the 1.58 picture the Earth is presented as abused and to be defended, and thus the morally dualistic gods-versus-demons dynamic has an entry, even though as far as overpopulation is concerned the relevant abuse would be by numbers, not by behaviour. If the two states are 'broken' and 'mended', the former is necessarily morally defective.

The ambiguity of the *avatāra* function (in favour of a warrior cull, and in favour of a Pāṇḍava victory) is maintained through most of the war. The battle is kept going, and the death-count thus maximised, by the Pāṇḍava successes against Bhīṣma, Droṇa, Karṇa, and Śalya, any one of whom could otherwise have led the Kauravas to victory. The success against Droṇa also has the effect – a salutary one from the perspective of the depopulation function – of helping to provoke the night massacre. In the mace duel between Bhīma and Duryodhana (Mbh 9.54–60), with the cull largely complete and the Earth largely satisfied already, perhaps either combatant could win. Indeed, if the question here is which king, Yudhiṣṭhira or Duryodhana, should be the first and defining king of the *kaliyuga*, then Duryodhana, the incarnation of Kali, is the obvious choice. This late in the *mahāyuga*, the bad should be in the ascendant. But at the same time, because the problem was that the Earth was suffering, and because that problem has by this point largely been solved regardless of who wins, the Earth's rescue is necessarily a victory of good over evil. And perhaps this would mean that Bhīma should win the duel, even were he not Kṛṣṇa's cousin and Arjuna's big brother.

But the Earth is not yet fully satisfied, and Bhīma's victory helps to move things on in this regard, for the way in which Duryodhana was felled helps to provoke Aśvatthāman to avenge his own father Droṇa's perfidious death by perpetrating the night massacre in part as an act of fealty to Duryodhana, who when he hears about it thinks he is the equal of Indra, and dies happy (10.9.19–55; Johnson 1998: 49–52). The Earth's satisfaction is arguably not fully accomplished until the Yādavas have been destroyed at Prabhāsa in 16.4 (Sharma 2020: 189–193); at 16.9.29 Vyāsa seems to suggest that Kṛṣṇa only stayed alive as long as it took him to relieve the Earth's burden. The destruction of the Yādavas at Prabhāsa is connected to the Kurukṣetra war of decades earlier through Kṛṣṇa's promise to Arjuna at the end of the *Bhagavadgītā* ('I will deliver you from all evils, don't worry', *ahaṃ tvā sarvapāpebhyo mokṣayiṣyāmi mā śucaḥ* ‖ Bhg 18.66cd, trans. Cherniak 2008: 301; see Hudson 1996: 70–72, 81–82), and through Gāndhārī's curse of Kṛṣṇa (Mbh 11.25.35–45), and through its being sparked off by ill-feeling over conduct during the war (16.4.16–27).

To sum up Chapter 5. We began by differentiating two functions of the *avatāra* within the general passages on the *avatāra* concept: one function is to restore *dharma*, the other is to relieve the Earth's burden. We looked at the story of the origin of Death (12.248–250) and related it to the latter function, and to the end of the *kṛtayuga*. The other function fits the end of the *kaliyuga*. We then looked in detail at the *Mahābhārata*'s various accounts of why the Kurukṣetra *avatāra* was necessary – the accounts of the divine plan. These accounts were compared and were resolved into the two *avatāra* functions, only one of which fits the demonic involvement in the Kurukṣetra generation. Insofar as both functions are illustrated, there is a paradox or tension between two poles (effectively between the two extremities of the *mahāyuga*), as one might expect at this intermediate *dvāpara–kaliyuga* transition. We then discussed the cosmic tendencies towards *jāmi* and *pṛthak* (similarity and difference) in the Brāhmaṇas. We framed those tendencies within the *mahāyuga* dynamic (with overpopulation as a problem of *jāmi* and low *dharma* as a problem of *pṛthak*) and in terms of the ritual that is performed to hold Prajāpati together at every junction-point in time, which seems to include the treatment for both *jāmi* and *pṛthak*, and thus to incorporate both functions of the *avatāra*. We explored the gendering of these two tendencies or extremities, but only briefly because their gendering, perhaps because it is so theologically curious, is ambiguous. We brought back, from Chapter 4, the idea of time-shifts as automatic, and queried the utility of the ritual model for explaining the *mahāyuga* cycle. In the final section of the chapter we surveyed the events of the Kurukṣetra generation in light of the two *avatāra* functions, one driving towards depopulation, the other towards restoration of *dharma*. Although both aspects are evident and the text is thus to an extent ambiguous, the depopulation is perhaps more obviously effective, which would be in keeping with the Earth's usual involvement in the initial complaint, and in keeping also with the fact that *dharma* does not increase at the *dvāpara–kaliyuga* transition. The idea I propose in Chapter 6, however, relates only to the function of rebooting *dharma*.

CHAPTER 6

Transition to the *Kṛtayuga*

This chapter moves forward in time from the Kurukṣetra war step by step, keeping the *yuga* cycle in view. This means moving outward through the *Mahābhārata*'s frame stories. Our trajectory in this chapter is as per Figure 14.

Kurukṣetra war	start of *kaliyuga* (1,200 yrs)
Janamejaya and the snake sacrifice	↓
Śaunaka's *satra*	↓
other Śaunaka *satra*s	↓
ancient audience	↓
	end of *kaliyuga*
modern audience	

Figure 14: Trajectory of Chapter 6.

Janamejaya and the *yuga*s

The *Mahābhārata*'s presentation of the events that it locates at the *dvāpara–kaliyuga* transition is, in the first instance, a presentation made to King Janamejaya at his snake sacrifice a few generations after those events. Janamejaya should thus locate himself within the *kaliyuga*. Janamejaya could think he is in the main body of the *kaliyuga*, or still in its dawn period. But if the Kurukṣetra war marked the *dvāpara–kaliyuga* transition, since when Parikṣit has been born, come of age, ruled for sixty years (1.45.15), and died, and Janamejaya, who was just a boy when Parikṣit died (1.40.6–7), has likewise come of age, then by the time of the snake sacrifice there cannot be much of the dawn period left, if any.

At the end of the snake sacrifice, as previously noted, Vyāsa describes the *yugānta* to Janamejaya (Hv 116–117). The context for this presentation is set by Janamejaya's comments on the Kurukṣetra war. Janamejaya asks why, since Vyāsa knows the future, he allowed the Pāṇḍavas to undertake the *rājasūya*

How to cite this book chapter:
Brodbeck, S. 2022. Divine Descent and the Four World-Ages in the *Mahābhārata* – or, Why Does the Kṛṣṇa *Avatāra* Inaugurate the Worst *Yuga*?. Pp. 141–163. Cardiff: Cardiff University Press. DOI: https://doi.org/10.18573/book9.f. Licence: CC-BY-NC-ND 4.0

ritual that led to the war (Hv 115.14–23). Vyāsa says that they never asked him what was going to happen, so he did not tell them, and that it would not have made any difference even if he had (Hv 115.24–25). In order to demonstrate to Janamejaya that knowing the future does not make any difference, Vyāsa reveals to him that Indra will attack his future horse-sacrifice, and that Janamejaya cannot avert this, and that he will be the last *kṣatriya* to perform the rite (vv. 26–35). Janamejaya asks if the tradition of performing horse sacrifices will subsequently be revived (v. 38), and Vyāsa says it will, by 'a certain army-commander, a brahmin descended from Kaśyapa' (*kaścit senānīḥ kāśyapo dvijaḥ*, v. 40). All this is in the future, but still in the *kaliyuga*.

Continuing forward in time, Vyāsa now mentions the *yugāntadvāra*, 'the entrance that leads into the end of the *yuga*' (Hv 115.42c). When Vyāsa here starts speaking about the future *yugānta*, he cannot intend to give a general account of the *kaliyuga*, since the *kaliyuga* is already in progress. He must be speaking more specifically, about the end of the *kaliyuga*.

Chapter 115 ends as follows:

> *tadāprabhṛti hāsyante nṛṇāṃ prāṇāḥ purākṛtīḥ* |
> *vinivartiṣyate loke vṛttānto vṛttimatsv api* ‖ Hv 115.43 ‖
> *tadā sūkṣmo mahodarko dustaro dānamūlavān* |
> *cāturāśramyaśithilo dharmaḥ pravicaliṣyati* ‖ 44 ‖
> *tadā hy alpena tapasā siddhiṃ yāsyanti mānavāḥ* |
> *dhanyā dharmaṃ cariṣyanti yugānte janamejaya* ‖ 45 ‖
>
> From then on [i.e. after the future *yugāntadvāra*], people's lives will no longer include their former activities. People will abandon their practices, even the people who have a profession. *Dharma* will totter in those days: it will be rooted in charity and lax about the four *āśrama*s, but though subtle it will be maximally consequential. In those days people will attain salvation through meagre efforts, Janamejaya; so the people who practise *dharma* at the end of the *yuga* are lucky.
>
> (*Harivaṃśa* 115.43–45)

We recall, as Janamejaya presumably does, that charity (*dāna*) is said to be the most appropriate form of *dharma* in the *kaliyuga* (Ms 1.85–86; Mbh 12.224.26–27; see also 12.252.8). Not just at the end of the *kaliyuga*, but for the whole *kaliyuga*. So here Vyāsa has apparently slipped into talking about the *kaliyuga* in general. In Hiltebeitel's interpretation of these *Harivaṃśa* verses (which I share), this '*yugadharma* of giving ... here as elsewhere probably denotes *bhakti* religiosity' (Hiltebeitel 2011b: 583) – that is, it denotes the devotional *yoga* that Kṛṣṇa taught to Arjuna in the *Bhagavadgītā*.

Janamejaya replies:

> *āsannaṃ viprakṛṣṭaṃ vā yadi kālaṃ na vidmahe* |
> *tasmād dvāparavidhvaṃsād yugāntaṃ spṛhayāmy aham* ‖ Hv 116.1 ‖

prāptā vayaṃ hi taṃ kālam anayā dharmatṛṣṇayā |
prāptā vayaṃ ca dharmaṃ svaṃ sukham alpena karmaṇā ‖ 2 ‖
prajāsamudvegakaraṃ yugāntaṃ samupasthitam |
pranaṣṭadharmaṃ dharmajña nimittair vaktum arhasi ‖ 3 ‖

We do not know whether that time is close at hand or far away. But since the *dvāpara* has finished, I am eager for the end of the *yuga*. If we are alive at that time it is because of our desire for religious merit, because at that time we can attain religious merit for ourselves easily, through meagre efforts.

Knower of propriety, you should describe, through its signs, the arrived-at end of the *yuga*, when creatures are put to fright and *dharma* is lost.

(*Harivaṃśa* 116.1–3)

Here Janamejaya seems to affirm that the word *yugānta* has been used ambiguously by Vyāsa. The *kaliyuga* is in progress, and so the new religious dispensation, according to which Janamejaya's salvation will be relatively easy, should already be in operation; and yet Vyāsa has spoken of it (and will do again at 117.13) as something that pertains to the future *yugānta*. Accordingly, Janamejaya is 'eager for' that *yugānta*, which he might reasonably have thought he was already in. His reference to 'the arrived-at end of the *yuga*' (*yugāntaṃ samupasthitam*, 116.3b) is ambiguous in a way that reflects the ambiguity Vyāsa has already introduced: Janamejaya could be asking about the *yugānta* that has already arrived (i.e. the *kaliyuga*), or about what the *yugānta* will be like **when** it arrives (i.e. the *kaliyugānta*). This ambiguity fits with his comment that he does not know how close the *yugānta* is.

In asking for a description of the *yugānta*, Janamejaya is asking for a reprise of what Mārkaṇḍeya twice presented to Yudhiṣṭhira in the previous *yuga*, once as a description of the end of the day of Brahmā, and once as a description of the end of the *mahāyuga* (3.186.24–55 and 3.188.14–84, discussed in Chapter 2). But this time, to make sense of the future tense, we will want to interpret it as a description of the end of the *kaliyuga*. Although Mārkaṇḍeya's memorable descriptions are placed several generations ago, both Janamejaya and Vyāsa have heard them recently, at the snake sacrifice that has just finished. So even without imagining a proto-text in which, for example, Vyāsa's speech to Janamejaya might have been delivered shortly before the *kaliyuga* began, we have some licence for reading Vyāsa's description of the *yugānta* as an improvised repurposing of something that originally had a rather different sense.

Vyāsa's description of the *yugānta*, like Mārkaṇḍeya's two long descriptions of the same, is a series of brief descriptions, with many verses also containing a temporal marker. In Vyāsa's description in Hv 116, as a rule he keeps things ambiguous: the time he describes is *yugānte* ('at the end of the *yuga*', vv. 5, 7, 8, 33), *yugakṣaye* ('when the *yuga* is waning', vv. 6, 9, 10, 12, 13, 14, 17, 26, 29, 30), *antagate yuge* ('when the *yuga* comes to its end', v. 16), *yuge kṣīṇe* ('when the *yuga* is worn out', vv. 18, 28), *nirgate yuge* ('when the *yuga* dies', v. 19), *yugasyānte* ('at the end of the *yuga*', v. 21), *yugānte samanuprāpte* ('when the end of the *yuga* is reached', v. 22), *tad yugāntasya lakṣaṇam* ('that is the sign of the end of the *yuga*', v. 23), *gate yuge* ('when the *yuga* is spent', v. 25), *yugāpakramaṇe* ('when the *yuga* is passing away', v. 27), *yugānte pratyupasthite* ('when the end of the *yuga* comes', vv. 31, 32), *yugānte samupasthite* ('when the end of the *yuga* comes along', v. 34), and *kāle kṣīṇe* ('when time has worn out', v. 40). But as in the earlier accounts from Mārkaṇḍeya to Yudhiṣṭhira, in addition to these ambiguous markers there is also at least one indication that the description is of the *kaliyuga* in general (which in this instance Janamejaya is already in, where Yudhiṣṭhira was not quite in it yet). Here in Vyāsa's speech those indications are at Hv 116.19 and 36:

> *na te dharmaṃ cariṣyanti mānavā nirgate yuge* |
> *ūṣarābahulā bhūmiḥ panthāno nagarāntarā* |
> *sarve vāṇijakāś caiva bhaviṣyanti kalau yuge* ‖ Hv 116.19 ‖
>
> People will not follow *dharma* when the *yuga* dies. The soil will become very salty, there will be nothing in the towns but roads, and everyone will be selling something, in the *kaliyuga*.
>
> (*Harivaṃśa* 116.19)
>
> *nakṣatrāṇi vihīnāni viparītā diśas tathā* |
> *saṃdhyārāgo 'tha digdāho bhaviṣyaty apare yuge* ‖ Hv 116.36 ‖
>
> [The planets] will not visit the constellations, the directions will be inverted, and the twilight will burn a crimson colour, in the latest/worst *yuga*.
>
> (*Harivaṃśa* 116.36)

Where the *kaliyuga* in general is specified, perhaps it is specified only for the details in those particular sentences.

Janamejaya asks for more:

> *janamejaya uvāca* |
> *eṣaṃ vilulite loke manuṣyāḥ kena pālitāḥ* |
> *nivatsyanti kimācārāḥ kimāhāravihāriṇaḥ* ‖ Hv 117.1 ‖
> *kiṃkarmāṇaḥ kimīhantaḥ kiṃpramāṇāḥ kimāyuṣaḥ* |
> *kāṃ ca kāṣṭhāṃ samāsādya prapatsyanti kṛtaṃ yugam* ‖ 2 ‖
>
> Janamejaya said:
> When the world is out of joint like this, who will protect the people? How will the people living (at that time) behave? What will they do for food? What will they do for pleasure? What will their rites be like? What

> will their ambitions be? What will their standards be? How long will they live? And what course will they take to reach the *kṛtayuga*?
>
> (*Harivaṃśa* 117.1–2)

Janamejaya himself uses the future tense here. Vyāsa now describes the transition from the *kaliyuga* to the *kṛtayuga*, which Janamejaya will not live to see (Hv 117, discussed below).

Vyāsa's full account to Janamejaya begins in the *kaliyuga*, moves forward into the future from there, and ends by describing the *kali–kṛtayuga* transition. But in the main body of his *yugānta* account Vyāsa describes things apparently being more parlous than Janamejaya is used to them being. So it may seem, even more than it did in Mārkaṇḍeya's accounts, that the transition from the *kaliyuga* to the *kṛtayuga* involves things first getting worse than they were in the majority of the *kaliyuga*, even though – exceptionally in terms of *yuga* transitions – the level of *dharma* will rise overall in the transition. The idea that there is a dharmic trough at the end of the *kaliyuga* (and not just across the whole *kaliyuga*) may or may not be due to Vyāsa's repurposing of Mārkaṇḍeya's *yugānta* description; but if it is, it is no less of an idea for all that. Thus if *dharma* is on one leg during the *kaliyuga*, during the dusk of the *kaliyuga* it would be on less than one leg, as suggested by the mention of *dharma* being not just badly compromised but actually lost (*pranaṣṭadharmaṃ*, Hv 116.3), before the bull gets up onto all four legs again during the dawn of the *kṛtayuga*. Figure 15 presents this in graph form (the nadir at 0.5 is arbitrary).

A dharmic trough at this ascending transition would in some ways resemble the trough that we have seen hypothesised at descending *yuga*-transitions on account of a perceived instability at *yugānta*s (as per Figure 10 in Chapter 4 above). But here, because it is an ascending transition, the trough additionally encapsulates the idea that things have to hit rock bottom before they can start improving. Though resembling it, Figure 15 is independent of Figure 10, in that it is theoretically possible (and probably simpler) for the *mahāyugānta* to work differently from how the descending *yugānta*s work. It is also necessary that this transition work differently, since here there is a whole *mahāyuga*'s worth of deterioration to reverse. So when the line on the graph moves back up, it moves far beyond the height from which it last fell. This could not be imagined as one might imagine a dropped ball bouncing; here one would have to throw the ball forcefully at the ground. In imagining the difference between the *mahāyugānta* and the other *yugānta*s the bull metaphor helps, because the fall off the last leg would be different from the loss of the fourth, third, or even second leg; the issue reduces to a binary, leg/s or no legs. Remaining standing somehow throughout vicissitudes is the heroic, victorious bull; falling to the ground would be the failing, sacrificed bull.

The last part of the *kaliyuga* is also in a special position because the reduction of the level of the complex variable by one is effected three times. As discussed in Chapter 5, the scenario at the *dvāparayugānta* mimics the scenario

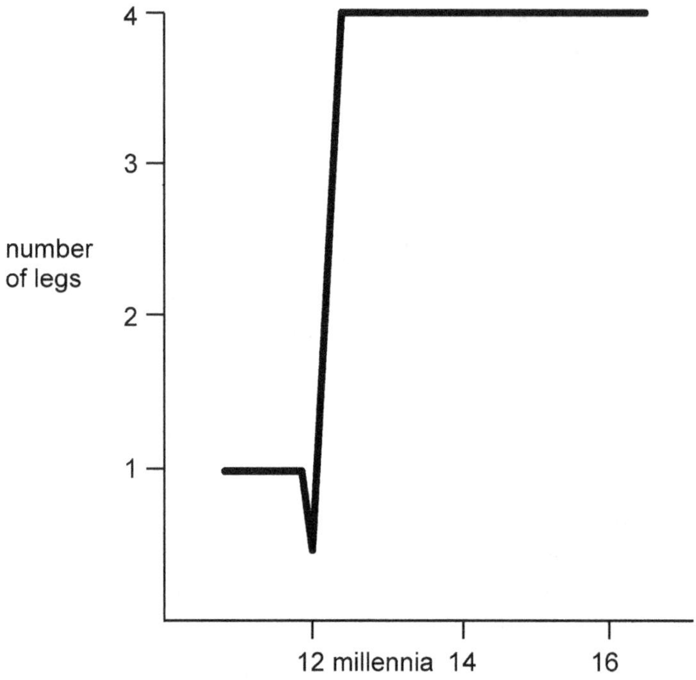

Figure 15: *Kali* to *Kṛta* Transition (with Trough).

at the *kṛtayugānta*: Earth is overburdened and is thus succoured. The *kaliyuga* can thus be a synecdoche for the combined *tretā–dvāpara–kaliyuga* unit: like that unit, it begins with an operation that aids the Earth, and ends with an operation that restores *dharma*. In this regard, the main structural difference between the *kaliyuga* and the combined *tretā–dvāpara–kaliyuga* unit is that the latter is internally divided into portions with diminishing levels of *dharma*. The scenario shown in Figure 15 applies such a division also to the *kaliyuga* itself, facilitated by the differentiation of the dusk from the main body of the *yuga*. The general trend is for *dharma* to keep decreasing until it increases, and a *kaliyugānta* trough is in keeping with that trend.

The king and the *yugas*

Janamejaya is told more about the past than he is about the future. As per our title question, Janamejaya is entitled to wonder how it can be that the Kurukṣetra *avatāra*, in whose low-*dharma* wake he lives, is said to have had, as its basic purpose, a restoration of *dharma*. The discussions of *yugas* and *avatāras* in the earlier chapters of this monograph have largely been pursued on the basis of passages that Janamejaya hears; and so, thus far, Janamejaya has potentially been at the same level of understanding of these concepts as we have.

The situation is complicated because, as mentioned briefly in Chapter 2, the *yuga* cycle, whereby the four *yuga*s succeed each other repeatedly in the same order, is not the text's only way of viewing the four *yuga*s. The *yuga* is also said to depend upon the king – which would be of interest to King Janamejaya – and Thomas has argued that this should be taken literally (Thomas 2007). When a king makes it a *kṛtayuga*, this is not just him ruling unexpectedly well during one of the generally more dharmically compromised *yuga*s; it actually is a *kṛtayuga*. We can understand this readily in terms of a king like Kalkin, who, despite being born in a *kaliyuga*, as if by sheer force of will bucks the trend and makes it be the next *kṛtayuga*. But it is harder to understand the idea of the king making the *kṛtayuga* if he does not do so, as Kalkin does, exactly 1,200 years after the *kaliyuga* began, and thus, as it were, with the assistance of time.

The idea that the king defines the *yuga* would be obviously compatible with the four-*yuga* cycle if a long period of excellent kings were followed by a shorter period of good kings, then an even shorter period of mediocre kings, then an even shorter still period of bad kings. But this does not fit with the alleged locations of specific king-made *kṛtayuga*s within the four-*yuga* cycle. One of the notable *kṛtayuga*-making kings was Bhīṣma, even though he was not really king (1.102.5; for others see p. 114 n. 63 above); and this was during, or at least in the immediate lead-up to, the *dvāpara–kaliyuga* transition. Was this due to *yugānta* instability? And although Bhīṣma tells Yudhiṣṭhira that the king makes the age (see e.g. 12.70) partly to encourage Yudhiṣṭhira to be the best king he can, and although Yudhiṣṭhira, being Dharma incarnate, is an excellent king, he rules at the beginning of the *kaliyuga*. Janamejaya rules in the *kaliyuga* too, despite being told the ancestral story at least partly in order to encourage him too to be an excellent king, which at the end of the text he seemingly is (Hv 118.39–41).

There is thus a conflict between the four-*yuga* cycle and the idea that the king makes the age. The situation is assisted, in a way, by the fact that there are other kingdoms. When it is a *kṛtayuga* across the Kuru realm under Bhīṣma's regency, it would presumably not be a *kṛtayuga* in every other kingdom. So what *yuga* would it be overall? Is there a cosmic average at any given time? Kane puts it nicely when he says that 'It is the king who can by his conduct introduce the characteristics of one yuga into another' (Kane 1973: 892).

The Vedic rituals that present the king and his kingdom or polity as a microcosm of the totality (as per our discussions of the *rājasūya* in Chapter 5; Thomas 2007: 190–197) seem not to consider the plurality of kingdoms. The Vedic grasping at totality within one context seems to rely on that context being the only one there really is. Thus there would be no 'now' in any other kingdom corresponding to the 'now' of this kingdom; they would be in different time-systems. But if the scenario is enlarged and kingdoms are plural within one time-system, then because they may be extremely plural indeed, the scaling between the local kingdom and the wider cosmos is potentially a scaling so large that any number of locally enormous massacres could be dissolved into it. In this perspective, Kurukṣetra could be averaged out, however many *kṣatriya*s died there.

This we already know. Look around and you will see a great range of behaviours. Whatever *yuga* it might be, it is not the case that everyone has to be equally dharmic. The limits of that are wide, and it is hard to imagine them being wider, even if the texture were different. Kurukṣetra, the field of *dharma*, occurs every day for many people, in a world where *dharma* is a struggle. And so Vyāsa says:

> *āśīs tu puruṣaṃ dṛṣṭvā deśakālānuvartinī* |
> *yuge yuge yathākālam ṛṣibhiḥ samudāhṛtā* ‖ Hv 117.49 ‖
> *iha dharmārthakāmānāṃ vedānāṃ ca pratikriyā* |
> *āśiṣaś ca śubhāḥ puṇyās tathaivāyur yuge yuge* ‖ 50 ‖
>
> In *yuga* after *yuga*, whatever the location in time, the seers look at a person and pronounce a blessing that is suited to that place and time. And in this world, in *yuga* after *yuga*, attention to *dharma*, profit, pleasure, and the Vedas is always rewarded by pleasant and holy blessings, and long life.
>
> (*Harivaṃśa* 117.49–50)

This statement relativises judgement of individuals according to the *yuga* (space collapsing into time as if different *yuga*s were to operate in parallel people), but the principles are the same throughout. It is a microcosmic version of the king making the age. 'When the world is running down, you make the best of what's still around' (The Police).

This relativistic angle can also help us to address a point raised by Biardeau: 'How can the restoration of *dharma* be understood if the law of karma is supposed to be respected? ... the socio-cosmic rhythm of the degradation of *dharma* fits ill with the interweaving of good and bad individual karmas'[70] (Biardeau 1976: 122–123). Births early in the *kṛtayuga* must be due to good karma, but how would one generate such good karma in the *kaliyuga* where people live relatively adharmic lives? The answer is that in the *kaliyuga*, because of the uncongenial environment, a little *dharma* can have a large karmic effect (Hv 115.44–45; 116.2; 117.13).

[70] 'Comment comprendre la restauration du *dharma* si l'on veut respecter la loi du *karman*? ... le rythme sociocosmique de la dégradation du *dharma* s'accorde mal avec l'entrecroisement des bons et des mauvais *karman* individuels'

In the *Mahābhārata* story, teachings on kingship are dispensed by Bhīṣma, Vidura, and Saṃjaya to the blind Dhṛtarāṣṭra and the perverse Duryodhana, and there they fall largely on deaf ears. But Bhīṣma, Vidura, and Saṃjaya's teachings to Yudhiṣṭhira – most particular Bhīṣma's – help Yudhiṣṭhira to be a better king; and then Vaiśaṃpāyana and Vyāsa's teachings to Janamejaya, which include all the teachings that helped Yudhiṣṭhira (and all those that might have helped Dhṛtarāṣṭra and Duryodhana but did not), help Janamejaya to be a better king. The way that Yudhiṣṭhira's education continues into Janamejaya's education means that it can also continue, along with Janamejaya's, into the education of any later kings who hear the text that tells Janamejaya's story. Because the king is the paradigm of the householder and also of any individual (Biardeau 1981: 88 n. 18; Adluri and Bagchee 2016: 104; Brodbeck 2017b: 133–135), that text can also edify Śaunaka and the guests at his *satra*, and the seers who hear it from Ugraśravas, and anyone who hears the *Mahābhārata* (which is for all *varṇa*s and genders; Black 2007: 54–56). The *Mahābhārata* message that the king makes the *yuga* means that one must consistently aim for top levels of appropriate *dharma* from oneself, whatever *yuga* it was for the previous king, and whatever *yuga* it is for parallel kings. But also, because this royal message is earthed in the Kurukṣetra event at the *dvāpara–kaliyuga* transition, its transmission is a phenomenon peculiar to the *kaliyuga*.

Vyāsa's transition account

We return to our title problem that if *dharma* progressively declines across a *mahāyuga* then the action of the *avatāra*, in order to restore and reboot *dharma* (as per Bhg 4.7–8, quoted earlier), should take effect at the *kali–kṛtayuga* transition. In dharmic terms, the *avatāra* represents that flick back up. So how can it come at the end of the *dvāparayuga*? Solving the Earth's overpopulation problem would not, and does not, appear to restore *dharma*. Even if Yudhiṣṭhira is a good king and cannot rule until after the *kṣatriya* cull, still he does not rule for long. The same problem occurs if an *avatāra* is imagined at the end of the *kṛtayuga* or the *tretāyuga*. Thus although Rāma Dāśarathi is traditionally placed at the *tretā–dvāparayuga* transition (12.326.78–81), this location does not sit well with the idea that after defeating Rāvaṇa he ruled perfectly for thousands of years (12.29.46–54; Hv 31.129–139).

In Chapter 5 we developed an understanding whereby the double nature of the *avatāra*'s function with respect to the *mahāyuga* means that the *avatāra*'s appearance cannot completely be located at either of the points to which those two functions theoretically correspond, because that would leave the other function significantly out of the account. Hence if the *avatāra* that represents both functions is located at an intermediate *yugānta*, it could somehow fit both functions, even if not really fitting the dharmic function at all.

In this section, we will try to see whether nonetheless, in answer to the title question, and prioritising the dharmic function as per the *Bhagavadgītā* statement, we might envisage the rebooting of *dharma* at the *kali-kṛtayuga* transition as a delayed effect of the appearance of the Kurukṣetra *avatāra*. We will thus attempt to sketch a literal way out of our impasse, by focusing upon the *kali-kṛtayuga* transition. This is to take the dharmic reboot as a *mahāyuga* moment overshadowing the intermediate *yugāntas*.

We return, then, to the *kali-kṛtayuga* transition, which was the topic at the end of Vyāsa's description of the *yugānta*. Mārkaṇḍeya described the *kali-kṛtayuga* transition to Yudhiṣṭhira in terms of the deeds of Kalkin the brahmin king, who mended the world forcefully, swiftly, and totally (3.188.89–189.6). We might call this the text's messianic view of the *kali-kṛtayuga* transition. When Vaiśaṃpāyana listed Viṣṇu's *avatāras* at Hv 31, he mentioned the future *avatāra* Kalkin (Hv 31.148); he did not at that point mention Kalkin's deeds or any connection with the *yugas*, but Janamejaya was already familiar with those.

But the messianic view of the *kali-kṛtayuga* transition is not the text's only view (González-Reimann 2002: 129–132). In Hv 117, Vyāsa describes the end of the present *kaliyuga* to Janamejaya without mentioning Kalkin:

vyāsa uvāca ǀ
ata ūrdhvaṃ cyute dharme guṇahīnāḥ prajās tataḥ ǀ
śīlavyasanam āsādya prāpsyante hrāsam āyuṣaḥ ǁ Hv 117.3 ǁ
āyurhānyā[71] *balaglānir balaglānyā vivarṇatā* ǀ
vaivarṇyād vyādhisaṃpīḍā nirvedo vyādhipīḍanāt ǁ 4 ǁ
nirvedād ātmasaṃbodhaḥ saṃbodhād dharmaśīlatā ǀ
evaṃ gatvā parāṃ kāṣṭhāṃ prapatsyanti kṛtaṃ yugam ǁ 5 ǁ ...
tadā vicalite dharme janāḥ śeṣapuraskṛtāḥ ǀ
śubhāny evācariṣyanti dānasatyasamanvitāḥ ǁ 10 ǁ ...
kaṣāyopaplave kāle jñānavidyāpraṇāśane ǀ
siddhim alpena kālena yāsyanti nirupaskṛtāḥ ǁ 13 ǁ ...
āyus tatra ca martyānāṃ paraṃ triṃśad bhaviṣyati ǀ
durbalā viṣayaglānā rajasā samabhiplutāḥ ǁ 38 ǁ
bhaviṣyati tadā teṣāṃ rogair indriyasaṃkṣayaḥ ǀ
āyuḥprakṣayasaṃrodhād dhiṃsā coparamiṣyati ǁ 39 ǁ
śuśrūṣavo bhaviṣyanti sādhūnāṃ darśane ratāḥ ǀ
satyaṃ cāpi prapatsyanti vyavahārāpaśaṅkayā ǁ 40 ǁ
bhaviṣyanti ca kāmānām alābhād dharmaśīlinaḥ ǀ
kariṣyanti ca saṃkocaṃ svapakṣakṣayapīḍitāḥ ǁ 41 ǁ
evaṃ śuśrūṣavo dāne satye prāṇābhirakṣaṇe ǀ
catuṣpādapravṛttaṃ ca dharmam āpsyanti mānavāḥ ǁ 42 ǁ
tesāṃ dharmābhimānānāṃ guṇeṣu parivartatām ǀ
svādu kiṃ nv iti vijñāya dharma eva svadiṣyati ǁ 43 ǁ

[71] At Hv 117.4a Vaidya has *āyurhārnyā*, but Dandekar corrects this as a typo (Vaidya 1969: 772; Dandekar 1971–1976, vol. 5: 220).

yathā hāniḥ kramaprāptā tathā vṛddhiḥ kramāgatā |
pragṛhīte tato dharme prapatsyanti kṛtaṃ punaḥ ‖ 44 ‖

Vyāsa said:
When *dharma* has fallen away, the only way is up from there. In those days the people will have no redeeming features. Through getting into ruinous habits some will have shorter lives, through having shorter lives some will lose their strength, through lack of strength some will lose their colour, through lack of colour some will be plagued by ailments, through being pained by ailments some will become disaffected with worldly affairs, through becoming disaffected some will come to understand the soul (*ātman*), and through that understanding some will get into virtuous habits. Following the highest course in this way, they will then reach the *kṛtayuga*.

... In those days, when *dharma* has fallen away, only the people who prioritise the little *dharma* that remains will still be touched by truth and charity, and will do good deeds.

... At the time of the ochre affliction (*kaṣāyopaplave*),[72] when wisdom and learning are destroyed, people who remain pure will attain salvation (*siddhim*) quite quickly.

... In those days, a person's lifespan will be thirty years at the most. People will be weak and riddled with impurity, their faculties fragile. In those days their powers will be sapped by sickness, and they will renounce violence in an attempt to stop their lives dwindling away. They will become keen to learn from living saints (*sādhūnāṃ*) and obsessed with catching sight of them, and they will neglect their businesses and pursue truth. By not gratifying their desires they will get into virtuous habits, and when they are troubled by the deaths of people close to them they will become humble. And in this way, people who are attentive to charity, truth, and the preservation of life will arrive at a *dharma* that stands on all fours. Those who are proud of their good works (*dharma*) might roam around in the realm of the senses asking what tastes good, but virtue (*dharma*) will be the only thing that really tastes good. As decay comes about step by step, so does growth, and when *dharma* is accepted once more, the *kṛtayuga* will come round again.

(*Harivaṃśa* 117.3–5, 10, 13, 38–44)

[72] Vyāsa says that at the *yugānta*, '*śūdra*s who follow the Buddha of the Śākyas will practise their *dharma* dressed in ochre robes (*kāṣāyavāsasaḥ*), with shaved heads, white teeth, and unconquered senses' (*śukladantājitākṣāś ca muṇḍāḥ kāṣāyavāsasaḥ* | *śūdrā dharmaṃ cariṣyanti śākyabuddhopajīvinaḥ* ‖ Hv 116.15; compare Eltschinger 2012: 46 n. 94). Thereafter Vyāsa uses the word *kaṣāya* on five occasions apparently as a shorthand for the *yugānta* (Hv 117.11, 12, 13, 14, 45).

In this account, rather than being effected from above by a single messianic figure, the *kṛtayuga* is effected from below. González-Reimann calls this 'a more "democratic" alternative' (González-Reimann 2002: 131).

Vyāsa's transition account fits with what Vaiśaṃpāyana says in Mbh 12.336 about the power of *bhakti*. In that *Nārāyaṇīya* passage, Vaiśaṃpāyana refers back to the *dharma* that was taught to Arjuna in the *Bhagavadgītā* (12.336.8–9). Before creation, Nārāyaṇa imparted this *dharma* to Brahmā, saying:

> *dharmaṃ ca matto gṛhṇīṣva sātvataṃ nāma nāmataḥ* ǀ
> *tena sarvaṃ kṛtayugaṃ sthāpayasva yathāvidhi* ǁ 12.336.27 ǁ
>
> Receive the *dharma* that is called Sātvata from me, and with it make the *kṛtayuga* just as it should be.
>
> (12.336.27)

Thus that creation began with a *kṛtayuga*. In the present creation, as the *Nārāyaṇīya* passage relates, the same *dharma* – here called *ekāntidharma*, the *dharma* of those with a single focus – has been taught again, to humans, in the *kaliyuga*. It has been taught, for example, to Janamejaya by Vaiśaṃpāyana, who learned about it from Vyāsa (12.336.57; see also the mention of the *sātvataṃ vidhim* at 6.62.39, p. 49 above). In the *Nārāyaṇīya* passage Vaiśaṃpāyana now says:

> *yady ekāntibhir ākīrṇaṃ jagat syāt kurunandana* ǀ
> *ahiṃsakair ātmavidbhiḥ sarvabhūtahite rataiḥ* ǀ
> *bhavet kṛtayugaprāptir āśīḥkarmavivarjitaiḥ* ǁ 12.336.58 ǁ
>
> If the world were filled with people of single devotion (to Nārāyaṇa), son of Kuru, who practiced non-injury (*ahiṃsā*), who knew the soul (*ātman*), and who had a good disposition towards all beings, [then] the Kṛta Yuga would begin, and wishes (would be granted) without the need for (ritual) acts.
>
> (12.336.58, trans. González-Reimann 2002: 131)

And now, in his *Harivaṃśa* account quoted above, Vyāsa has explained to Janamejaya, in general terms, how this will happen.

Now we can ask whether the coming of the *kṛtayuga* could be a delayed result effected, long after the actual *avatāras* have died, through Vyāsa's full story of the Kurukṣetra *avatāra* – that is, through the *Mahābhārata*. Von Stietencron mentions the salvific effects not just of 'direct incarnation on earth', but also of 'words spoken by holy men' (von Stietencron 2005b: 45). But those are not specifically words about an incarnation, and their envisaged effects are for individuals. What we have in mind is rather a general effect upon the level of dharmic behaviour, and thus the *yuga*, caused by a specific *avatāra* text that has *avatāra* Kṛṣṇa Vāsudeva's *Bhagavadgītā* message at its heart.

Janamejaya's education, as passed on to Śaunaka, the seers, and us, includes the story of the Kurukṣetra *avatāra* as a story of the past. That story was put together by Kṛṣṇa Vyāsa, who helped to make it happen at the time. Not just a story, it also contains detailed teachings on cosmology, theology, and soteriology, among other things. It was taught to Vyāsa's various disciples. And it was performed for Janamejaya by Vyāsa's disciple Vaiśaṃpāyana, in Vyāsa's presence, at the snake sacrifice. Vyāsa introduced Vaiśaṃpāyana's performance at 1.54.22, interjected within it at 12.335 (Hiltebeitel 2006: 243–249; Brodbeck 2009b: 236 n. 12), and, after Vaiśaṃpāyana's performance had had its effect in the immediate context of the snake sacrifice by helping Janamejaya to make peace with the snakes and his father Parikṣit (15.43.4–17), Vyāsa concluded it with commentary at Hv 115–117. That performance, largely delivered by Vaiśaṃpāyana but credited in toto to Vyāsa, helped Janamejaya to become a fine king – not least by performing a horse sacrifice (as did his great forebears, Yudhiṣṭhira and so on).

At Janamejaya's horse sacrifice, Indra took the form of the suffocated horse and had sex with Janamejaya's wife Vapuṣṭamā. Janamejaya, furious, dismissed his priests and was going to dismiss his wife too, but he reconsidered after hearing a speech by *gandharva* king Viśvāvasu (Hv 118.24–38). Viśvāvasu's words, as part of the *Mahābhārata*, are credited to Vyāsa too. At the end we hear this of Janamejaya:

na ca viramati viprapūjanān na ca vinivartati yajñaśīlanāt |
na ca viṣayaparirakṣaṇāc cyuto 'sau na ca parigarhati vapuṣṭamāṃ ca ‖
Hv 118.41 ‖
vidhivihitam aśakyam anyathā hi kartuṃ yad ṛṣir acintyatapāḥ purābravīt saḥ |
iti narapatir ātmavāṃs tadāsau tad anuvicintya babhūva vītamanyuḥ ‖ 42 ‖

He never stops receiving brahmins,
he never stops performing rituals,
he never stops protecting the realm,
and he never finds fault with Vapuṣṭamā.

The sensible king stayed free of angst
by remembering what Vyāsa said earlier.
The inconceivably austere seer had claimed
that what fate fixes can't be changed.

(*Harivaṃśa* 118.41–42)

The full performance of his royal duties, even during the *kaliyuga*, is something that Janamejaya should aspire to achieve; and it is something that kings after him should all the more aspire to achieve, facilitated as they are by his example, thanks to this text. And insofar as kingship stands in for householdership and for individual comportment in general, with Vyāsa's text aimed at the widest audience, it may seem that we shall overcome, and the *kṛtayuga* will come again, through Vyāsa's story.

In considering this possibility, we must acknowledge and stress that Kṛṣṇa Vyāsa, like Kṛṣṇa Vāsudeva, is Nārāyaṇa (12.334.9; 12.337.4–5; 12.337.42–43, quoted earlier, p. 50; Kātre 1934: 105–107; Hiltebeitel 1976: 61;[73] Sullivan 1999: 69–71; Sutton 2000: 164; Saindon 2007: 311, 315–318). To that extent, Vyāsa is effectively part of the Kurukṣetra *avatāra*. Vyāsa facilitates the full divine plan not just by doing so many things to allow-cum-help the Kurukṣetra war to happen (fathering sons from Vicitravīrya's widows, directing and supervising the Pāṇḍavas, advising Drupada about Draupadī's marriage, etc.), but also by subsequently putting the story of the Kurukṣetra war together and promulgating it.

Vyāsa's account of the *kali–kṛtayuga* transition (quoted above) is self-effacing in that it does not dwell on the effect of his text. His account of the Kurukṣetra war is also self-effacing in that it does not dwell upon his identity with Viṣṇu (it is difficult enough that Viṣṇu is both Kṛṣṇa and Baladeva, as Vyāsa mentions to Drupada at 1.189.31). But the *Mahābhārata* is Viṣṇu's text in being **about** Viṣṇu as Kṛṣṇa, and in being **by** Viṣṇu as Vyāsa.

In Vyāsa's account, the transition to the *kṛtayuga* is facilitated by the conditions prevailing in the *kaliyuga*. It is because people are so depraved that they finally develop wisdom. The *Mahābhārata* is about a war that happened at the *dvāpara–kaliyuga* transition – without the Kurukṣetra *avatāra* there would be no *Mahābhārata* – but it is also about the story of that war, and the transformative power of that story, whose audience is unrestricted. The power of the text is due, among other things, to its movement beyond Janamejaya into general distribution. The *Mahābhārata* was perhaps the first Sanskrit text to be widely available; it is a textual resource for the *kaliyuga*, and its availability is one of the *kaliyuga*'s salient conditions. As Koskikallio explains (1994: 261–263, 265–266), the way it manages to be such a resource is by setting out an allegedly revived religious orientation appropriate to the other conditions of the *kaliyuga*, with a focus on charity, *bhakti*, and the faithful fulfilment of one's own duties and *yoga* regardless of the failings of others, through the example and teachings of Kṛṣṇa and Vyāsa, who were Viṣṇu himself.

Thus the divine intervention at the *dvāpara–kaliyuga* transition can rescue the Earth through depopulation while *dharma* is still declining, and it can effect the transition to the next *kṛtayuga* twelve hundred years later, in keeping with the *avatāra* principle as Kṛṣṇa states it, through the intermediate instrument of the *Mahābhārata* itself. Speaking as Viṣṇu-Nārāyaṇa, Kṛṣṇa says:

---

[73] For the nominal connection between the several Kṛṣṇas, see Hiltebeitel 1976: 60–62; Hiltebeitel 1984; Hiltebeitel 1985.

ye tu dharmyāmṛtam idaṃ yathoktaṃ paryupāsate |
śraddadhānā matparamā bhaktās te 'tīva me priyāḥ ‖ Bhg 12.20 ‖

Those faithful *bhaktas* who are intent on me as their highest goal, and who resort to this dharmic nectar that I have uttered, are especially dear to me.

(*Bhagavadgītā* 12.20, trans. Cherniak 2008: 265, adapted)

This would be because by doing so, they perform their proper duties without attachment and participate in Kṛṣṇa's *avatāra* purpose of restoring *dharma*, and they are *bhaktas* by belonging in that sense. Kṛṣṇa is, after all, the paradigm of the type of actor that he urges Arjuna and everyone else to be (Brodbeck 2003). A similar kind of delayed dharmic effect brought about by textual means might be imagined in other *mahāyugas* too, through the effect of the stories of other *avatāras*.

The sketched scenario provides a cosmic explanation for the *Mahābhārata*'s repeated focus upon its own importance and efficacy, which is, in a way, the point of the story of Janamejaya – hearing Vyāsa's tale enabled him to make peace with the snakes – and which is also stressed by the various verses that describe the benefits of engagement with the text as a whole, or specific parts of it. The following two verses from the *Mahābhārata*'s closing passage evoke a *kṛtayuga*:

idaṃ mahākāvyam ṛṣer mahātmanaḥ paṭhan nṛṇāṃ pūjyatamo bhaven naraḥ |
prakṛṣṭam āyuḥ samavāpya durlabhaṃ labheta sarvajñaphalaṃ ca kevalam ‖ Hv 118.43 ‖ ...
purāṇam etac caritaṃ mahātmanām adhītya buddhiṃ labhate ca naiṣṭhikīm |
vihāya duḥkhāni vimuktasaṅgaḥ sa vītarāgo vicared vasuṃdharām ‖ 49 ‖

This is the great seer Vyāsa's great poem.
People who study it become most praiseworthy,
live lives of rare length and distinction,
and receive the reward of total omniscience. ...

This is the ancient tale telling of great characters,
after pondering which a person attains the perfect perspective,
leaves sorrows and attachments behind,
and moves over the jewel-bearing earth free of desires.

(*Harivaṃśa* 118.43, 49)

Such verses might be seen merely as tools to keep the texts they are attached to alive and in use. From this angle, as Taylor puts it, such verses would 'serve to attract and maintain religious capital in a crowded, devotional marketplace, where the survival of a tradition relies on the financial and material resources provided by a devout audience to a body of expert purāṇic practitioners' (Taylor 2012: 93). But such an understanding underplays the nature of the claim being made about this text: namely, that it has the extraordinary power to change people in specific ways. This is the main story of the *Mahābhārata*. The text changed Janamejaya, and it can change you (Hegarty 2012: 54–64). Hudson puts it nicely:

> The fact that these two outer frames [the Naimiṣa Forest frame and the snake sacrifice frame] contextualize the epic's narration tells us something about the *Mahābhārata*'s relation to time. Since these stories that tell the circumstances (the where, when, why, and by whom) of the epic's first two telling are contained in the *Mahābhārata*, they are also ... *part* of the *Mahābhārata*. If we take this insight and extend it logically, the design of the epic suggests that whenever, wherever, or whoever tells or receives the story of the great Bhāratas becomes part of the *Mahābhārata*. In other words, through the art of its design, the text explodes the boundary between interiority and exteriority.
>
> (Hudson 2013: 165)

In the sketched scenario, after doing its work for a millennium or so, the powerful *Mahābhārata* would eventually change so many people so much that it would be *kṛtayuga*.

An objection to the sketched scenario is that although it can potentially account for the rebooting of *dharma* at the *kali–kṛtayuga* transition, it cannot account for the fact that when *dharma* is rebooted onto all fours, lifespan too is quadrupled at that same point, such that it can be said, hyperbolically, that death is absent in the *kṛtayuga*. This objection can only be countered by referring to the textual indications, mentioned in Chapter 2, that lifespan and *dharma* are intrinsically correlated. It is said on two occasions that when lifespan is reduced, *dharma* is reduced as a consequence (12.224.65; 12.230.14); and this causal effect is said to operate in the other direction too. In the *Harivaṃśa*'s account of Earth's problem, the reason why human population has grown so large is that because human beings are behaving so very dharmically, they do not fear Death (Hv 41.16). Hence when Earth comes to heaven to complain about the situation, she comes in company with the emaciated and suffering god Death (Hv 41.23; 43.66; 44.1). So just as reducing lifespan can reduce *dharma* at the first three *yuga*-transitions, so increasing *dharma* can increase lifespan at the final *yuga*-transition. Lifespan and *dharma* are two aspects of one complex variable. The complexity of the variable means that our attempts to understand the interaction between two of its various aspects in terms of plausible causality are unlikely to be satisfactory, and will certainly be incomplete. So although it might seem that the *kṛtayuga* could be brought about because the people become Nārāyaṇa-*bhakta*s, this kind of consequentialist account is really not adequate to the task.

To sum up regarding Janamejaya. He knows that the *dvāpara-kaliyuga* transition was just a few generations ago, so he knows that the *kali-kṛtayuga* transition is still a long way off. In terms of the *yuga*s as made by the king (Thomas 2007), when Janamejaya rules righteously in the years following his horse sacrifice (Hv 118.39–42), he can be living in the *kaliyuga* while at the same time making a local *kṛtayuga*. Prompted by what he has heard about the *kali-kṛtayuga* transition, he can imagine a future king who will make the new *kṛtayuga*, as Kalkin does in Mārkaṇḍeya's account, and/or he can imagine the *kṛtayuga* being made by future people more widely, through a groundswell of *dharma*, *bhakti*, and charity, in accordance with the message of the *Mahābhārata* and of the *Bhagavadgītā* within it.

The ancient audience and the *yuga*s

We now move beyond Janamejaya to consider Śaunaka, the next listener out. Śaunaka hears the story an unspecified period of time after the snake sacrifice.

The storyteller Ugraśravas arrives at Śaunaka's *satra* ritual in Naimiṣa Forest (Mbh 1.4). Ugraśravas was at Janamejaya's snake sacrifice, and he heard what Janamejaya heard there. He is received by Śaunaka, and he soon tells Janamejaya's full story (ending at Hv 118), including exactly what Janamejaya was told at and after the snake sacrifice.

Are Śaunaka and his guests still in the *kaliyuga*? Yes, they are. Although Ugraśravas does not tell Śaunaka how long ago it was that Janamejaya's snake sacrifice occurred, it does not seem to have been hundreds of years ago. Indeed it could not have been, for Ugraśravas, who was at the snake sacrifice, would only have a *kaliyuga* lifespan of a hundred years. And if Śaunaka is still in the *kaliyuga*, then the seers who are there at Śaunaka's *satra* or *satra*s in Naimiṣa Forest would still be in the *kaliyuga* too.

What do I mean by saying 'Śaunaka's *satra* or *satras*'? Well, when at the beginning of the *Mahābhārata* Ugraśravas addresses the seers at Śaunaka's *satra*, he – Ugraśravas – refers to his performance at Śaunaka's *satra* as something that took place in the past (Mbh 1.2.29–30, 70–71; Kosambi 1946: 111; Brodbeck 2009b: 244–245 n. 40). It seems that Śaunaka's *satra* was iterated. Beyond Śaunaka himself, but still in a ritual and narrative frame, there are seers who are about to hear what Śaunaka previously heard. Accordingly, the Śaunaka *satra* does not just occupy one particular point in the *kaliyuga*; it occupies an extended but unspecified period within the *kaliyuga*, during which the alleged audience of the text is expanding.

Now we can consider the *Mahābhārata*'s actual ancient audience: the early audience of the *Mahābhārata* as reconstituted by the critical editors and retrojected; the audience that the *Mahābhārata*-as-we-have-it was presented to. That audience is presented by the text as the audience of seers at the most recent of the iterated Śaunaka *satras*.[74] It is also presented as an audience of all genders and social classes, despite the fact that the story is overwhelmingly about great and well-born men.

The *Mahābhārata*, in all its aspects discussed above, was about this ancient audience, presented to this audience, and thus conditioned by this audience. By saying 'conditioned by', I do not imply that a previous and similar audience's reaction latterly fed back (though it may have done) into the ancient editing of the text that we have. I mean that the ancient audience, as an intended receiver, was a precondition of the text's existence in that form. In the same way, this monograph is conditioned by the audience that I imagine and know for it. We have here come to the ancient audience by working outwards through the *Mahābhārata*'s interlocutory frame stories until we fell off the edge of the text. But this audience conditions what is most innermostly framed as much as it conditions all the frames. The distinction between frame and framed is an artifice, a literary fiction – more broadly, an artistic fiction (Brodbeck 2016: 391–393).

Is the ancient audience still in the *kaliyuga*? Yes, it is, unless more than a millennium has passed between Janamejaya's snake sacrifice and the ancient audience, which seems unlikely. But nonetheless a considerable period of time has obviously passed since the snake sacrifice, and the *kaliyuga* might be quite far advanced by this stage. It would certainly be much further advanced than it was for Janamejaya and Śaunaka.[75]

The material about the *yugānta* that was presented to Yudhiṣṭhira and Janamejaya must be understood with the ancient audience in mind. The ancient audience was looking forward to the transition to the *kṛtayuga*, perhaps facilitated by Kalkin, or perhaps, Kalkin's appearance not forthcoming, in a scenario more akin to Vyāsa's account. Eltschinger says that 'Mārkaṇḍeya's teachings ... clearly reflect the belief that a thousand-year *kali-yuga* would imminently come to its end' (Eltschinger 2012: 44). But that belief cannot be Mārkaṇḍeya's belief at the time of his speech to Yudhiṣṭhira, since that was shortly before the *kaliyuga* started; it cannot be Yudhiṣṭhira's belief shortly after the war, when he asks Bhīṣma how one can stand firm 'with Law dwindling away as the Ages pass'

[74] If it is the same Ugraśravas at all of the Śaunaka *satras*, then this cannot cover much of the *kaliyuga*. But there is some scope for slippage into subsequent generations, since Ugraśravas continues the role and stories of his father Lomaharṣaṇa, and so the storyteller is always by implication the son-of-the-storyteller, with *sūta* and *sauti* being used to label him interchangeably. If he is a *sauti* because of his *sūta* father, then his sons can be *sauti*s because of theirs. By having Śaunaka relate to Ugraśravas through the always absent Lomaharṣaṇa, the text allows the iterated 'Śaunaka *satras*' to cover a potentially long period. This also means that the *Mahābhārata* can be backdated – that is, pretending to be older than it actually is. If the text may seem to suggest that the audience had grandfathers who heard more or less the same tale, perhaps they did not.

[75] Fleet notes that 'The popular view divides the Kaliyuga into six eras', citing the *Ain-i-Akbari* and various Hindu almanacs (Fleet 1911: 680); but this would be the 432,000-year *kaliyuga*.

(*yugakṣayāt parikṣīṇe dharme*, 12.138.1, trans. Fitzgerald 2004a: 529); and it cannot be Janamejaya's belief, since he lived just a few generations after that. It must be the belief of the text's presenters and ancient audience (González-Reimann 2009: 417, 422; González-Reimann 2013: 109; Bronkhorst 2015: 32–33, 37).[76] The ambiguity of the term *yugānta*, which refers to the *kaliyuga* in general and/or to the end of the *kaliyuga*, allows the text's accounts of the *yugānta* to work in different contexts that the text places centuries apart.

The *kaliyugānta* could already be setting in at the time the audience hears about it. The conversation between Janamejaya and Vyāsa at Hv 115–117 contains the text's most 'recent' account of the *yugānta* (generations after Mārkaṇḍeya's account), and although it describes the *yugānta* in the future tense, it could describe conditions prevailing at the time of the *Mahābhārata*'s distribution. Various scholars have connected the *Mahābhārata*'s descriptions of the *yugānta* with socio-political conditions at or before the time of the *Mahābhārata*'s distribution. This has often been done in parallel reference to similar issues for various Purāṇas (see Dwivedi 1977; Yadava 1979; Sharma 1982; Bailey 2008: 28–35).

Eltschinger notes that

> [T]he *Mārkaṇḍeya* section of the *Mahābhārata* as well as the *Yugapurāṇa*, both likely to have been composed or at least updated during the first two and a half centuries CE, consider foreign, *mleccha* rule as the hallmark of the *kali-yuga* and/or of its final period (*yugânta*).
> (Eltschinger 2012: 29–30)

The references to foreign rule fit the dating of the text, with Indo-Greeks, Indo-Scythians (Śakas), Indo-Parthians (Pahlavas), Kuṣāṇas, and Indo-Sassanians ruling in the north-west of the subcontinent between the second century BCE and the fourth century CE (Thapar 2000: 953–955; Thapar 2002: 213–225; González-Reimann 2013: 106–107). For *mleccha*s (barbarians) see 3.186.29–30; 3.188.29, 37, 45, 52, 70; Eltschinger 2012: 37; Bronkhorst 2015: 30; Eltschinger 2020: 47–48. In the *Yugapurāṇa*, the Śaka *mleccha*s are said to have severely attenuated male populations (though it is presented in the future tense; *Yugapurāṇa* 64–65, 82–86). Granoff comments on 'the very ancient identification of the *mleccha* or outsider with the demons, an identification that occurs as early as the *Śatapatha Brāhmaṇa*' (Granoff 1984: 292; *Śatapatha Brāhmaṇa* 3.2.1.24).

Foreign rule is one thing, Buddhists are another (González-Reimann 2009: 416). The *Mahābhārata* refers explicitly to Buddhists. Vyāsa says that at the

---

[76] Compare what Kane said (before the critical edition was complete): 'there is not a single [extant] work which thinks that the era of perfection may dawn in the very near future' (Kane 1973 [1946]: 886).

yugānta, '*śūdras* who follow the Buddha of the Śākyas will practise their religion dressed in ochre robes' (Hv 116.15; see p. 151 n. 72 above). Vyāsa also mentions 'many different kinds of sages who should never be sages' (*abhāvino bhaviṣyanti munayo bahurūpiṇaḥ* ‖ Hv 117.19cd). The *eḍūkas* that Mārkaṇḍeya refers to in Mbh 3 could be Buddhist sites (Mbh 3.188.64–66; Allchin 1957; Biardeau 1976: 132; Eltschinger 2012: 40; Bailey 2012: 687–688). And there are handful of references to *pāśaṇḍas* ('heretics', 3.186.43; 3.189.9; 12.138.40; 12.211.4, Wynne 2009: 385; 12.292.20; 13.24.56, 67). Again, these references broadly fit the (post-Buddhist, post-Aśokan) dating of the text.

Vyāsa makes the following prediction to Janamejaya:

> *audbhido bhavitā kaścit senānīḥ kāśyapo dvijaḥ* ।
> *aśvamedhaṃ kaliyuge punaḥ pratyāhariṣyati* ‖ Hv 115.40 ‖
> *tadyuge tatkulīnaś ca rājasūyam api kratum* ।
> *āhariṣyati rājendra* ...
>
> In the *kaliyuga* a certain army commander, a brahmin descended from Kaśyapa, will burst onto the scene and revive the horse sacrifice once again. In the same *yuga*, the same man from the same family will also offer the *rājasūya* rite, your supreme majesty ...
>
> (*Harivaṃśa* 115.40–41c)

This is Puṣyamitra, the first monarch in the historical Śuṅga dynasty, who removed the last Mauryan king and ruled in the first half of the second century BCE (Tsuchida 2009: 12–20; Tsuchida 2010: 9–14; Fitzgerald 2004a: 121–122). This event was in the future at the time of Janamejaya, but in the past at the time of the *Mahābhārata*'s distribution. The *yugānta* begins only some time after this character's appearance (Hv 115.42).

We noticed some ambiguities when we tried to locate Janamejaya precisely with respect to the *kaliyuga* (was he in its main body when he had his conversation with Vyāsa, or its dawn?) and with respect to the *yugānta* (when Vyāsa described the *yugānta*, was this the *kaliyuga* in general, or just its last part?). Vyāsa's repurposed description of the *yugānta* in the future tense seemed to indicate the scenario illustrated in Figure 15, whereby the last part of the *kaliyuga* is even worse than the main body of that *yuga*. But once we bring the ancient audience centre-stage, this ambiguity regarding Janamejaya is no longer such a problem, because what matters is the location of the audience. From their point of view, the question of whether Figure 15 is an accurate representation is somewhat academic. More striking is the impression that the *yugānta* conditions described in the future by Vyāsa now obtain in the present, and thus that the next change to occur will be a huge increase in the level of *dharma*. Vyāsa's account of the *kali–kṛtayuga* transition is thus far more relevant to the ancient audience than it was to Janamejaya, its immediate addressee.

The idea that the *Mahābhārata*'s ancient audience felt the *kaliyugānta* to be imminent, incipient, or actual depends upon the number of years. The *kaliyuga* is twelve hundred years long. So if the *kṛtayuga* had not yet begun, the audience must be placed – and must have placed themselves – not more than twelve hundred years after the Kurukṣetra war.

Had the numbers been understood as per the Purāṇic scheme where the *yuga*s are measured in years of the gods (and so the *kaliyuga* is 432,000 human years long), the end of the *kaliyuga* would still be a great distance in the future at the time of the *Mahābhārata*'s ancient audience, and so it would not make sense for the signs of the *kaliyugānta* to depict conditions resembling those at the time of the text's presentation. But as discussed in Chapter 2, the *Mahābhārata* numbers are in human years. Purāṇas commonly present future-tense *yugānta* descriptions that their ancient audiences would have recognised as descriptions of their present *kaliyuga*; but if in those Purāṇas the *kaliyuga* is said to last 432,000 years, such a *yugānta* cannot be interpreted as the *kaliyugānta*. In the *Mahābhārata* it can, and so when ancient audiences recognised the *Mahābhārata*'s *yugānta* descriptions as descriptions of their present, this implied – and was intended to imply – the imminent arrival of the next *kṛtayuga*.

In addition to the multiplication of the *yuga* durations by 360, a further aspect of the post-*Mahābhārata* tradition is the dating of the start of the *kaliyuga* in 3102 BCE. This dating is that of a conjunction of all the planets, an *exeligmos* (Pingree 1963: 239; see p. 44 above; Fleet 1911: 494–495, 679; van der Waerden 1978).[77] Pingree wrote to Gombrich that '*Only* astronomers from the fifth century AD on and their imitators begin the Kaliyuga on 17/18 February 3101; others (including the author of *Mahābhārata* XII) give no specific date' (Gombrich 1975: 140 n. 9). The *Mahābhārata* gives no specific date.

In the *Mahābhārata*, the beginning of the *kaliyuga* coincided with the Kurukṣetra war.[78] Other sources say that it coincided with Yudhiṣṭhira first taking up the throne of Indraprastha, or with the death of Kṛṣṇa some thirty-six years after the Kurukṣetra war, or with Yudhiṣṭhira's final abdication of the throne of Hāstinapura (Fleet 1911: 676–681 and special note B; on Kṛṣṇa's death see also Biardeau 1976: 146–147). If the *yuga* durations were numbered in divine years, then whichever of these narrative events it might mark, the

[77] Van der Waerden argues that 'the Hindu astronomers learnt about the conjunction of 3102 B.C. from the Persians', and that 'the "Persian System" with its conjunction of 3102 B.C. ... was ultimately derived from Hellenistic sources' (van der Waerden 1978: 374, 377).

[78] On the dating of the war, see Kane 1973: 902–923: 'attempts to settle the exact date of the Mahābhārata war on the strength of the astronomical materials contained therein are dismal failures' (p. 904); 'the astronomical passages ... are hopelessly inconsistent and ... no certain chronological conclusion can be drawn therefrom' (p. 923). In terms of the *exeligmos*, the salient line is this one: 'in the heavens the seven great planets converged in a blaze of light' (*dīpyamānāś ca saṃpetur divi sapta mahāgrahāḥ* ‖ 6.17.2cd, trans. van Buitenen 1981: 51).

dating of the beginning of the *kaliyuga* in 3102 BCE would still leave the end of the *kaliyuga* in the distant future. It would be as per Fleet's reckoning:

> [W]e are still in only the 'dawn' of the Kali age: this dawn lasts for 36,000 years; and the daytime of the age, with all its depraved characteristics fully developed, will not begin until A.D. 32,899.
>
> (Fleet 1911: 484)[79]

If, alternatively, the *yuga* durations were numbered in human years (as they are), then a dating of 3102 BCE for the start of the *kaliyuga* would place the early audiences of the *Mahābhārata* in the following *kṛtayuga*. As Gombrich says, 'once the beginning of the *kali yuga* was dated by astronomers at 3102 BC, simple arithmetic showed the epic bards that the *kali yuga* would already be over if it lasted only 1,200 years' (Gombrich 1975: 121). So this can help to explain the switch to numbering in years of the gods – and also the interpretive backdating of this switch into the *Mahābhārata* itself.

The *yuga* numbers make more sense if the Kurukṣetra war is seen as having occurred a millennium or so ago at the time of the early audiences. If the early audiences were in the common era, then 3102 BCE would be too early for the Kurukṣetra war. The drama of the *kaliyuga* in the *Mahābhārata* would be spoiled by placing the war there, whether or not the *yuga* durations were reckoned in divine years. So the 3102 BCE dating must be foreign to the text. González-Reimann dates that dating to the fifth century CE (González-Reimann 2014: 359).

The *Mahābhārata*'s descriptions of the future *yugānta* include commentary on events that were comparatively recent at the time of the text's distribution. This is what McGinn calls 'history disguised as prophecy' (McGinn 1979: 7; Eltschinger 2012: 31–32). But if the *kaliyuga* began at Kurukṣetra and was ending or soon to end, that sets quite a narrow chronological window for the ancient audience, within which the *yuga* aspect of the text would have had an urgent resonance. From this perspective, in terms of the title question, the Kurukṣetra *avatāra* would have to be placed at the *dvāpara–kaliyuga* transition so that the early audiences, this many years later, could be in or approaching the *kaliyugānta*.

After the ancient audience, the audience continues, eventually including ourselves. At some stage the switch to reckoning in divine years seems inevitable, even if that switch disarms the palpable urgency of the text's location in time: the imminence of the transition into *kṛtayuga*. That millenarian urgency defines the text and then, after a time, breaks it.

[79] See also Kane 1973: 923–926; Biardeau 1976: 122 ('the authors of our texts, and with them all the India of their time, were situated right at the beginning of the *kaliyuga*, that is, several hundred thousand human years away from the final cataclysm', 'les auteurs de nos textes, et avec eux toute l'Inde de leur temps, se situent au tout début de l'âge Kali, c'est-à-dire à plusieurs centaines de milliers d'années humaines du cataclysme final').

When we receive the text in the twenty-first century, we know we are still in the *kaliyuga*, since people do not live for four hundred years. But we also know that the Kurukṣetra war must be set more than twelve hundred years ago, since at the time of the text's first presentation, which was more than twelve hundred years ago, the war was already some distance in the past.

The fact that the text does not date the Kurukṣetra war means that its ancient audience are at liberty to imagine it having occurred a thousand years ago, or a little bit more. But they cannot imagine it having occurred more than twelve hundred years ago. Some audience members might imagine the start of the *kṛtayuga* to be more imminent than others, but the general effect is millenarian (Bronkhorst 2015: 30 n. 5). But it cannot continue to be so. After a few hundred years of the text being available in this form, it would lose that effect. In this it differs from, for example, Christian millenarianism, where the second coming of Christ can still be anticipated as imminent.

The relevant dating for the *Mahābhārata* is a relative dating: the dating of the audience member relative to the undated Kurukṣetra war. In terms of absolute dating, the above discussions would tend to suggest a date after Puṣyamitra and a good deal of *mleccha* rule, but before the Gupta period had fully settled in ('millenarian expectations continued until the early Guptas in the fourth century CE', Bronkhorst 2015: 41).

In this chapter, we began by locating Janamejaya a few generations after the Kurukṣetra war, early in the *kaliyuga*. We looked at Vyāsa's account, to Janamejaya, of the *yugānta* to come. We considered the implications, for Janamejaya and others, of the idea that the king makes the *yuga*. We studied Vyāsa's account of the transition to the next *kṛtayuga*, and we discussed the idea that the *Mahābhārata* delivered to Janamejaya might be a definitive work for the *kaliyuga*, a text inspired by the Kurukṣetra *avatāra* – its basic subject – to bring about, in time, the next *kṛtayuga*. In the final section of the chapter we zoomed the camera progressively out from Janamejaya, considering Śaunaka, and the seers, and then, more particularly, the ancient audience of the reconstituted *Mahābhārata*. For members of that audience, according to the *Mahābhārata*'s *yuga* scheme where the years are numbered in human years, there was the exquisite drama of their approaching the *mahāyugānta* itself. This drama, which has been mentioned by previous scholars but never detailed in its narrative operations, affects the text's basic orientation, freezes it within a specific time-window, and makes the *yuga* cycle a crucial aspect of what it is about.

CHAPTER 7

Conclusion

The project of this monograph is as per the title question: Why does the Kṛṣṇa *avatāra* inaugurate the worst *yuga*? In Chapter 3 we set up the question, and in Chapter 4 we discussed and problematised one possible answer: that the Kṛṣṇa *avatāra* does what an *avatāra* is required to do at any *yugānta*, which is to drag the bull up, from its latest collapse, onto the number of legs appropriate for the new *yuga*. In Chapter 5 we proposed another possible answer: that the Kṛṣṇa *avatāra* represents the dynamic of the *mahāyuga* as a whole, with two opposing *avatāra* functions superimposed, as it were. In Chapter 6, by focusing on Vyāsa's depiction of the *mahāyuga* transition in Hv 117, we envisioned the *Mahābhārata* itself as a vehicle for facilitating and prompting the *kali–kṛtayuga* transition in the near future, through its early audiences. That vision is broken now, in the twenty-first century, after such a passage of time. We now know that the *yuga* theory, as the *Mahābhārata* presents it, is wrong. But the idea that the king (or whoever) makes the *yuga* lives on.

In terms of the *mahāyuga* cycle as explored in Chapter 5, if there was too much *jāmi* at the start of the *mahāyuga*, and so Death had to be introduced in order to wobble the bull,[80] why does the space beyond the midpoint have to be so fully explored? Why, seeking non-extremity, would one go to the opposite extreme? Would one not correct back to the midpoint as soon as one had gone noticeably past it? Thus the bull could perhaps thereafter alternate between three and two legs. But bulls have four legs. And within human range as described by the text, there are four *yugas*, not two.

Can we locate the extremities within a wider context? The range from 4 to 1 might seem to be quite a gentle range, given how much lower than 1 and

[80] That reminds me of an old joke, playing on the word 'weebles'. Great winds kept blowing the cows over, but not the bulls. The cows asked the bulls why. The bulls replied: 'We bulls wobble but we don't fall down.' Weebles are a variety of egg-shaped self-righting children's toy.

How to cite this book chapter:
Brodbeck, S. 2022. Divine Descent and the Four World-Ages in the *Mahābhārata* – or, Why Does the Kṛṣṇa *Avatāra* Inaugurate the Worst *Yuga?*. Pp. 165–175. Cardiff: Cardiff University Press. DOI: https://doi.org/10.18573/book9.g.

how much higher than 4 some things can go. If we imagine a bull we can also imagine a spider, a centipede, or a snake. But the point of the bull's legs is that at first it is four out of four, with total plentitude, as it seems most proper for that beast to be, and that is why the gods complain about the humans, and that is also why the Earth complains, and why total plenitude can only obtain for forty per cent of the time. But that is a pretty good score. Forty per cent is a pass. And the fact that the stable nadir is the totality-as-four divided by four supplies some kind of security at the bottom end. By analogy with money (compare Seaford 2020: 17–37, 317–346), if the poorest people had a quarter as much wealth as the richest, that would look, from our point of view, as if it were a relatively economically equal society. In any case, in the *Mahābhārata* scheme there is faithful protection, by God, of the range between 4 and 1; and given that 4 tends towards infinity, who are we to say how far beyond the midpoint 1 might be? The same problem of extremities is present anywhere in a terrestrial hemisphere with regard to the year: if you stay in the same place and experience the year, the days get longer and shorter in a repeating cycle, and that is what the year is, there. However much difference there is between the lengths of the longest and the shortest days in that particular place as compared to other places, they are the longest and the shortest days there all the same, and it is the same year. Whatever stories we hear from whatever travellers, there is no way of knowing quite how thankful we should be; but we know that we should be thankful.

Avatāra revisited

In terms of theology, we must reflect on the differences between the implications of the instability theory, the representation theory, and the text-as-transformer theory. These three theories are not altogether incompatible with each other. But they are different approaches to the problem.

In the instability scenario, every *yugānta* requires an *avatāra* to destroy the demon and pull time across the gap. God's involvement is as a celestial mechanic, turning up reactively to replace a broken part. The *kaliyugānta* requires an *avatāra* just as any other *yugānta* does, but in a puzzlingly different way, since here the replacement part is not only better than it is anywhere else, but also takes longer to break again.

In the representation scenario, no *yugānta* requires an *avatāra*, but any *yugānta* can collect *avatāra* stories in terms of the *mahāyuga* dynamic as a whole. In this scenario we have found it hard to move from the textual accounts to a precise conceptualisation of what the *avatāra* actually does individually and causally within the world, and so we might prefer to think that time's progress through the *yuga*s could be smooth and unproblematic, as per the *yuga* machine, given God's constant *yoga* of sheer gravity and rotation (Figure 11). This is a theology different from that of the celestial mechanic.

In the text-as-transformer scenario, the *avatāra* provides the subject and voice for a text that eventually prompts the transition to the next *mahāyuga*. The *avatāra* would be required once per *mahāyuga*, and would be concerned only with the last of the four *yuga* transitions. But would the *avatāra* really be required? The point is the existence of the text and the power of the story that it carries (the story about, among other things, its own origin). Could the text and its power obtain independently of the actual truth of the story it presents? And beyond the idea of a delayed effect brought about through eventual mass conversion, what are the theological implications? Would there be just one *avatāra* per *mahāyuga*? At Hv 40.34–36 Nārāyaṇa, asleep apparently since the start of the *mahāyuga*, wakes up at the end of the *dvāparayuga*. Or would there be three *avatāra*s per *mahāyuga* as per the instability theory, with the third of these doing double duty in also bringing about the *kaliyugānta* later on, without any need for Kalkin? Or would the textual diffusion of the alleged *avatāra* at the *dvāparayugānta* into mass religious effect at the *kaliyugānta* imply a widening of the *avatāra* idea, beyond specific mythologised instances, into the population at large? If so, this would be compatible with the *yuga* machine, the text being, as it were, the bending of the twangy bar by the peg, priming it with molecular potential energy. But because of the intimate involvement of the masses, this would be a human theology from within the machine.

In terms of *avatāra* theology, the nature of the complex variable that changes from *yuga* to *yuga* is perplexing, because what has to happen at each *yuga* transition is very peculiar and specific, and it is hard to imagine any story being able to explain the required change in straightforward terms. In the representations of the *avatāra* function of reducing the Earth's burden, an eighteen-day cull of *kṣatriya*s is asked to stand in for a shift in the level of lifespan, *dharma*, and whatever else. It can only do that symbolically, because in the short term it would only mean that those particular *kṣatriya*s would suddenly be dead. How would it make everyone henceforth die younger? Likewise, in the instability theory the *avatāra* stories require the demon to stand as a symbol or impression of what the *avatāra* acts against. But how can such a strange level-control be adjusted by the physical defeat of a demon? Within each story, the presented problems can only be solved by Viṣṇu in response to their presentations. But what would the actual problem be at the end of a *yuga*? When the level is no longer correct for the time, it must change. To present this problem-and-change narratively, with such a complex variable, is impossible. The narrative will focus on causation, which can only be applied by singling out one aspect of the variable. So even if we suspend disbelief and allow the killing of a demon to stand for a general increase in *dharma*, or a cull of *kṣatriya*s to stand for a general decrease in lifespan, still we would have to suspend disbelief again, and in a different way, to think that that would mean an equal change in all the other aspects or parameters that make up the complex variable. This second suspension of disbelief is encouraged by the various verses where a shift in one parameter is said to cause a corresponding shift in another. But although such verses show that the poets appreciated the implications of the *yuga* scheme, they cannot serve as an aid to comprehension; the causal story of what happens at a *yuga* transition breaks down. The last causal story to remain is the story of the text and the people it works through; but even then it is not credible in causal terms. We cannot believe that if everyone kept trying to follow Kṛṣṇa's advice and example and so everyone became four times as dharmic, that would mean people would live to four hundred years of age – still less that they would be four times as large, or that nearly five thousand years after that, all those changes would be reversed by a specific fraction. The problem is as intractable to solution by mass human conversion as it is to solution by specific *avatāra* action: either way, we cannot imagine what needs to change being changed causally from within the machine. What happens at *yuga* transitions has to be part of what is always already being done to and through the machine from without.

Here we can take recourse in the notion of two forms of *brahman*, time and the timeless (*kāla* and *akāla*), as mentioned in the *Maitrī Upaniṣad* (see pp. 128–129 above; Shulman 2014: 46, 65–66; Cohen 2020). As Hawking showed, time comes into existence with the universe; there is no 'before' the universe (Hawking 1988). If we imagine multiple universes, it is as misleading to think of them as consecutive as it is to think of them as parallel. But if the *Mahābhārata*'s theology requires there to be something outside time, this can be the *akāla brahman*, which, by dint of what it is, sets the terms for what happens, structurally, within time and as time.

From an *akāla* perspective (if we can talk of such a thing), any stories of Viṣṇu's *avatāra*s are myths, and those famous characters alive at the time of the Kurukṣetra war are not *avatāra*s in any special sense. Viṣṇu is incarnated as Kṛṣṇa, but while he acts within time as Kṛṣṇa, he is acting equally at all other points too, as if uniformly from within and without, through everything and everyone. If there is something holy here, it is not here in any greater measure at certain points than at others. The stories of God doing something in particular are always partial and incomplete. Whatever Viṣṇu might be portrayed as doing in incarnated form, he is also in an important sense not doing it, because it is always something he would have been doing anyway, even in non-incarnated form; thus the transition to the *kṛtayuga* can happen with or without Kalkin.

> *na me pārthāsti kartavyaṃ triṣu lokeṣu kiṃ cana* |
> *nānavāptam avāptavyaṃ varta eva ca karmaṇi* ‖ Bhg 3.22 ‖
> *yadi hy ahaṃ na varteyaṃ jātu karmaṇy atandritaḥ* |
> *mama vartmānuvartante manuṣyāḥ pārtha sarvaśaḥ* ‖ 23 ‖
> *utsīdeyur ime lokā na kuryāṃ karma ced aham* |

> I have no task at all to accomplish in these three worlds, Pārtha. I have nothing to obtain that I do not have already. Yet I move in action. If I

were not to move in action, untiringly, at all times, Pārtha, people all around would follow my lead. These people would collapse if I did not act ...

(*Bhagavadgītā* 3.22–24b, trans. van Buitenen 1981: 83)

And whatever Viṣṇu might not be portrayed as doing in incarnated form – because, for example, it is what he is apparently acting against – is always something that he is also doing in equal measure. Everything is all God. We are all God (Ginsburg 1994: 27). The mythology of isolated *avatāras* is picturesque and exemplary and makes for good stories, but theologically it is misleading.

Viṣṇu's wholesale presence throughout the cosmos is expressed repeatedly. When Arjuna requests to hear about Kṛṣṇa's divine self-manifestations (*divyā hy ātmavibhūtayaḥ*, Bhg 10.16b), Kṛṣṇa describes himself as the superlative member of every set – as Viṣṇu among the Ādityas, the sun among illuminations, and so on.

yad yad vibhūtimat sattvaṃ śrīmad ūrjitam eva vā ǀ
tat tad evāvagaccha tvaṃ mama tejoṃśasaṃbhavam ǁ Bhg 10.41 ǁ

You should know that whatever being has splendor, glory or might is made from a spark of my brilliance.

(*Bhagavadgītā* 10.41, trans. Cherniak 2008: 247)

In this frame, the divine is opposed to the demonic (*dvau bhūtasargau loke 'smin daiva āsura eva ca* ǀ Bhg 16.6ab). But while this kind of description is fitting insofar as the cosmos works dialectically through the tension between one polarity and another, it is only part of the story. Before listing his divine manifestations, Kṛṣṇa says that he is responsible for both poles of any opposition – fear and fearlessness, fame and infamy (Bhg 10.4–5). Moreover, the ability to see both poles of any opposition as radically equal is the hallmark of the perspective for which the sages strive, the attainment of which indicates that one has, as it were, graduated beyond the cosmos: 'the undeluded, free from the opposites called pleasure and pain, go to the permanent place' (*dvaṃdvair vimuktāḥ sukhaduḥkhasaṃjñair gacchanty amūḍhāḥ padam avyayaṃ tat* ǁ Bhg 15.5cd). The successful *yogin* 'doesn't object to clarity, activity or confusion when they appear ... nor long for them when they disappear' (*prakāśaṃ ca pravṛttiṃ ca moham eva ca pāṇḍava* ǀ *na dveṣṭi saṃpravṛttāni na nivṛttāni kāṅkṣati* ǁ Bhg 14.22, trans. Cherniak 2008: 277, as are other imminent translations). Such a *yogin* 'is equable in pain and pleasure' (*samaduḥkhasukhaḥ*, 14.24a), 'has the same attitude towards clods of earth, stones, and gold' (*samaloṣṭāśmakāñcanaḥ*, 14.24b), 'is indifferent to pleasant and unpleasant things, and to being praised or blamed, and to honor and dishonor, [and] behaves the same towards friendly and antagonistic parties' (*tulyapriyāpriyo dhīras tulyanindātmasaṃstutiḥ* ‖ *mānāvamānayos tulyas tulyo mitrāripakṣayoḥ* | 14.24–25).

> *sarvabhūteṣu yenaikaṃ bhāvam avyayam īkṣate* |
> *avibhaktaṃ vibhakteṣu taj jñānaṃ viddhi sāttvikam* ‖ Bhg 18.20 ‖
>
> Know that the knowledge by which one perceives the indestructible reality as a unity in all creatures, undivided among the divided, is *sattva* knowledge.
>
> (*Bhagavadgītā* 18.20, trans. Cherniak 2008: 293)

This being the case, the principle of *avatāra*, insofar as it is apparently the concentration of God in one place rather than another, must be provisional and perspectival.

The spreading and inclusive nature of the *avatāra* idea is evident not just within but also beyond the *Mahābhārata*, for example in the so-called 'Vaiṣṇava Purāṇas', where many characters who are not said to be *avatāras* of Viṣṇu in the *Mahābhārata* are re-presented as such (Sutton 2000: 156–166), and in the Purāṇa and other genres more widely, where other characters unmentioned in the *Mahābhārata* are said to be *avatāras*. '[T]he *avatāra* theory is open-ended, allowing for numerous future and present incarnations as well as the past incarnations celebrated in the epics and the *purāṇas*' (Granoff 1984: 301 n. 1). In principle anyone can be an *avatāra*; and sometimes an *avatāra* can appear for just one person. In this inclusive sense, the idea of *avatāra* would not have anything to do with the *yuga* theory except in a localised, microcosmic way – for example, in the way that a good king would make it, in his prime, the *kṛtayuga* for his realm, wherever he might be in the *mahāyuga* (Thomas 2007). An *avatāra* killing some demons, or a good king making it a local *kṛtayuga*, can be accommodated as long as the *dharma* average fits the *yuga*. But there is more than this, because if the concept of *avatāra* is a guarantee that time will be as time should be at any given point in the *mahāyuga*, then the boosting of *dharma* celebrated by the *Bhagavadgītā*'s statement of the *avatāra* function is only one aspect of the story: the aspect that keeps the complex variable at level 1 or above. Equally important is the amoral aspect – the other function of the *avatāra* – that keeps the complex variable at level 4 or below, and that makes it fall down through the levels as it should. Once the *avatāra* concept is seen to include both functions, there is no need for *avatāras* to be morally good (this is perhaps particularly true in the case of Kṛṣṇa); and the *avatāra* task of making time be as time should be is a task discharged collectively, at all times, by all the inhabitants of the universe, by manifesting the precise balance of qualities that they find themselves to have. If, as per Vyāsa's transition account, when it is the new *kṛtayuga* it is so insofar as people have become dramatically more dharmic (and long-lived), then by the same token, when it is the new *tretāyuga* (or *dvāparayuga*, or *kaliyuga*) it is so insofar as people have become slightly but significantly more adharmic (and short-lived).

Time

Hudson says of the *Mahābhārata* that 'transforming our understanding of time is at the heart of its ethical project of refiguring our understanding of suffering' (Hudson 2013: 147). I think this is right. Hudson then discusses what she calls two 'theories of time' in the *Mahābhārata*: the *yuga* theory (pp. 149–156) and the *kālavāda* (literally 'talk about time', pp. 156–163). The *yuga* theory is as described in the present monograph, especially in Chapter 2. The *kālavāda* is the genre of commentary on the sheer power of time to change things inexorably, to revolve and reverse what used to be the case (Barua 1921: 199–212; Vassilkov 1999). The law of time (*kāladharman*) is the law of death, and time is always cooking or ripening creatures (root *pac*), driving them towards the madness of their doom. Time is thus to be blamed for untimely death. Hudson identifies two *kālavāda* sub-genres in the *Mahābhārata*: the lament (Hudson 2013: 157–159), and the argument against grief (pp. 160–163). The lament is an exclamation about the awesome power of time to effect changes, as if casually, that will have enormous existential implications – a power that stands in contrast to the utter powerlessness of those who suffer those implications. The argument against grief is the proposition that because the facts of time are such brute, irrevocable, and universal facts, responding to them with grief is inappropriate and unhelpful. As Hudson points out, the *yuga* theory and the *kālavāda* have very different contexts, the former being macrocosmic, the latter microcosmic (pp. 163–164).

But Hudson implies that the *kālavāda* is more integral to the *Mahābhārata* than the *yuga* theory is (Hudson 2013: 164). She joins González-Reimann in sidelining the *yuga* theory, although she does not make the historical claim that it was a comparatively recent addition into an expanding *Mahābhārata*, instead resting on judgements of the scope of its play within the narrative. Hudson says that 'there are only two extensive discussions of the *yugas* in the *Mahābhārata*' (Hanūmat's and Mārkaṇḍeya's), and that 'Neither is located "in the thick of things," that is, in the midst of the heat of the action of the central narrative' (p. 151). That is an obscure judgement, and it looks as if, following González-Reimann, Hudson does not want to engage the *yuga* theory with the *Mahābhārata* narrative. She discourages such engagement by exaggerating the marginality of the *yuga* theory. She has a similar view of the *avatāra* theory, referring to Sutton, who says that 'despite the centrality of Kṛṣṇa to the theism of the narrative, in didactic terms the notion of *avatāra* remains a peripheral concept' (Sutton 2000: 166; Hudson 2013: 200 n. 94).

In this monograph we have taken up these two subjects, *yuga* and *avatāra*, and tried to understand them in light of each other, and in light of the text as a whole. They are not peripheral, though in the ongoing wake of Hopkins's scheme of hypothetical *Mahābhārata* expansion we have only been able to show this by employing a resolutely synchronic method. Such a method requires the text to include the *Harivaṃśa*, without which, as it happens, many of the *Mahābhārata*'s crucial passages on these subjects would be missing.

The *Mahābhārata* is trying, as Hudson suggests, to transform our understanding of time. And the *avatāra* and *yuga* ideas, and the locations of the Kurukṣetra war and the early audiences in relation to the *yuga* cycle, are some of the tools it uses. Hudson is interested in 'the epic's who-dunnit quest, posed in the form of riddle-questions, of why things went so horribly wrong' (Hudson 2013: 156), which is a quest performed on the level of what we might call human wisdom ethics. But hand in hand with this focus upon the human aspect, Hudson sidelines the divine context of the Kurukṣetra war, which involves also its temporal context within the *yuga* cycle (pp. 138–139 n. 132). In doing so she weakens the resonances of the long-form inevitability of how time works, and in common with many prior scholars she weakens the resonances of the words that are used in the context of the incarnated gods doing their job as humans. The word for inevitability used in connection with the events of the dicing scene and the Kurukṣetra war is often *daiva*, which in this context is usually best translated (see Biardeau 1976: 143) as 'the business of the gods' or even 'the secret of the gods', since it pertains directly to the plan detailed at 1.58–61, whose crucial actors are incarnated divinities. This aspect of the word *daiva* – that is, the divine plan – is neglected by Fitzgerald's translation of *daiva* as 'fate' at 11.8.17–31 (quoted above, pp. 131–133) and elsewhere. It is also neglected by Shulman 1992, by Hudson, and by Black 2021 (see Brodbeck 2022: 205–206). Where the word is *kāla* rather than *daiva* (Hudson 2013: 170), this would have a similar resonance (as at Bhg 11.32).

Hudson hopes that by means of *Mahābhārata* study a person might 'no longer be subject to the sorrow that time brings'; might be 'no longer swayed by the strong emotional responses that time's ravages cause'; might 'in essence move beyond time in the sense that he or she would no longer be psychologically terrorized by time' (Hudson 2013: 175). In this respect, according to our discussions in Chapter 6, it might make a difference **when** the text is studied. Nonetheless, I think that what Hudson evokes here is probably something similar to what Kṛṣṇa suggests to Arjuna as the *bhaktiyoga* of non-attached action in the *Bhagavadgītā*. If this is something that is achieved by the text through its own strategies of manipulating the audience, then it is indeed a very good trick. The transformative power of the text is an emergent emphasis of the foregoing monograph, as it is of Hudson's; but Hudson does not credit the *daiva* perspective in its *yuga* context, which can somehow explain the event of all those men dying. The *yuga* cycle can frame some kind of explanation for massive violent bloodshed which is otherwise hard to make sense of.

Sometimes terrible things happen, and that has always been the case. Sometimes in wars the numbers are barely credible, and each of the people who died had a mother, and other relatives. People die in large numbers in all kinds of other ways too, not just in wars; but when they die in wars it cannot be called an accident, it seems like human self-harm, and it calls for detailed review. That is part of what is happening when Vaiśampāyana tells Janamejaya about the Kurukṣetra war that happened at the *dvāparayugānta*, or when schoolchildren are taught about the first and second world wars. Large-scale wars perhaps lend themselves to being viewed as watersheds in history; but the story of the Kurukṣetra war differs from the standard story of either world war by including the divine perspective, which purports to explain the war irrespective of analysis at the human level of the characters involved (their ethical situations, their ethical or unethical decisions, and so on). For reasons that are fairly fully explained, it had to be the case that all those men died there. It was an exceptional case. The story of the Kurukṣetra war also has (or at least had) implications for the future, in the drama of the *mahāyuga* wearing on towards and into the *mahāyugānta*. And this is all part of the *kālavāda*. So I would like to dissolve the distinction that Hudson makes between the *yuga* theory and the *kālavāda*: the *yuga* theory has technical aspects, but it is a central part (as at 12.230) of the central *kālavāda* discourse.

Return to the title question

In this monograph I have tried to engage with the text and previous scholarship in an attempt to answer the title question as well as is conveniently possible for me. To what extent I have presented a novel response to the question is for the reader to judge. It is novel at least in being presented explicitly in monograph form, but it is hampered by my ignorance of much relevant scholarship on many of the subjects touched upon. My answer is not easily stated, because it involves two incommensurable understandings of the *avatāra*, a representational understanding (as per Chapter 5) and a causal understanding (as per Bhg 4.8, the instability theory, and the text-as-transformer theory), neither of which are up to the task, but neither of which can easily be transcended, given the narrative medium of the *Mahābhārata*'s textual presentation from its specific location within spacetime and the discursive medium of my own presentation from its. So instead of a single answer, here, by way of summary, is a cumulative set of six partial answers, or aspects of the answer. Where they repeatedly say 'The Kṛṣṇa *avatāra* inaugurates the worst *yuga* because ...', the 'because' means not 'so that' or 'in order that', but 'on account of the fact that'. The intent of the title question was not to ask after the purpose of the Kṛṣṇa *avatāra* so much as to ask how an *avatāra* could occur at this particular moment, given the friction between the *avatāra* idea at Bhg 4.8 and the condition in which Kṛṣṇa left time.

1. The Kṛṣṇa *avatāra* inaugurates the worst *yuga* because shortly after the Earth registered her official complaint (as per 1.58 and Hv 40–45), the *dvāparayuga* expired and the *kaliyuga* began. The precise timing of the Earth's complaint was due to the particular complexity and sensitivity of her affliction. Despite being juxtaposed with its beginning, the *avatāra* does not make the *kaliyuga* happen. Any *yuga* transition involves a change in the level of *dharma* (and lifespan, and so on), but no causal, narrative, or

mythical dramatisations of the change could hope to capture the complexity of the variable whose level is changing. The various markers that the text applies to this *dvāpara–kaliyuga* moment – dharmic decay, dharmic rescue, demonic activity, divine descent, overpopulation, class massacre, Kṛṣṇa-*bhakti*, and so on – do not all sit easily together (some would speculate on the recentness of their combination), and even together they can only gesture towards what a *yuga* transition would realistically involve.

2. Nonetheless, at the *dvāpara–kaliyuga* transition the level is changing, and stories about that are inevitable. The Kṛṣṇa *avatāra* inaugurates the worst *yuga* because although many reported *avatāras* are nothing to do with transitions between ages of humanity or society (the apparently cosmogonic *avatāras*, for example, have hardly been mentioned in this monograph), nonetheless if there are any *avatāras* at all, then a transition between *yugas* is an appropriate place for an *avatāra* to be, since it involves something special and complicated happening to time, akin to what happens when time starts or ends. The rationale of the *avatāra* as a mode of divine action is to operate on time, and temporal difference within the cosmos is registered paradigmatically at *yuga* transitions.
3. The Kṛṣṇa *avatāra* inaugurates the worst *yuga* because the *dvāpara–kaliyuga* transition is one of the two transitions which do not register a change in the direction of change, and so are appropriate points at which to represent a composite view of the *mahāyuga* cycle as a whole and the dynamics of the two *avatāra* functions that govern it. This aspect of the Kṛṣṇa *avatāra* is potentially shared with the two Rāma *avatāras* at the *tretā–dvāparayuga* transition, but the following aspects are particular to the Kṛṣṇa *avatāra*, at least as far as Viṣṇu's *avatāras* are concerned.
4. The Kṛṣṇa *avatāra* inaugurates the worst *yuga* because Kṛṣṇa's life spanned the previous and the current *yugas*, and the current *yuga* – the one that Janamejaya, Śaunaka, the ancient audience, and we ourselves are in – must be the worst *yuga*, since lifespan is a hundred years and so on. Compared to Viṣṇu's other famous *avatāras* (with the possible exception of Kalkin), Kṛṣṇa is quite proximate to Janamejaya, Śaunaka, and the ancient audience, in time and in existential quality. In this respect Kṛṣṇa has something in common with the other members of the *avatāra* team of 1.58–61 and Hv 43 that he does not have in common with the other *avatāras* of Viṣṇu. In this aspect God has a special relationship with how the text's primary listeners found the world non-negotiably to be.
5. The Kṛṣṇa *avatāra* inaugurates the worst *yuga* because, as the most perfect recipient of *bhakti*, Viṣṇu-Nārāyaṇa is particularly important in that *yuga*. This aspect has to do with the soteriological peculiarities of life during the *yugānta*, which apply to the text's ancient audience.

6. The Kṛṣṇa *avatāra* inaugurates the worst *yuga* because the *Mahābhārata*'s transformative story of Viṣṇu being Kṛṣṇa at Kurukṣetra at the start of that *yuga*, and of him teaching Arjuna about Arjuna and himself in the *Bhagavadgītā*, is a large part of how that *bhakti* works. Through what it does in the *kaliyuga*, the *Mahābhārata* helps to get the world ready for the *kṛtayuga* to come. But the *Mahābhārata* cannot cause the *kṛtayuga* to come, because although it can potentially account for a dramatic rise in *dharma*, it cannot realistically do the same for lifespan, bodily size, and so on. In this aspect the *avatāra* plants a seed which takes 1,200 years to bear fruit.

Opinions will no doubt differ on questions such as how neocolonial this monograph might be, but I hope that I have assembled the most relevant passages, and I hope that if I have told their story badly, they may tell it better themselves by being discussed here, and others may tell it better after me. There is much more to be done (for example, on the two Rāmas at the *tretā–dvāparayuga* transition). The key passages for answering the title question are the accounts of the Earth's problem, which have a gendered resonance with the human story of Draupadī's complaint following the first dicing match. The text shows the scene with the Earth from various angles, and one of them is to conflate the two functions of the *avatāra* up front in the 1.58 account. Hiltebeitel contextualises this *Mahābhārata* scene historically in the wake of 'India's second urbanization' (Hiltebeitel 2018: 246–263), but the mythology of the Earth's complaint has a new resonance for us in the twenty-first century, in the days of climate change following centuries of industrial pollution and exploitation. I have not explored that avenue. Nor have I sought to apply the *yuga* scheme to the present day, except insofar as you or I, dear reader, will be lucky to live to be a hundred, and so if we were in a *yuga*, it would be the *kaliyuga*. I suppose, against the numbers in *Genesis*, that all our ancestors would have been in that same *kaliyuga* too, since I do not expect many of them lived to be more than a hundred either. I have not advocated that you or anyone else convert yourself to Kṛṣṇa's yogic method as described in the *Bhagavadgītā* in order to hasten the *kṛtayuga*, but I would generally encourage the making of local *kṛtayuga*s, within reason. I hope that these research results are of interest to scholars of world theology, world literature, theoretical cosmology, Hinduism, and religious studies. The productive bipolarity sketched in Chapter 5 can be elaborated indefinitely through cosmogony, reproductive phenomenology, psychotherapy, Sāṃkhya philosophy, *yoga* praxis, and so on.

Outro: 'Who Knows where the Time Goes?', by Sandy Denny.

Glossary of Sanskrit Words

adharma	poor behaviour
agnicayana	a Vedic rite involving the construction of a large altar
agnihotra	(morning and evening) worship of fire
ahaṃkāra	'I-maker', ego
akāla	timeless
antakāla	end-time
āśrama	way or stage of life
asura	demon, antigod
avatāra	'crossing-down', divine descent, manifestation
avataraṇa	'crossing-down', divine descent, manifestation; taking-down, removal
avyakta	unmanifest
bala	strength, power
bhakta	devotee
bhakti	devotion, sharing
bhaktiyoga	discipline of devotion
bhārāvataraṇa	removal of a burden
brahman	the impersonal absolute
caturyuga	(cycle of) four world-ages
daitya	a type of demon descended from Diti
daiva	divine, of the gods, the business of the gods
dāna	charity

dānava	a type of demon descended from Danu
dharma	duty, proper behaviour, meritorious behaviour
divya	divine
dvāpara	name of the penultimate world-age, a dice throw, and a divine being
dvāparayuga	the penultimate world-age
dvāparayugānta	the end, or last part, of the penultimate world-age
gandharva	a type of semidivine being associated with music and lovemaking
gavām ayana	'course of the cows', a Vedic rite
guṇa	quality, any of the three qualities making up the psycho-physical world
jāmi	similarity, relatedness
jñāna	knowledge
kāla	time, death
kālavāda	discourse about time
kali	name of the final world-age, a dice throw, and a divine being
kalidvāra	entrance into the final world-age
kaliyuga	the final (and worst) world-age
kaliyugānta	the end, or last part, of the final world-age
kalpa	a full cycle of the world, from creation to destruction
kalpabheda	differentiation of one cycle of the world from another
karmayoga	discipline of dutiful action
kaṣāya	ochre-coloured
khila parvan	supplementary book
kṛṣṇa	dark
kṛta	name of the first world-age and a dice throw
kṛtayuga	the first (and best) world-age
kṛtayugānta	the end, or last part, of the first world-age
kṣatra	the military and ruling class
kṣatriya	a member of the military and ruling class
mahābhūta	gross element, great being
mahākalpa	great world-cycle
mahāyuga	cycle of four world-ages
mahāyugabheda	differentiation of one cycle of four world-ages from another
mahāyugānta	the end, or last part, of a cycle of four world-ages
manvantara	period of time supervised by a Manu
māyā	illusion, transcendental power
mleccha	foreigner, barbarian, outsider
niṣāda	tribal person, savage
nivṛtti	disengagement, quiescence
pāda	foot, quarter-verse
parvan	book

prādurbhāva	manifestation
prakṛti	psychophysical substance
pralaya	end of the world
pravṛtti	engagement, activity
pṛthak	difference, differentiation
purāṇa	ancient lore; a genre of texts
puruṣa	soul, spiritual principle
puṣya	name of the final world-age and an asterism
rajas	the quality of passion and drive
rājasūya	a Vedic royal rite
rākṣasa	monster, demon
sahasrānte	at the end of a thousand
saṃdhi	junction, transition
saṃdhyā	junction, transition
satra	extended ritual session
sattva	the quality of clarity
sātvata	a member of Kṛṣṇa's community; associated with Kṛṣṇa's people
sātvata vidhi	the religion or method of Kṛṣṇa's people
satya	truth, truthfulness; name of the first world-age
sauptika	relating to sleep; attack on the sleeping; name of a book (Mbh 10)
saura	solar
sauti	descendant of a storyteller
śūdra	member of the servile class
sūta	storyteller
tad ekam	'that one'; precosmic entity
tamas	the quality of inertia
tapas	asceticism, disciplined self-deprivation
tiṣya	name of the final world-age and an asterism
tretā	name of the second world-age and a dice throw
tretāyuga	the second world-age
tretāyugānta	the end, or last part, of the second world-age
triguṇa	the three qualities making up the psychophysical world
triloka	three worlds, triple world
triyuga	three world-ages, of three world-ages
upākhyāna	story, substory
varṇa	class, type, occupational social class
vāyuprokta	promulgated by (the wind-god) Vāyu
vedāṅga	any one of the six 'limbs' or auxiliary sciences of the Veda
yajamāna	sacrificer, ritual patron
yajña	(sacrificial) ritual
yakṣa	a type of semidivine being associated with terrestrial nature

yoga	discipline, personal praxis
yogin	disciplined practitioner
yuga	age, eon, world-age, world-cycle
yugadharma	meritorious action appropriate to the world-age
yugānta	the end, or last part, of the age
yugāntadvāra	entrance into the last part of the age

Bibliography

A Midsummer Night's Dream: see https://myshakespeare.com/midsummer-nights-dream/act-1-scene-1

Adams, T 2021 Judith Kerr was right, time flies for adults, but childhood lasts half a lifetime. *The Guardian*, 9 May. https://www.theguardian.com/commentisfree/2021/may/09/judith-kerr-right-times-flies-for-adults

Adluri, V & J Bagchee 2014 *The nay science: A history of German Indology*. New York: Oxford University Press.

Adluri, V & J Bagchee 2016 Bloß Glaube? Understanding academic constructions of bhakti in the past century. In: E Francis & C Schmid (eds.), *The archaeology of bhakti II: Royal bhakti, local bhakti*. Pondicherry: Institut Français de Pondichéry. pp. 79–126.

Allchin, F R 1957 Sanskrit *Eḍūka* – Pāli *Eluka*. *Bulletin of the School of Oriental and African Studies* 20: 1–4.

Allen, N 2006 Just war in the *Mahābhārata*. In: R Sorabji & D Rodin (eds.), *The ethics of war: Shared problems in different traditions*. Aldershot: Ashgate. pp. 138–149.

Allen, N 2019 *Arjuna-Odysseus: Shared heritage in Indian and Greek epic*. London: Routledge.

Āpastamba Dharmasūtra: see Olivelle 2000.

Āryabhaṭṭīya: see Shukla & Sarma 1976.

Bailey, G 1985 *Materials for the study of ancient Indian ideologies: Pravṛtti and nivṛtti*. Turin: Indologica Taurinensia.

Bailey, G 2008 On the significance of the *Mahābhārata* as a cultural artefact in early historical India (400BCE–400CE). *Indologica Taurinensia* 34: 13–37.

Bailey, G 2012 *Sthavirabuddhayaḥ* in the Mārkaṇḍeyasamāsyaparvan of the Mahābhārata: Problems in locating critiques of Buddhism in the Mahābhārata. In: F Voegeli, V Eltschinger, D Feller, M P Candotti, B Diaconescu, & M Kulkarni (eds.), *Devadattīyam: Johannes Bronkhorst felicitation volume.* Bern: Peter Lang. pp. 685–701.

Balkaran R 2022 The *Bhagavad Gītā* and beyond: Synchronic strategy for Sanskrit narrative literature. *Religions of South Asia* 15(2) (for 2021): 120–141.

Balslev, A N 1984 An over-all view of the problem of time in Indian philosophy. *Indologica Taurinensia* 12: 39–48.

Barua, B 1921 *A history of pre-Buddhistic Indian philosophy.* Calcutta: Calcutta University Press.

Belvalkar, S K (ed.) 1947 *The Bhīṣmaparvan, being the sixth book of the Mahābhārata, the great epic of India, for the first time critically edited.* Poona: Bhandarkar Oriental Research Institute.

Belvalkar, S K (ed.) 1954 *The Śāntiparvan, being the twelfth book of the Mahābhārata, the great epic of India, for the first time critically edited. Part III: Mokṣadharma, A.* Poona: Bhandarkar Oriental Research Institute.

Bhagavadgītā: see *Mahābhārata* 6.23–40.

Bhandarkar, R G 1965 [1913] *Vaiṣṇavism, Śaivism and minor religious systems.* Varanasi: Indological Book House.

Biardeau, M 1976 Études de mythologie hindoue (IV). *Bulletin de l'École Française d'Extrême-Orient* 63: 111–262. Reprinted in M Biardeau, *Études de mythologie hindoue II: Bhakti et avatāra*, Pondicherry: École Française d'Extrême-Orient, 1994. pp. 1–145.

Biardeau, M 1981 The salvation of the king in the *Mahābhārata. Contributions to Indian Sociology* (new series) 15(1–2): 75–97.

Biardeau, M 1994 [1981] *Hinduism: The anthropology of a civilization*, trans. Richard Nice. Delhi: Oxford University Press.

Biardeau, M 1997 Some remarks on the links between the epics, the Purāṇas and their Vedic sources. In: G Oberhammer (ed.), *Studies in Hinduism: Vedism and Hinduism.* Vienna: Verlag der Österreichischen Akademie der Wissenschaften. pp. 69–177.

Black, B 2007 Eavesdropping on the epic: Female listeners in the *Mahābhārata.* In: S Brodbeck & B Black (eds.), *Gender and Narrative in the Mahābhārata.* London: Routledge. pp. 53–78.

Black, B 2021 *In dialogue with the Mahābhārata.* London: Routledge.

Bowlby, P 1991 Kings without authority: The obligation of the ruler to gamble in the *Mahābhārata. Studies in Religion/Sciences Religieuses* 20(1): 3–17.

Bowles, A (trans.) 2008 *Mahābhārata book eight: Karṇa, volume two.* Clay Sanskrit Library. New York: New York University Press / J J C Foundation.

Bowles, A 2019 The *gṛhastha* in the *Mahābhārata*. In: P Olivelle (ed.), *Gṛhastha: The householder in ancient Indian religious culture*. New York: Oxford University Press. pp. 173–203.

Brahmāṇḍapurāṇa: *The Brahmānda Purāna*, trans. G V Tagare. Delhi: Motilal Banarsidass, 1983.

Brinkhaus, H 2001 Āścaryaparvan and prādurbhāva in the Harivaṃśa. *Journal of Indian Philosophy* 29(1–2): 25–41.

Brinkhaus, H 2021 Parallel passages in the *Harivaṃśa*, the *Matsyapurāṇa* and the *Brahmāṇḍa-Vāyu* core. In: I Andrijanić & S Sellmer (eds.), *Mythic landscapes and argumentative trails in Sanskrit epic literature: Dubrovnik International Conference on the Sanskrit Epics and Purāṇas, DICSEP publications*. Zagreb: Croatian Academy of Sciences and Arts. pp. 277–298.

Brockington, J L 1992. *Hinduism and Christianity*. Basingstoke: Macmillan.

Brockington, J L 1998. *The Sanskrit epics*. Leiden: Brill.

Brodbeck, S 2003 Kṛṣṇa's action as the paradigm of *asakta karman* in the *Bhagavadgītā*. In: R Czekalska & H Marlewicz (eds.), *2nd International Conference on Indian Studies: Proceedings*. Cracow: Jagiellonian University Institute of Oriental Philology. pp. 85–112.

Brodbeck, S 2006 Review of *Pancha-kanya: The five virgins of Indian epics*, by P Bhattacharya. *South Asia Research* 26(1): 101–105.

Brodbeck, S 2007 Gendered soteriology: Marriage and the *karmayoga*. In: S Brodbeck & B Black (eds.), *Gender and narrative in the Mahābhārata*. London: Routledge. pp. 144–175.

Brodbeck, S 2009a Husbands of earth: Kṣatriyas, females, and female kṣatriyas in the *Strīparvan* of the *Mahābhārata*. In: R P Goldman & M Tokunaga (eds.), *Epic undertakings: Papers of the 12th World Sanskrit Conference, vol. 2*. Delhi: Motilal Banarsidass. pp. 33–63.

Brodbeck, S 2009b *The Mahābhārata patriline: Gender, culture, and the royal hereditary*. Farnham: Ashgate.

Brodbeck, S 2011 Analytic and synthetic approaches in light of the critical edition of the *Mahābhārata* and *Harivaṃśa*. *Journal of Vaishnava Studies* 19(2): 223–250.

Brodbeck, S 2012 Solar and lunar lines in the *Mahābhārata*. *Religions of South Asia* 5 (for 2011): 127–152.

Brodbeck, S 2014 On the lineal significance of the *rājasūya* in the *Mahābhārata*. *Indologica Taurinensia* 38 (for 2012): 27–63.

Brodbeck, S 2016 Upākhyānas and the Harivaṃśa. In: V Adluri & J Bagchee (eds.), *Argument and design: The unity of the Mahābhārata*. Leiden: Brill. pp. 388–427.

Brodbeck, S 2017a Libretto for *Viśvāmitra and Nandinī*. In: J M Hegarty & S Brodbeck, 'An appreciation of, and tribute to, Will Johnson on the occasion of his retirement'. *Asian Literature and Translation* 4(1): 17–31.

Brodbeck, S 2017b Mapping masculinities in the Sanskrit *Mahābhārata* and *Rāmāyaṇa*. In: I Zsolnay (ed.), *Being a man: Negotiating ancient constructs of masculinity*. London: Routledge. pp. 125–149.

Brodbeck, S 2018a Triśaṅku, Hariścandra, and the rājasūya. In: S Brodbeck, A Bowles, & A Hiltebeitel (eds.), *The churning of the epics and Purāṇas: Proceedings of the epics and Purāṇas section at the 15th World Sanskrit Conference*. Delhi: Dev Publishers. pp. 264–283.

Brodbeck, S 2018b The Upaniṣads and the *Bhagavadgītā*. In: S Cohen (ed.), *The Upaniṣads: A complete guide*. London: Routledge. pp. 200–218.

Brodbeck, S 2019a Translating Vaidya's *Harivaṃśa*. *Asian Literature and Translation* 6(1): 1–187.

Brodbeck, S (trans.) 2019b *Krishna's lineage: The Harivamsha of Vyāsa's Mahābhārata*. New York: Oxford University Press.

Brodbeck, S 2021a What difference does the *Harivaṃśa* make to the *Mahābhārata*? *Journal of the American Oriental Society* 141(1): 73–92.

Brodbeck, S 2021b The end of the Pāṇḍavas' year in disguise. *Journal of Hindu Studies* 13(3): 320–346.

Brodbeck, S 2022. Review of *In dialogue with the Mahābhārata*, by B Black. *Religions of South Asia* 15(2) (for 2021): 204–206.

Bronkhorst, J 2015 The historiography of Brahmanism. In: B-C Otto, S Rau, & J Rüpke (eds.), *History and religion: Narrating a religious past*. Berlin: De Gruyter. pp. 27–44.

Bühler, G (trans.) 1886 *The laws of Manu translated with extracts from seven commentaries*. Sacred Books of the East. Oxford: Clarendon Press.

van Buitenen, J A B (trans.) 1973 *The Mahābhārata, book 1: The book of the beginning*. Chicago: University of Chicago Press.

van Buitenen, J A B (trans.) 1975 *The Mahābhārata, book 2: The book of the assembly hall; book 3: The book of the forest*. Chicago: University of Chicago Press.

van Buitenen, J A B (trans.) 1978 *The Mahābhārata, book 4: The book of Virāṭa; book 5: The book of the effort*. Chicago: University of Chicago Press.

van Buitenen, J A B (trans.) 1981 *The Bhagavadgītā in the Mahābhārata: A bilingual edition*. Chicago: University of Chicago Press.

Burgess, J 1893 Notes on Hindu astronomy and the history of our knowledge of it. *Journal of the Royal Asiatic Society of Great Britain and Ireland* (2nd series) 25(4): 717–761.

Cherniak, A (trans.) 2008 *Mahābhārata book six: Bhīṣma, volume one, including the 'Bhagavad Gītā' in context*. Clay Sanskrit Library. New York: New York University Press / J J C Foundation.

Cherniak, A (trans.) 2009 *Mahābhārata book six: Bhīṣma, volume two*. Clay Sanskrit Library. New York: New York University Press / J J C Foundation.

Church, C D 1971 The Purāṇic myth of the four *yugas*. *Purāṇa* 13(2): 151–159.

Cohen, S 2020 Time in the Upaniṣads. *Religions* 11(2, p. 60): 1–12.

Coleman, T 2017 Avatāra: An overview of scholarly sources. *Journal of Vaishnava Studies* 26(1): 5–23.
Couture, A 1999 The problem of the meaning of Yoganidrā's name. *Journal of Indian Philosophy* 27(1–2): 35–47. Reprinted in Couture 2015: 144–159.
Couture, A 2001 From Viṣṇu's deeds to Viṣṇu's play, or Observations on the word avatāra as a designation for the manifestations of Viṣṇu. *Journal of Indian Philosophy* 29(3): 313–326. Reprinted in Couture 2017: 426–445.
Couture, A 2006 Dharma as a four-legged bull: A note on an epic and Purāṇic theme. In: R Panda & M Mishra (eds.), *Voice of the Orient: A tribute to Prof Upendranath Dhal*. Delhi: Eastern Book Linkers. pp. 69–76.
Couture, A 2010 Avatāra. In: K A Jacobsen (ed.-in-chief), *Brill's encyclopedia of Hinduism*, vol. 2: 701–705. Leiden: Brill.
Couture, A 2011 Kubjā, la bossue redressée par Kṛṣṇa. *Comptes rendus des séances de l'Académie des Inscriptions et Belles-Lettres* (2011)(2): 1013–1051. For English translation ('Kubjā, the hunchbacked woman straightened up by Kṛṣṇa'), see Couture 2015: 214–259.
Couture, A 2015 *Kṛṣṇa in the Harivaṁśa, vol. 1: The wonderful play of a cosmic child*. Delhi: D K Printworld.
Couture, A 2017 *Kṛṣṇa in the Harivaṁśa, vol. 2: The greatest of all sovereigns and masters*. Delhi: D K Printworld.
Couture, A & C Schmid 2001 The *Harivaṃśa*, the goddess Ekānaṃśā, and the iconography of the Vṛṣṇi triads. *Journal of the American Oriental Society* 121(2): 173–192.
Currie, B 2012 Hesiod on human history. In: J Marincola, L Llewellyn-Jones, & C Maciver (eds.), *Greek notions of the past in the archaic and classical eras: History without historians*. Edinburgh: Edinburgh University Press. pp. 37–64.
Dahlmann, J 1899 *Genesis des Mahābhārata*. Berlin: Felix L Dames.
Dandekar, R N (gen. ed.) 1971–1976 *The Mahābhārata text as constituted in its critical edition*. 5 vols. Poona: Bhandarkar Oriental Research Institute.
Dejenne, N 2009 *Triḥsaptakṛtvaḥ*: The significance of the number 'thrice seven' in the Rāma Jāmadagnya myth of the *Mahābhārata*. In: R P Goldman & M Tokunaga (eds.), *Epic undertakings: Papers of the Twelfth World Sanskrit Conference, vol. 2*. Delhi: Motilal Banarsidass. pp. 65–78.
Derrett, J D R 1959 *Bhū-Bharaṇa, Bhū-Pālana, Bhū-Bhojana*: An Indian conundrum. *Bulletin of the School of Oriental and African Studies* 22(1): 108–123.
Dhand, A 2004 The subversive nature of virtue in the *Mahābhārata*: A tale about women, smelly ascetics, and God. *Journal of the American Academy of Religion* 72(1): 33–58.
Dimmitt, C & J A B van Buitenen (ed. and trans.) 1978 *Classical Hindu mythology: A reader in the Sanskrit Purāṇas*. Philadelphia: Temple University Press.
Doniger O'Flaherty, W 1976 *The origins of evil in Hindu mythology*. Berkeley: University of California Press.

Doniger O'Flaherty, W (trans.) 1994 [1975] *Hindu myths: A sourcebook translated from the Sanskrit*. Penguin Classics. Delhi: Penguin Books.

Dumézil, G 1995 [1968–1973] *Mythe et épopée I. II. III*. Paris: Gallimard.

Dumont, P-E (trans.) 1951 The special kinds of Agnicayana (or special methods of building the fire-altar) according to the Kaṭhas in the Taittirīya-Brāhmaṇa: The tenth, eleventh, and twelfth prapāṭhakas of the third kāṇḍa of the Taittirīya-Brāhmaṇa with translation. *Proceedings of the American Philosophical Society* 95(6): 628–675.

Dundas, P 2002 *The Jains*, 2nd edn. London: Routledge.

Dwivedi, R K 1977 A critical study of the changing social order at yugānta: or The end of Kali age (with special reference to the *Mahābhārata*). In: L Gopal (ed.-in-chief), *D D Kosambi commemoration volume*. Varanasi: Banaras Hindu University. pp. 276–297.

Eckermann, J P 1850 *Conversations of Goethe with Eckermann and Soret*, trans. J Oxenford, vol. 2. London: Smith, Elder & Co.

Edgerton, F (trans.) 1965 *The beginnings of Indian philosophy: Selections from the Rig Veda, Atharva Veda, Upaniṣads, and Mahābhārata*. London: George Allen & Unwin.

Eggeling, J (trans.) 1978 [1885] *The Śatapatha-Brāhmaṇa according to the text of the Mādhyandina school*, part 4. Sacred Books of the East. Delhi: Motilal Banarsidass.

Eldredge, N & S J Gould 1972 Punctuated equilibria: An alternative to phyletic gradualism. In: T J M Schopf (ed.), *Models in paleobiology*. San Francisco: Freeman Cooper. pp. 82–115.

Eliade, M 1977 Mythologies of death: An introduction. In: F E Reynolds & E H Waugh (eds.), *Religious encounters with death: Insights from the history and anthropology of religions*. University Park: Pennsylvania State University Press. pp. 13–23.

Eltschinger, V 2012 Apocalypticism, heresy and philosophy. In: P Balcerowicz (ed.), *World view and theory in Indian philosophy*. Delhi: Manohar. pp. 29–85.

Eltschinger, V 2020 On the early history of the Brahmanical yugas. In: P W Kroll & J A Silk (eds.), *'At the shores of the sky': Asian studies for Albert Hoffstädt*. Leiden: Brill. pp. 38–53.

Etz, D V 1993 The numbers of Genesis V 3–31: A suggested conversion and its implications. *Vetus Testamentum* 43(2): 171–187.

Falk, H 1986 *Bruderschaft und Würfelspiel: Untersuchungen zur Entwicklungsgeschichte des vedischen Opfers*. Freiburg: Hedwig Falk.

Feller, D 2004 *The Sanskrit epics' representation of Vedic myths*. Delhi: Motilal Banarsidass.

Filliozat, J 1957 Ancient relations between Indian and foreign astronomical systems. *Journal of Oriental Research* (Madras) 25: 767–775.

Filliozat, J 1970 Influence of Mediterranean culture areas on Indian science. *Indian Journal of the History of Science* 5(2): 326–331.

Fitzgerald, J L 2002 The Rāma Jāmadagnya 'thread' of the *Mahābhārata*: A new survey of Rāma Jāmadagnya in the Pune text. In: M Brockington (ed.), *Stages and transitions: Temporal and historical frameworks in epic and Purāṇic literature. Proceedings of the second Dubrovnik International Conference on the Sanskrit Epics and Purāṇas*. Zagreb: Croatian Academy of Sciences and Arts. pp. 89–132.

Fitzgerald, J L (trans.) 2004a *The Mahābhārata, book 11: The book of the women; book 12: The book of peace, part one*. Chicago: University of Chicago Press.

Fitzgerald, J L 2004b Mahābhārata. In: S Mittal & G Thursby (eds.), *The Hindu world*. New York: Routledge. pp. 52–74.

Fleet, J F 1888 *Inscriptions of the early Gupta kings and their successors*. Corpus Inscriptionum Indicarum, vol. 3. Calcutta: Superintendent of Government Printing.

Fleet, J F 1911 The Kaliyuga era of B.C. 3102. *Journal of the Royal Asiatic Society of Great Britain and Ireland* (2nd series) 43(2): 479–496; 43(3): 675–698.

Frauwallner, E 1953 *Geschichte der indischen Philosophie*, vol. 1. Salzburg: Otto Müller.

Frauwallner, E 1973 *History of Indian philosophy*, vol. 1, trans. V M Bedekar. Delhi: Motilal Banarsidass.

Frauwallner, E 2003 *Geschichte der indischen Philosophie*, vol. 1, ed. A Pohlus. Aachen: Shaker Verlag.

Frazer, J G 1919 *Folk-lore in the Old Testament: Studies in comparative religion, legend and law*, vol. 1. London: Macmillan.

Ganguli, K M (trans.) 1970 [1883–1896] *The Mahabharata translated into English prose from the original Sanskrit text*. Delhi: Munshiram Manoharlal. First edition credited to Roy, the publisher.

Gautama Dharmasūtra: see Olivelle 2000.

van der Geer, A, M Dermitzakis, & J de Vos 2008 Fossil folklore from India: The Siwalik hills and the *Mahābhārata*. *Folklore* 119 (April): 71–92.

Genesis: *The Holy Bible, containing the Old and New Testaments: Revised Standard Version* (pp. 1–47). New York: Collins. Copyright dates 1952 (Old Testament), 1946 (New Testament).

van Gennep, A 1960 *The rites of passage*. Chicago: University of Chicago Press.

Geslani, M, B Mak, M Yano, & K Zysk 2017 Garga and early astral science in India. *History of Science in South Asia* 5(1): 151–191.

Ginsburg, A 1994 *Howl and other poems*. San Francisco: City Lights Books.

Gombrich, R 1975 Ancient Indian cosmology. In: C Blacker & M Loewe (eds.), *Ancient cosmologies*. London: George Allen & Unwin. pp. 110–142.

Gönc Moačanin, K 2021 *Nālopākhyāna* revisited. In: I Andrijanić & S Sellmer (eds.), *Mythic landscapes and argumentative trails in Sanskrit epic literature: Dubrovnik International Conference on the Sanskrit Epics and Purāṇas, DICSEP publications*. Zagreb: Croatian Academy of Sciences and Arts. pp. 93–123.

Gonda, J 1954 *Aspects of early Viṣṇuism*. Utrecht: A Oosthoek's Publishing Company.

Gonda, J 1984 *Prajāpati and the year*. Amsterdam: North-Holland Publishing Company.

González-Reimann, L 1988 *Tiempo cíclico y eras del mundo en la India*. Mexico City: Colegio de Mexico.

González-Reimann, L 1989 The ancient Vedic dice game and the names of the four world ages in Hinduism. In: A F Aveni (ed.), *World archaeoastronomy: Selected papers from the 2nd Oxford International Conference on Archaeoastronomy, held at Merida, Yucatan, Mexico*. Cambridge: Cambridge University Press. pp. 195–202.

González-Reimann, L 1993 La finalidad de la encarnación de Visnu como Krsna de acuerdo con el *Bālacarita* de Bhāsa. *Estudios de Asia y África* 28(1): 7–20.

González-Reimann, L 2002 *The Mahābhārata and the yugas: India's great epic poem and the Hindu system of world ages*. New York: Peter Lang.

González-Reimann, L 2009 Cosmic cycles, cosmology, and cosmography. In: K A Jacobsen (ed.-in-chief), *Brill's encyclopedia of Hinduism*, vol. 1. Leiden: Brill. pp. 411–428.

González-Reimann, L 2010 Time in the *Mahābhārata* and the time of the *Mahābhārata*. In: S Pollock (ed.), *Epic and argument in Sanskrit literary history: Essays in honor of Robert P Goldman*. Delhi: Manohar. pp. 61–73.

González-Reimann, L 2013 The coming golden age: On prophecy in Hinduism. In: S Harvey & S Newcombe (eds.), *Prophecy in the new millennium: When prophecies persist*. Farnham: Ashgate. pp. 105–122.

González-Reimann, L 2014 The *yugas*: Their importance in India and their use by Western intellectuals and esoteric and New Age writers. *Religion Compass* 8(12): 357–370.

Gospel According to Mark: see Nestle & Aland 1988.

Gospel According to Matthew: see Nestle & Aland 1988.

Granoff, P 1984 Holy warriors: A preliminary study of some biographies of saints and kings in the classical Indian tradition. *Journal of Indian Philosophy* 12(3): 291–303.

Gupta, A S 1969 The Purāṇic theory of yugas and kalpas – a study. *Purāṇa* 11(2): 304–323.

Hacker, P 1960 Zur Entwicklung der Avatāralehre. *Wiener Zeitschrift für die Kunde Sud- und Ostasiens* 4: 47–70. Includes summary in English, pp. 68–70.

Hara, M 1973 The king as a husband of the earth (*mahī-pati*). *Asiatische Studien/Études Asiatiques* 27(2): 97–114.

Harivaṃśa: *The Harivaṃśa, being the khila or supplement to the Mahābhārata, for the first time critically edited*, ed. P L Vaidya. Poona: Bhandarkar Oriental Research Institute, 1969-1971.

Hawking, S 1988 *A brief history of time: From the big bang to black holes*. New York: Bantam Books.

Hawthorne, S M 2017 Origin myths and temporal orders. In: S M Hawthorne (ed.), *Gender: God*. Macmillan Interdisciplinary Handbooks. Farmington Hills, Michigan: Macmillan Reference USA. pp. 247–262.

Heesterman, J C 1957 *The ancient Indian royal consecration*. The Hague: Mouton.
Hegarty, J M 2006a Extracting the *kathā-amṛta* (elixir of story): Creation, ritual, sovereignty, and textual structure in the Sanskrit Mahābhārata. *Journal of Vaishnava Studies* 14(2): 39–60.
Hegarty, J M 2006b Encompassing the sacrifice: On the narrative construction of the significant past in the Sanskrit *Mahābhārata*. *Acta Orientalia Vilnensia* 7(1–2): 77–118.
Hegarty, J M 2012 *Religion, narrative and public imagination in South Asia: Past and place in the Sanskrit Mahābhārata*. London: Routledge.
Hellwig, O 2019 Dating Sanskrit texts using linguistic features and neural networks. *Indogermanische Forschungen* 124(1): 1–45.
Herrmann, W 1977 Human mortality as a problem in ancient Israel. In: F E Reynolds & E H Waugh (eds.), *Religious encounters with death: Insights from the history and anthropology of religions*. University Park: Pennsylvania State University Press. pp. 161–169.
Hesse, H 2000 [1943] *The glass bead game (magister ludi)*, trans. R & C Winston. London: Vintage.
Hiltebeitel, A 1976 *The ritual of battle: Krishna in the Mahābhārata*. Ithaca, New York: Cornell University Press.
Hiltebeitel, A 1984 The two Kṛṣṇas on one chariot: Upaniṣadic imagery and epic mythology. *History of Religions* 24(1): 1–26.
Hiltebeitel, A 1985 Two Kṛṣṇas, three Kṛṣṇas, four Kṛṣṇas, more Kṛṣṇas: Dark interactions in the *Mahābhārata*. *Journal of South Asian Literature* 20(1): 71–77. Reprinted in Sharma 1991: 101–109.
Hiltebeitel, A 2001 *Rethinking the Mahābhārata: A reader's guide to the education of the dharma king*. Chicago: University of Chicago Press.
Hiltebeitel, A 2006 The *Nārāyaṇīya* and the early reading communities of the *Mahābhārata*. In: P Olivelle (ed.), *Between the empires: Society in India 300 BCE to 400 CE*. New York: Oxford University Press. pp. 227–255.
Hiltebeitel, A 2011a The archetypal design of the two Sanskrit epics. In: A Hiltebeitel, *Reading the fifth Veda: Studies on the Mahābhārata. Essays by Alf Hiltebeitel, volume 1*, ed. V Adluri & J Bagchee. Leiden: Brill. pp. 111–129.
Hiltebeitel, A 2011b *Dharma: Its early history in law, religion, and narrative*. New York: Oxford University Press.
Hiltebeitel, A 2012 Between history and divine plan: The *Mahābhārata*'s royal patriline in context. *Religions of South Asia* 5 (for 2011): 103–125.
Hiltebeitel, A 2018 *Freud's Mahābhārata*. Delhi: Oxford University Press.
Hoban, R 1987 *The Medusa frequency*. London: Jonathan Cape.
Hopkins, E W 1901 *The great epic of India: Its character and origin*. New York: Charles Scribner's Sons.
Hudson, D 1996 Arjuna's sin: Thoughts on the *Bhagavad-Gītā* in its epic context. *Journal of Vaishnava Studies* 4(3): 65–84.
Hudson, E T 2013 *Disorienting dharma: Ethics and the aesthetics of suffering in the Mahābhārata*. New York: Oxford University Press.

Huntington, R M 1960 A study of Purāṇic myth from the viewpoint of depth psychology. PhD thesis, University of Southern California.

Huntington, R M 1964 Avatāras and yugas: An essay in Purāṇic cosmology. *Purāṇa* 6(1): 7–39.

Inden, R 1998 [1978] Ritual, authority, and cyclic time in Hindu kingship. In: J F Richards (ed.), *Kingship and authority in South Asia*. Delhi: Oxford University Press. pp. 41–91.

Jacobi, H 1908 Ages of the world (Indian). In: J Hastings (ed.), *Encyclopedia of religion and ethics*, vol. 1. Edinburgh: T & T Clark. pp. 200–202.

Jacobsen, T (ed. and trans.) 1939 *The Sumerian king list*. Chicago: University of Chicago Press.

Jaiminīya Brāhmaṇa: *Jaiminīya Brāhmaṇa of the Sāmaveda*, ed. R Vira & L Chandra. Sarasvati Vihara Series. Nagpur: International Academy of Indian Culture, 1954.

Jerome, J K 1889 *Three men in a boat (to say nothing of the dog)*. Bristol: J W Arrowsmith.

Johnson, W J (trans.) 1998 *The Sauptikaparvan of the Mahābhārata: The massacre at night*. Oxford World's Classics. Oxford: Oxford University Press.

de Jong, J W 1985 The over-burdened earth in India and Greece. *Journal of the American Oriental Society* 105(3): 397–400.

Kane, P V 1973 [1946] *History of dharmaśāstra (ancient and mediæval religious and civil law)*, vol. 3, 2nd edn. Poona: Bhandarkar Oriental Research Institute.

Karve, I 1991 [1969] *Yuganta: The end of an epoch*, 2nd edn. First published in Marathi. Hyderabad: Orient Longman (Disha Books).

Kātre, S L 1934 Avatāras of God. *Allahabad University Studies* 10: 37–130.

Katz, R C 1985 The *Sauptika* episode in the structure of the *Mahābhārata*. *Journal of South Asian Literature* 20(1): 109–124. Reprinted in Sharma 1991: 130–149.

Katz, R C 1989 *Arjuna in the Mahābhārata: Where Kṛṣṇa is, there is victory*. Columbia: University of South Carolina Press.

Kaul, S 2022 Temporality and its discontents or *Why time needs to be retold*. In: S Kaul (ed.), *Retelling time: Alternative temporalities from premodern South Asia*. London: Routledge. pp. 1–10.

Keith, A B (trans.) 1920 *Rigveda Brahmanas: The Aitareya and Kauṣītaki Brāhmaṇas of the Rigveda, translated from the original Sanskrit*. Cambridge, Massachusetts: Harvard University Press.

Kinjawadekar, R (ed.) 1929 *Mahabharatam with the commentary of Nīlakantha. 1 Adiparva, illustrated*. Poona: Chitrashala Press.

Kloetzli, W R 2013 *Myriad* concerns: Indian macro-time intervals (*yugas*, *sandhyās* and *kalpas*) as systems of number. *Journal of Indian Philosophy* 41(6): 631–653.

Knight, C 1995 *Blood relations: Menstruation and the origins of culture*. New Haven, Connecticut: Yale University Press.

Kosambi, D D 1946 The Parvasaṁgraha of the Mahābhārata. *Journal of the American Oriental Society* 66(2): 110–117.

Koskikallio, P 1994 When time turns: Yugas, ideologies, sacrifices. *Studia Orientalia* (Helsinki) 73: 253–271.

Kuiper, F B J 1960 The ancient Aryan verbal contest. *Indo-Iranian Journal* 4(4): 217–281.

Laine, J W 1989 *Visions of God: Narratives of theophany in the Mahābhārata.* Vienna: De Nobili Research Library.

Lanman, C R 1978 [1884] *A Sanskrit reader: Text and vocabulary and notes.* Cambridge, Massachusetts: Harvard University Press.

Leslie, J 1996 [1994] Menstruation myths. In: J Leslie (ed.), *Myth and myth-making: Continuous evolution in Indian tradition.* Richmond: Curzon. pp. 87–105. First published in R Porter & M Teich (eds.), *Sexual knowledge, sexual science: The history of attitudes to sexuality* (Cambridge: Cambridge University Press).

Lingat, R 1962 [1961] Time and the dharma (on *Manu* I, 85–86). *Contributions to Indian Sociology* 6: 7–16. First published in French in *Journal Asiatique* 249: 487–495.

Lipner, J J 1993 Seeking others in their otherness. *New Blackfriars* 74 (#869): 152–165.

Lipner, J J 2017 *Hindu images and their worship with special reference to Vaiṣṇavism: A philosophical-theological inquiry.* London: Routledge.

Long, J B 1977 Death as a necessity and a gift in Hindu mythology. In: F E Reynolds & E H Waugh (eds.), *Religious encounters with death: Insights from the history and anthropology of religions.* University Park: Pennsylvania State University Press. pp. 73–96.

Lüders, H 1907 *Das Würfelspiel im alten Indien.* Berlin: Weidmannsche Buchhandlung.

Macdonell, A A 1895 Mythological studies in the Rigveda, II: The mythological basis in the Rigveda of the dwarf and boar incarnations of Viṣṇu. *Journal of the Royal Asiatic Society of Great Britain and Ireland* (2nd series) 27(1): 165–189.

Macdonell, A A 1897 *Vedic mythology.* Strasburg: Karl J Trübner.

Macdonell, A A & A B Keith 1912 *Vedic index of names and subjects*, vol. 1. London: John Murray.

McGinn, B 1979 *Visions of the end: Apocalyptic traditions in the Middle Ages.* New York: Columbia University Press.

Mahābhārata: *The Mahābhārata for the first time critically edited*, ed. V S Sukthankar et al. Poona: Bhandarkar Oriental Research Institute, 1933–1971.

Maitrī Upaniṣad: *The Maitrāyaṇīya Upaniṣad: A critical essay, with text, translation and commentary*, by J A B van Buitenen. The Hague: Mouton, 1962.

Mankad, D R 1941–1942 The yugas. *Poona Orientalist* 6(3–4): 206–216.

Mankad, D R 1942 The manvantara. *Indian Historical Quarterly* 18: 208–230.

Manusmṛti: see Olivelle 2006.

Matchett, F 2001 *Kṛṣṇa: lord or avatāra? The relationship between Kṛṣṇa and Viṣṇu in the context of the avatāra myth as presented by the Harivaṃśa, the Viṣṇupurāṇa and the Bhāgavatapurāṇa*. London: Routledge.

Matsyapurāṇa: *The Matsya Puranam*, trans. A Taluqdar. Allahabad: Pāṇini Office, 1916–1917.

Mayor, A 2000 *The first fossil hunters: Paleontology in Greek and Roman times*. Princeton: Princeton University Press.

Meiland, J (trans.) 2007 *Mahābhārata book nine: Śalya, volume two*. Clay Sanskrit Library. New York: New York University Press / J J C Foundation.

Miller, H 1952 *The books in my life*. Norfolk, Connecticut: James Laughlin.

Minkowski, C Z 2000 Nīlakaṇṭha's cosmographical comments in the Bhīṣmaparvan. *Purāṇa* 42(1): 24–40.

Minkowski, C Z 2004 Competing cosmologies in early modern Indian astronomy. In: C Burnett, J P Hogendijk, K Plofker, & M Yano (eds.), *Studies in the history of the exact sciences in honour of David Pingree*. Leiden: Brill. pp. 349–385.

Mitchiner, J E 1978 The evolution of the manvantara theory as illustrated by the saptarṣi manvantara traditions. *Purāṇa* 22(1): 7–37.

Mitchiner, J E (ed. and trans.) 2002 *The Yuga Purāṇa*, 2nd edn. Kolkata: Asiatic Society.

Monier-Williams, M 1899 *A Sanskrit-English dictionary, etymologically and philologically arranged, with special reference to cognate Indo-European languages*, 2nd edn. Oxford: Clarendon Press.

Nestle, E, K Aland, et al. (eds.) 1988 *Novum Testamentum Graece*, 26th edn. Stuttgart: Deutsche Bibelgesellschaft.

Olivelle, P (ed. and trans.) 1998 *The early Upaniṣads: Annotated text and translation*. Delhi: Munshiram Manoharlal.

Olivelle, P (ed. and trans.) 2000 *Dharmasūtras: The law codes of Āpastamba, Gautama, Baudhāyana, and Vasiṣṭha*. Delhi: Motilal Banarsidass.

Olivelle, P (ed. and trans., with the editorial assistance of S Olivelle) 2006 *Manu's code of law: A critical edition and translation of the Mānava-Dharmaśāstra*. Delhi: Oxford University Press.

Pañcaviṃśa Brāhmaṇa: *Pañcaviṃśa-Brāhmaṇa, the Brāhmaṇa of twenty five chapters*, trans. W Caland. Bibiotheca Indica. Calcutta: Asiatic Society of Bengal, 1931.

Parpola, A 1975–1976 Sanskrit *kālá-* «time», Dravidian *kāl* «leg», and the mythical cow of the four yugas. *Indologica Taurinensia* 3–4: 361–378.

Parpola, A 1979 On the symbol concept of the Vedic ritualists. In: H Biezais (ed.), *Religious symbols and their functions*. Uppsala: Almqvist & Wiksell. pp. 139–153.

Patnaik, P, S C Chatterjee, & D Suar (eds.) 2009 *Time in Indian culture: Diverse perspectives*. Delhi: D K Printworld.

Piatigorsky, A 1993 *Mythological deliberations: Lectures on the phenomenology of myth*, ed. A Cantlie. London: School of Oriental and African Studies.

Pingree, D 1963 Astronomy and astrology in India and Iran. *Isis* 54(2) (#176): 229–246.

Plofker, K 2009 *Mathematics in India*. Princeton: Princeton University Press.
Proferes, T N 2007 *Vedic ideals of sovereignty and the poetics of power*. New Haven, Connecticut: American Oriental Society.
Przyluski, J 1938 From the great goddess to Kāla. *Indian Historical Quarterly* 14: 267–274.
Reich, T C 2011 Ends and closures in the *Mahābhārata*. *International Journal of Hindu Studies* 15(1): 9–53.
Ṛgveda: *The Rigveda, the earliest religious poetry of India*, trans. S W Jamison & J P Brereton. New York: Oxford University Press, 2014.
Rocher, L 1975 Review of *Das heliozentrische System in der griechischen, persischen und indischen Astronomie*, by B L van der Waerden. *Journal of the American Oriental Society* 95(1): 142.
Rocher, L 1980 A note on the Sanskrit gerund. In: J Bingen, A Coupez, & F Mawet (eds.), *Recherches de linguistique: Hommage à Maurice Leroy*. Brussells: Université Libre de Bruxelles. pp. 181–188.
Roebuck, V J (trans.) 2003 *The Upaniṣads*, revised edn. Penguin Classics. London: Penguin Books.
Roth, R 1860 *Über den Mythus von den fünf Menschengeschlechtern bei Hesiod und die indische Lehre von den vier Weltaltern*. Tübingen: Ludwig Friedrich Fues.
Roy, see Ganguli.
Saindon, M 2007 Quand Kṛṣṇa Dvaipāyana Vyāsa est considéré comme un *avatāra* de Viṣṇu. *Bulletin d'Études Indiennes* 22–23 (for 2004–2005): 307–321.
Śatapatha Brāhmaṇa: *The Satapatha-Brâhmana according to the text of the Mâdhyandina school*, trans. J Eggeling. Sacred Books of the East. Oxford: Clarendon Press, 1882–1900. For Sanskrit text, see http://gretil.sub.uni-goettingen.de/gretil.html
Sathaye, A 2016 Pride and prostitution: Making sense of the Mādhavī exhibit in the Mahābhārata museum. In: V Adluri & J Bagchee (eds.), *Argument and design: The unity of the Mahābhārata*. Leiden: Brill. pp. 237–274.
Satyamurti, C 2015 *Mahabharata: A modern retelling*. New York: W W Norton.
Scheuer, J 1982 Śiva dans le Mahābhārata. Paris: Presses Universitaires de France.
Schmid, C 2010 *Le don de voir: Premières représentations krishnaïtes de la région de Mathurā*. Paris: École Française d'Extrême-Orient.
Seaford, R 2020 *The origins of philosophy in ancient Greece and ancient India: A historical comparison*. Cambridge: Cambridge University Press.
Sharma, A (ed.) 1991 *Essays on the Mahābhārata*. Leiden: Brill.
Sharma, R S 1982 The kali age: A period of social crisis. In: S N Mukherjee (ed.), *India: History and thought. Essays in honour of A L Basham*. Calcutta: Subarnarekha. pp. 186–203.
Sharma, V 2020 The problem of indifference to suffering in the *Mahābhārata* tradition. *International Journal of Hindu Studies* 24(2): 177–197.

Shukla, K S & K V Sarma (eds. and trans.) 1976 *Āryabhaṭīya of Āryabhaṭa*. Delhi: Indian National Science Academy.

Shulman, D 1992 Devana and daiva. In: A W van den Hoek, D H A Kolff, & M S Oort (eds.), *Ritual, state and history in South Asia: Essays in honour of J C Heesterman*. Leiden: Brill. pp. 350–365.

Shulman, D 2014 Waking Aja. In: Y Bronner, D Shulman, & G Tubb (eds.), *Innovations and turning points: Toward a history of kāvya literature*. Delhi: Oxford University Press. pp. 35–70.

Slaje, W 1995 Ṛtú-, ṛ́tv(i)ya-, ārtavá-. Weibliche 'Fertilität' im Denken vedischer Inder. *Journal of the European Ayurvedic Society* 4: 109–148. Includes summary in English, pp. 147–148.

Smith, B K 1989 *Reflections on resemblance, ritual, and religion*. New York: Oxford University Press.

Smith, B K 1994 *Classifying the universe: The ancient Indian varṇa system and the origins of caste*. New York: Oxford University Press.

Smith, F M 2006 *The self possessed: Deity and spirit possession in South Asian literature and civilization*. New York: Columbia University Press.

Smith, J D (trans.) 2009 *The Mahābhārata: An abridged translation*. Penguin Classics. Delhi: Penguin Books.

Soifer, D A 1991 *The myths of Narasiṁha and Vāmana: Two avatars in cosmological perspective*. Albany: State University of New York Press.

Srinivasan, D 1981 Early Kṛṣṇa icons: The case at Mathurā. In: J G Williams (ed.), *Kalādarśana: American studies in the art of India*. Leiden: Brill. pp. 127–136.

von Stietencron, H 2005a [1985] Political aspects of Indian religious art. In: H von Stietencron, *Hindu myth, Hindu history: Religion, art, and politics*. Ranikhet: Permanent Black. pp. 7–30.

von Stietencron, H 2005b [1986] Calculating religious decay: The kaliyuga in India. In: H von Stietencron, *Hindu myth, Hindu history: Religion, art, and politics*. Ranikhet: Permanent Black. pp. 31–49.

Sukthankar, V S (ed.) 1933 *The Ādiparvan, being the first book of the Mahābhārata, the great epic of India, for the first time critically edited*. Poona: Bhandarkar Oriental Research Institute.

Sullivan, B M 1999 [1990] *Seer of the fifth Veda: Kṛṣṇa Dvaipāyana Vyāsa in the Mahābhārata*. Delhi: Motilal Banarsidass.

Sullivan, B M 2016 The tale of an old monkey and a fragrant flower: What the Mahābhārata's Rāmāyaṇa may tell us about the Mahābhārata. In: V Adluri & J Bagchee (eds.), *Argument and design: The unity of the Mahābhārata*. Leiden: Brill. pp. 187–205.

Sutton, N 2000 *Religious doctrines in the Mahābhārata*. Delhi: Motilal Banarsidass.

Śvetāśvatara Upaniṣad: see Olivelle 1998.

Taittirīya Brāhmaṇa: *Kṛṣṇayajurvedīyaṃ Taittirīyabrāhmaṇam*, ed. V S Godbole et al. Sanskrit Series, 37. Poona: Ānandāśrama, 1934.

Taylor, M 2012 Heavenly carrots and earthly sticks: How *phalaśruti* paratexts empower Purāṇic discourse. *Journal of Hindu Studies* 5(1): 92–111.

Taylor, M 2022 Time is born of his eyelashes: Purāṇic measurement and conceptions of time. In: S Kaul (ed.), *Retelling time: Alternative temporalities from premodern South Asia*. London: Routledge. pp. 75–88.

Thapar, R 2000 Millenarianism and religion in early India. In: R Thapar, *Cultural pasts: Essays in early Indian history*. Delhi: Oxford University Press. pp. 946–962.

Thapar, R 2002 *Early India from the origins to AD 1300*. London: Allen Lane.

Thomas, L 1988 Theories of cosmic time in the Mahābhārata. PhD thesis, University of Oxford.

Thomas, L 1996 Paraśurāma and time. In: J Leslie (ed.), *Myth and mythmaking: Continuous evolution in Indian tradition*. Richmond: Curzon. pp. 63–86.

Thomas, L 1997 The nature of the repetition in the Indian idea of cyclical time. In: P Connolly & S Hamilton (eds.), *Indian insights: Buddhism, Brahmanism and bhakti. Papers from the annual Spalding Symposium on Indian Religions*. London: Luzac Oriental. pp. 83–89.

Thomas, L 2007 Does the age make the king or the king make the age? Exploring the relationship between the king and the *yugas* in the *Mahābhārata*. *Religions of South Asia* 1(2): 183–201.

Trautmann, T R 1995 Indian time, European time. In: D O Hughes & T R Trautmann (eds.), *Time: Histories and ethnologies*. Ann Arbor: University of Michigan Press. pp. 167–197.

Truschke, A 2017 *Aurangzeb: The life and legacy of India's most controversial king*. Stanford, California: Stanford University Press.

Tsuchida, R 2009 Some reflections on the chronological problems of the *Mahābhārata*. *Studies in Indian Philosophy and Buddhism* 16(3): 1–24.

Tsuchida, R 2010 On the dynastic transition from the Śuṅgas to the Kāṇvāyanas. *Studies in Indian Philosophy and Buddhism* 17(3): 1–16.

Turner, V 1969 *The ritual process: Structure and anti-structure*. Chicago: Aldine.

Vaidya, P L (ed.) 1969 *The Harivaṁśa, being the khila or supplement to the Mahābhārata, for the first time critically edited. Volume I: Introduction, critical text and notes*. Poona: Bhandarkar Oriental Research Institute.

Vāsiṣṭha Dharmasūtra: see Olivelle 2000.

Vassilkov, Y 1999 *Kālavāda* (the doctrine of cyclical time) in the Mahābhārata and the concept of heroic didactics. In: M Brockington & P Schreiner (eds.), *Composing a tradition: Concepts, techniques and relationships. Proceedings of the first Dubrovnik International Conference on the Sanskrit Epics and Purāṇas*. Zagreb: Croatian Academy of Sciences and Arts. pp. 17–33.

Vāyupurāṇa: *The Vāyu Purāṇa*, trans. G V Tagare. Delhi: Motilal Banarsidass, 1987.

van der Veer, P 1999 Monumental texts: The critical edition of India's national heritage. In: D Ali (ed.), *Invoking the past: The uses of history in South Asia*. Delhi: Oxford University Press. pp. 134–155.

Verpoorten, J-M 1977 Unité et distinction dans les spéculations rituelles védiques. *Archiv für Begriffsgeschichte* 21(1): 59–85.

Vielle, C 1996 *Le mytho-cycle heroïque dans l'aire indo-européenne*, vol 1. Louvain: Peeters.

Viethsen, A 2009 The reasons for Viṣṇu's descent in the prologue to the Kṛṣṇacarita of the *Harivaṃśa*. In: P Koskikallio (ed.), *Parallels and comparisons: Proceedings of the fourth Dubrovnik International Conference on the Sanskrit Epics and Purāṇas*. Zagreb: Croatian Academy of Sciences and Arts. pp. 221–234.

Viṣṇupurāṇa: *The critical edition of the Viṣṇupurāṇam*, ed. M M Pathak. Vadodara: Oriental Institute, 1997–1999.

de Vreese, K 1948 The game of dice in ancient India (the vibhītaka game). In: J H Kramers et al. (eds.), *Orientalia Neerlandica: A volume of Oriental studies published under the auspices of the Netherlands Oriental Society*. Leiden: A W Sijthoff. pp. 349–362.

van der Waerden, B L 1978 The great year in Greek, Persian and Hindu astronomy. *Archive for History of Exact Sciences* 18(4): 359–383.

Willis, M 2009 *The archaeology of Hindu ritual: Temples and the establishment of the gods*. Cambridge: Cambridge University Press.

Witzel, M 2005 The Vedas and the epics: Some comparative notes on persons, lineages, geography, and grammar. In: P Koskikallio (ed.), *Epics, khilas, and Purāṇas: Continuities and ruptures. Proceedings of the third Dubrovnik International Conference on the Sanskrit Epics and Purāṇas*. Zagreb: Croatian Academy of Sciences and Arts. pp. 21–80.

Woods, J F 2001 *Destiny and human initiative in the Mahābhārata*. Albany: State University of New York Press.

Works and Days: *Hesiod, the Homeric hymns and Homerica, with an English translation*, ed. and trans. H G Evelyn-White (pp. 2–65). Loeb Classical Library. London: William Heinemann, 1914.

Wulff Alonso, F 2008 *Grecia en la India: El repertorio griego del Mahabharata*. Madrid: Ediciones Akal.

Wulff Alonso, F 2014 *The Mahābhārata and Greek mythology*, trans. A Morrow. Delhi: Motilal Banarsidass.

Wulff Alonso, F 2018 The fourth book of the Mahābhārata and its Greek sources. In: S Brodbeck, A Bowles, & A Hiltebeitel (eds.), *The churning of the epics and Purāṇas: Proceedings of the epics and Purāṇas section at the 15th World Sanskrit Conference*. Delhi: Dev. pp. 71–95.

Wynne, A (trans.) 2009 *Mahābhārata book twelve: Peace, volume three, 'The book of liberation'*. Clay Sanskrit Library. New York: New York University Press / J J C Foundation.

Yadava, B N S 1979 The accounts of the kali age and the social transition from antiquity to the Middle Ages. *Indian Historical Review* 5(1–2): 31–63.

Yokochi, Y 2001 The goddess in the Kṛṣṇa legend: Reconsidered. *Studies in the History of Indian Thought* 13: 38–62.

Yugapurāṇa: see Mitchiner 2002.

Index of Passages Cited

(Bold type indicates an indented quotation.)

A Midsummer Night's Dream
5.1 **64**

Āpastamba Dharmasūtra
2.8.10–11 43

Āryabhaṭṭīya
1.3–4 43
3.9 32

Bhagavadgītā, see under *Mahābhārata*

Brahmāṇḍapurāṇa
1.2.31.110 68–69

Gautama Dharmasūtra
23.32–34 35n
24.4–5 35n

Genesis
5.3–32 55–56
11.10–26 55–56

Gospel According to Mark
4.25 35

Gospel According to Matthew
13.12 35

Harivaṃśa, see under *Mahābhārata*

Jaiminīya Brāhmaṇa
1.117 117

Mahābhārata (Mbh, incl. Bhg and Hv)
1.1 47
1.1.11 **48**
1.1.28 15

Mahābhārata (Mbh, incl. Bhg and Hv) (*continued*)
1.1.36–38 15
1.2.1–8 48
1.2.3 65, 106n
1.2.9–10 **48**
1.2.29–30 157
1.2.69 9
1.2.70–71 157
1.2.233 9
1.4 157
1.15–17 65
1.40.6–7 141
1.45.15 141
1.54.22 153
1.57 17
1.57.72–73 **17**, 49
1.57.72 26, 66n
1.58–61 172, 174
1.58 64–65, 104–106, 109–110, 112–115, 120, 122, 127, 130, 133–139, 175
1.58.4–8 123n
1.58.8 **104**
1.58.30–34 **134**, 135
1.58.41–47 **105**
1.58.51–59.2 115
1.59.3 134
1.60.7 135
1.61 112, 133
1.61.1–60 134–136
1.61.72 131
1.61.80–81 131
1.61.82–87 135
1.61.95–98 123
1.62.7–10 114n
1.69.45–48 114n
1.90.45–96 82
1.91 127
1.94.1–17 114n
1.94.88 115
1.99.14 50n
1.101 127
1.102.5 114n, 147
1.155.44–45 124
1.189 106–110, 113–116, 120–122, 127, 130, 137
1.189.1–8 **106–107**
1.189.6 114, 116, 120
1.189.14 **108**
1.189.25–26 **108**
1.189.31 154
2.33.11–20 133
2.45.50 52
3.45.21 64
3.56.6–7 16
3.81.109 15
3.84.4 67
3.100.19–23 63
3.121.19 24
3.146–150 17
3.146.33 63
3.146.38 77
3.146.59 17
3.148 17–18
3.148.7 17, 26–27, 29, 66n, 98
3.148.9 **18**, 26, 66n, 98
3.148.11 97
3.148.16–33 66, 81
3.148.37 **48**
3.180 20
3.185 65
3.186–189 5, 18–22
3.186 73, 78
3.186.18–23 36, 39
3.186.24–55 19, 143
3.186.29–30 159
3.186.32 **19**, 26, 98
3.186.34–35 97n
3.186.43 19, 160
3.186.45 **19**
3.186.48 **19**
3.186.53 **19**

3.187.26–28	**91**
3.187.31	66, 70, 81
3.187.32	**69**, 70
3.188–189	26, 73, 78
3.188.4–7	**20**
3.188.10–13	**20–21**
3.188.10	16, 34
3.188.14–84	21, 143
3.188.15–17	**21–22**, **27–28**
3.188.29	159
3.188.37	21, 159
3.188.45	159
3.188.47	**21–22**
3.188.52	159
3.188.64–66	160
3.188.70	159
3.188.85–189.9	64, 150
3.189.9	160
3.189.13–14	**22**, 53
3.239.18–19	**136**
3.240.1–24	136–137
3.240.10–14	4, **136–137**
3.240.17	**136–137**
3.242.14–15	127
4.47.1–2	**68**
5.48.21	104
5.57.12–13	127
5.66.12–13	**128**
5.67.3–4	67
5.72.11–18	77–78
5.72.12	65–66, 77
5.139.29–51	127
5.154.4	127
5.158.16	**77**
6.7.6	23
6.11	22–24, 46n, 47
6.11.1	26
6.11.5–6	**23**
6.11.6	48
6.11.14	**48**
6.17.2	161n
Bhg 3.9–20	120
Bhg 3.22–24	**168–169**
Bhg 3.36–43	28
Bhg 4.5–7	56
Bhg 4.6–8	89, **90**
Bhg 4.7–8	**56**, 58, 60, 79, 149
Bhg 4.8	57, 66, 80, 173
Bhg 7.4–5	123
Bhg 8.17–19	15
Bhg 9.7	15
Bhg 9.8–10	124
Bhg 10.4–5	169
Bhg 10.16	169
Bhg 10.41	**169**
Bhg 11.18	90
Bhg 11.32	172
Bhg 12.20	**155**
Bhg 14.3	124
Bhg 14.22–25	169–170
Bhg 15.5	169
Bhg 15.7–8	123
Bhg 15.16–20	123
Bhg 16.6	169
Bhg 18.20	**170**
Bhg 18.66	139
6.61–62	102–104, 115, 121
6.61.61–63	**102–103**
6.61.67–68	**102–103**
6.62.7–10	**103**
6.62.26–27	**103–104**
6.62.39	**49**, 152
6.62.40	15, 66n
7.11.17–18	133
7.28.23–26	66
7.156.22	92
7.172.81	66n
7.172.86	66n
8.65.18	66n
9.54–60	139
9.59.21	**49**
10.8.64–67	124
10.9.19–55	139
11.8.17–31	**131–133**, 172
11.25.35–45	139
11.26.9–10	1, 102

Mahābhārata (Mbh, incl. Bhg and Hv) (*continued*)
12.12.27 77n
12.29.46–54 149
12.43.6 67
12.56–13.151 24
12.64.25 66n
12.70 147
12.138.1 158–159
12.138.40 160
12.139.13–23 78
12.168–353 24
12.200 24–25
12.200.34 **24**
12.200.43 **24**
12.201.9 15n
12.203.14–17 15
12.211.4 160
12.220.41 66n
12.221 109
12.224–247 25
12.224 25, 39
12.224.1 **25**, 26, 66n
12.224.16–18 **41–42**, 43
12.224.17 39–43
12.224.19–20 36, 42
12.224.22 34
12.224.24–25 97
12.224.26–27 142
12.224.27 25, 120
12.224.30 42
12.224.65 25, 27, 99, 156
12.224.68–69 66n
12.230 25, 173
12.230.14 25, 27, 99, 156
12.230.18 66n
12.248–250 28, 94–97, 115, 124, 140
12.248.13–14 **94–95**
12.249.3–4 **95**
12.250.34–36 28, **96**
12.252.8 142
12.291.14 15
12.292.20 160
12.299.1–14 15n
12.321–339 25–26, 49–50, 92–94, 152
12.323.50–51 65
12.326.71–97 63–65
12.326.77 65, 106n
12.326.78–81 149
12.326.82 **49**, 112
12.326.105 71
12.327 25–26, 30
12.327.53 66n
12.327.73 34
12.327.89 15, 71–72
12.328.19 66n
12.328.33 64
12.334.9 154
12.335 153
12.336 71, 152
12.336.27 **152**
12.336.58 **152**
12.337.4–5 154
12.337.29–34 3, **92–94**, 98, 112, 129
12.337.31 64
12.337.35–36 63
12.337.42–44 50n
12.337.42–43 **50**, 154
13.14.183 15
13.24.56 160
13.24.67 160
13.100 101
13.135.11 15
13.143.9 66
13.143.10–12 **91–92**
14.53.11–15 **90–91**
14.65–69 82
15.39.8 135n
15.43.4–17 153
16.4 139
16.9.29 64, 139
18.5 9
Hv 1.1–14 59
Hv 2.54 66n

Hv 3.57 66n
Hv 5–6 101
Hv 7 70
Hv 7.11 53
Hv 7.21 53
Hv 7.50–52 **71**
Hv 7.52–54 15
Hv 9.88–10.20 78
Hv 13.25–40 123, 127
Hv 13.39–40 **50**
Hv 13.39 65, 72
Hv 13.64 66n
Hv 14–19 27
Hv 23.30 15
Hv 30 59
Hv 30.15 66n
Hv 31 63–66, 150
Hv 31.68–92 65, 78
Hv 31.129–139 149
Hv *481 22
Hv 32–38 91, 104
Hv 32.10 52
Hv 32.17 15, 70
Hv 32.19 124
Hv 40–45 64, 110–116, 120, 122–123, 130, 136–137
Hv 40–43 115, 138
Hv 40 72n, 110, 124
Hv 40.34–36 83, 167
Hv 41 80, 110, 114
Hv 41.16 27, 113, 156
Hv 41.18–20 **111**
Hv 41.23 111, 113, 115, 156
Hv 42.14–53 101
Hv 42.51 **111**
Hv 43 111, 123, 127, 174
Hv 43.5 131
Hv 43.15–55 124
Hv 43.53–61 **50–51**, 52
Hv 43.58–59 81
Hv 43.63 131
Hv 43.66 113, 115, 156
Hv 43.69 **111**, 112
Hv 44 115, 135
Hv 44.1 113, 115, 156
Hv 44.4 131
Hv 47–48 124
Hv 58.45 70n
Hv 68.30 114n
Hv 71.22–35 102
Hv 79.35 114n
Hv 81.1–13 133
Hv 85.40–45 51–52
Hv 85.55–56 51, 98
Hv 85.59 **52**
Hv 85.62 98
Hv 91.21 113n
Hv 96.11–19 124
Hv 115–117 153, 159
Hv 115.14–23 133, 141–142
Hv 115.24–42 142
Hv 115.40–41 **160**
Hv 115.42 160
Hv 115.43–45 **142**, 148
Hv 116–117 5, 26, 75, 141
Hv 116 143–144
Hv 116.1–3 **142–143**
Hv 116.2 148
Hv 116.3 145
Hv 116.15 151n, 159–160
Hv 116.19 **144**
Hv 116.36 **144**
Hv 117 26, 145, 165
Hv 117.1–2 **144–145**
Hv 117.3–5 **150–151**
Hv 117.10 **150–151**
Hv 117.11–14 151n
Hv 117.13 143, 148, **150–151**
Hv 117.19 160
Hv 117.38–44 **150–151**
Hv 117.45–46 **29**, 30, 151n
Hv 117.49–50 66n, **148**
Hv 118 9, 157
Hv 118.24–38 153
Hv 118.39–41 147

Mahābhārata (Mbh, incl. Bhg and Hv) (*continued*)
Hv 118.41–42 **153**
Hv 118.43 **155**
Hv 118.49 **155**

Maitrī Upaniṣad
6.15 **128–129**, 168

Manusmṛti (Ms)
1.8–9 124
1.66–68 39
1.68–72 **13–14**, 15, 36, 43n, 46
1.81–86 **14–15**, 25–26, 34, 46, 97, 121, 142
3.45–47 35n
4.40–42 35n

Matsyapurāṇa
144.98–99 68–69

Pañcaviṃśa Brāhmaṇa
24.11.2 117

Ṛgveda
1.155.6 29
10.42.9 33
10.90 24
10.127 124

Śatapatha Brāhmaṇa
1.6.3.35 **117–118**
1.6.3.36 **119**
2.2.3.7 68
3.2.1.24 159
8.7.1.4 68
10.4.2 44–45
10.4.3 118
10.4.3.6 **118**
13.1.1.4 119

Śvetāśvatara Upaniṣad
1.10 123

Taittirīya Brāhmaṇa
2.2.7.1 117
3.10.9.1 117

Vāsiṣṭha Dharmasūtra
12.5 35n

Vāyupurāṇa
58.109–110 68–69

Viṣṇupurāṇa
2.3.19 23–24
3.2.56–59 66n
3.3.9–21 66n
4.24.20–21 69
6.3–4 71

Works and Days
109–201 54–55
174–175 55

Yugapurāṇa
12–13 52, 97
36 **138**
64–65 159
82–86 159

CPSIA information can be obtained
at www.ICGtesting.com
Printed in the USA
LVHW080726171022
730780LV00014B/1016

9 781911 653394